The First Twenty-One

Ray Warden

authorHOUSE

AuthorHouse™ UK
1663 Liberty Drive
Bloomington, IN 47403 USA
www.authorhouse.co.uk
Phone: 0800.197.4150

Published by AuthorHouse   11/04/2016

ISBN: 978-1-5246-6585-2 (sc)
ISBN: 978-1-5246-6584-5 (e)

PREFACE

Many years ago, probably around 30 or 40, I used to relate to friends and family some of the happenings to me when I was very young and then when I was growing up, and they seemed amazed that I was able to remember so far back and also in such detail. Now to me it seemed normal, as I think that when one has some sort of incident or situation that is profound in its entirety, then it is impressed into the brain whether it is something traumatic or joyful, it stamps itself into your memory bank. So as I've said, I was always being asked to try and write down my memories of certain times in my childhood and youth, but of course the biggest drawback was finding the time to be able to do it when you have a family and engaged in earning a living which was of course the priority, so other things took precedence.

So as the years rolled by, the children grew up and left to establish their own future lives, my wife and I retired, but sadly I lost her, which devastated me for a long time, but that was many years ago. So I found myself on my own, but I kept myself busy looking after our home and the garden, but I have reached the age now where one begins to reflect on the past and being that this year there seems to be so many anniversaries going on with regard to the 1st and 2nd world wars that I began to relate some stories to family and friends about what happened to our family during the 2nd world war, and again I was urged to put pen to paper, so I though why not, perhaps someone may be interested.

So armed with pencil and writing pads I began, now the amazing thing to me was that although my memory was pretty good, as people had commented, that as I began to write, a lot of things even became clearer and clearer, and as I was writing I began to re-live what I was writing, I was there inside my memory and even the smallest details were recalled, as I said I began writing by hand, and when I decided to type up all that I had written, even as I was typing I would think, 'oh yes that happened also', and so it went on. Like I'm doing at the moment!

Now all the things I have written are factual as far as they can be, the names, the people, places, perhaps one or two of the names are incorrect, perhaps to protect their identity!!! Not really, as I don't believe anyone could be embarrassed with the things I have written. So sue me! Amen.

THE FIRST 21

MY VERY FIRST RECOLLECTION OF life as it appeared to me, and etched itself into my memory was when I was about 2 or 3 years of age, Now to me it has always seemed rather remarkable for a child of that tender age to be able to imprison a situation or happening to memory, and to be able to retrieve it for future recollections at a much later stage in life. Imagine, I used to think to myself, just two or three years old and I can still remember what was happening all around me. I must have some sort of advanced memory bank in this tiny little brain of mine, could I possibly be a candidate for MENSA perhaps, but realistically, I don't think so. When I first told someone that I could recall things that happened to me when I was only very little, expecting gasps of astonishment and admiration, well the reaction was very deflating, with a rapid and somewhat deflating retort from some woman, "I can recall things from when I was only 6 months old", I didn't know whether to believe her or not, is that possible I thought, to remember things at 6 months of age?, probably just trying to upstage me!, Anyway, where was I, ah yes, my childhood recollections, one particular one, was when I was being pushed, and strapped into a pushchair, down the street where we lived, the recollection is not of the street or the surrounding, but of the person who was actually pushing me. How to say that the person who was dutifully taking me for a walk was the very first female that I fell in love with may sound rather ridiculous, but, as true as I am sitting here putting pen to paper, I did actually feel that emotion at that tender age. I cannot say that as I grew older that feeling for that particular person grew with me, no, it was just that particular emotion at that particular time, that sort of established my presence in this world, and kick started my memory bank, and indeed quite vividly.

Now obviously I did not know who that person was at that time, that was not established with names and facts until I was much older, but getting back to the pushchair, as I have said, I recall it quite vividly, I recall that I dressed in some sort of woolly hat and mittens, and it was one of those pushchairs that you sat facing forward, but I wasn't interested what was in front of me because I had twisted myself around, and was spellbound by the person who was pushing me, and the moment of looking at a pair of bare long legs, and short gym skirt, and jumper, and craning my neck back to look at that fresh young face and long auburn hair, stirred within me a feeling of warmth and closeness which I can only describe as probably the very first love of my life, and even now, 79 years later, I have only experienced that feeling a couple of times since, crazy you may think, but I can only state what was my earliest memories and feelings at the start of my life, and I do cherish them, as it probably set out the pattern for the rest of my life, but I must say in all fairness to the possible sceptics or critics, that that was the only recollection of any significance with the opposite sex, when I was a child, until much later on.

Bye the way, as I grew older, and with that memory still there, I made enquiries through my family as to who it was who used to take me for walks in my pushchair, and it turned out to be a young girl who was about 13yrs old, and who lived just opposite us in our street, and her family were friends of our family, well, everybody knew everybody else in those days, anyway, AVRIL was her name, she used to come home from school, and offer to take me for walks, which my mother was probably only too glad to get rid of me for a while, as evidently I was a bit of a handful to be stuck with all day long!, Actually AVRIL grew up to be a rather skinny, and unattractive woman as I recall, even when I was over twenty years of age she was still single, and hadn't met her man or settled down, but never the less the memory of when she was 14 yrs old, and I was in a pushchair will always stay with me, and I will always be grateful for the feelings which she was the first to stir up in me.

Perhaps now would b e the time to establish a little groundwork and facts to put you in the picture as to my background, and my recollections of my infancy and youth. Well to start with I was born on the 7th of July 1934, in a city which was famous for engineering and car manufacturing, and still is of course, Coventry. We lived in the Stoke area of the city, along the WALSGRAVE ROAD on Ball Hill, and as a family we were working class, and like all working class families in those days things were not always cosy or easy. Our house was a two up and two down in a row of terraced houses with a small garden. The houses were back to back in a terraced street, with an alley way along the backs of them. Life was very communal in those days, everybody knew everyone else, and people lived and died in their little terraced houses, and the biggest majority of them were rented from landlords. Families seemed to have 2 or 3 children, who would eventually grow up and leave home. But the parents would still live and eventually die in the same house. I say communal life existed as everyone seemed to know every other ones personnel business, not that it really mattered. As people didn't have a lot to hide anyway!. The communal life, sadly, seems to have vanished nowadays, or dying out.

I can recall those long hot summers when in the evenings practically the whole street would bring out their tables and chairs, and sit outside on the pavement in the front of their houses in the cool of the evening. Just sitting there, talking and gossiping with each other, then perhaps someone would bring out the old crank up gramophone, and some of the Dads would go down to the outdoor beer shop, and fetch some jugs of beer whist us kids played in the street, and the younger ones were probably asleep on their Mothers laps. Everyone would be out there until quite late, and the gas street lights would come on, and if it was payday, there would perhaps be some pie and mash, or faggots and peas from the corner shop, but you had to take your own dish!. My brother and I, who was a few years older than myself, and to whom I shall refer to from now on, as 'our kid', used to love those times, and we often talked about them when we met up in later years. Those pre-war days of patriotic family minded people unfortunately seem to be gone forever, a sadness which today's generations would benefit from.

My brother, Les, (our kid) was 5 years older than myself, and I think he hated me when we were young, as when I was probably 4-5 yrs old, and he would be around 10, and out with his mates, Mum used to say. "Now take Ray,(ME), with you, and look after him, and he would go "oh no Mum"

3

and moan that when I tag along with them, I would invariably mess my pants or something, and that I was a cry baby, I used to love going along with them though, it made me feel grown up, but it wasn't all that long afterwards before I had a gang of my own, yes, we grew up very quickly in those days, I suppose it was because we were war babies, as I was only 5 when war broke out, but more about the war later

My mother was the strong personality in the family, a Matriarch if you like, a devoted, strong, loyal person, who made do with very little money, but always managed to keep a full table, a clean tidy house, always warm with an open fire and grate, a big black metal thing, with a little oven type thing to keep things warm on each side. It was one of my jobs to black lead it once a week, you had a tin of what looked like black boot polish, and you brushed it on all over the metal parts of the grate

Mum was a strict disciplinarian, a few hefty smacks around the legs, or a clip around the ear saw to that!, but never the less a very warm and loving person when needed, and as practical as they come, plus being a very morally minded person, the first one you would run to if you had a problem. I wonder what she would think of me now, one thing for sure, she can be very proud of what she did and achieved in her life.

My Father was rather a quiet, take it as it comes sort of person, sometimes living in a world of his own, and never very talkative, a person of few words, but like my Mother a strict disciplinarian in a quiet strong way. If ever our Kid or I did anything wrong, or tried to talk back, he only had to reach for the belt on his trousers, which was a thick leather one with a huge brass buckle, and we would run a mile! But he never did actually take it off, as there no need to, we were gone!!. It was strange as he wore bracers, plus that thick leather belt ? I'm sure Mum and Dad used to laugh after we had done a bunk. Our Kid and I often used to laugh about that when we met up.

My Father served in the first world war as a aircraft mechanic, and he was very clever with his hands, He had his little workshop at the bottom of the garden, his shed, and he would spend hours in there making or repairing things, it was his little retreat and he didn't like to be disturbed, except if Mum took him a cup of tea sometimes, also woe betide anyone who touched his tools, he used to keep the shed padlocked, but I used to unscrew the hasp on the padlock if I wanted to used any of his tools, but

4

I really had to make sure I put everything back in its right place. Exactly as it was. I never did know what rank he held in the ROYAL FLYING CORPS as it was called in those days, also I am not sure whether or not he served in France, he never talked about the war, and if we asked him, Mum would say," now don't bother your Father" so we didn't. As I recall, my Father was sort of two people in one, As I have said, he was clever with his hands, he was a toolmaker, machine setter, and operator at one of the large engineering factories in the town, which was near the Cathedral, that factory played a big part in our lives during the 2nd world war, as I will explain later. As I've said he was a toolmaker, and the pride of his life was his box of instruments which he used for setting up machines. It was a highly polished Walnut case, like an attaché case, about 2ft square, and the inside was lined with purple velvet, and every instrument had its own recess to fit exactly into, it must have been worth a fortune, if ever he bought it home, you had to have special permission to look inside it, but not allowed to touch anything. It used to fascinate me, Sometimes when Dad came home from work in the evenings, I would wait for him at the end of the street, and he would let me sit on the saddle of his bike, and he would push me up the street as I steered it, then up the alley, and round to the back of the house, as I have said he was sort of two people, sometimes he was kind and thoughtful and I could feel close to him, yet other times his mood would change if something upset him, perhaps at work or something, Mum and Dad never had words, or arguments, so it probably was something to do with work, or the war. He would then retreat into himself, and shut himself off from the world to the extent he would lock himself in his shed, and mend or repair something. Either that or he would shut himself in the front room and you daren't talk to him, as you wouldn't get any reply probably, Mum would just say "leave your Dad alone, he just wants to quiet for a while" and she would take his meals into him. And when he went out, he would leave little notes for Mum. It never seemed to bother her though, she just carried on as normal. We grew up used to it I suppose, and Mum knew he would come around after a while

I sometimes wondered whether it was something to do with the war years, both the first world war, and perhaps something he experienced at that time, or the 2nd world war, and what people went through on the home front, during the Blitz. Our Kid and I used to discuss it when we met up in our later years, nowadays it's called Post Traumatic Stress. It would explain some of Dads moods.

Our kid and I used to fight when we were younger, but as we grew older there was always an understanding and comradeship between us, and that remained with us throughout our lives, and he was always my best friend, someone I could always confide in, even very personnel things, knowing he would listen, and give good advice if needed, it worked both ways as well. When we both grew up, and moved. I moved to another town, about 40 miles away, but I always went to see him once a month, and we would go and have a few beers, and a good chin wag, and catch up on the latest happenings to ourselves and our love lives, and have a dam good laugh until usually tears would be streaming down our faces. We used to save up all the jokes to tell each other when we met up. I likened a visit to see our Kid as a sort of relief valve when you were living some sort of pressurised life as I was sometimes., but going over to see him, and relaxing for a few hours in his company,it seemed to drain out of me, and as I drove home in the early hours, I felt a tremendous sense of relief and inward satisfaction. They say it does you good to get things of your chest now and again, and our Kids company, and his big ears seemed to do that for me. Oh yes, he had big ears !!

Now our Kid, as I remember him in childhood, was the brainy one in the family, he was good academically at school, a bit of a egg head in some respects, very clever with his hands, chemistry, modelling, handicrafts, metal work, you name it,he had a flair for it, When he started work at 14, he worked in a tool shop, making all sorts of things, he was a good welder so I was told and well advanced for his years, and could work without supervision, and follow drawings quite easily, as he was tall, he looked older than he was.

Anyway, came the winter of 1947, and it was the winter of all winters as far as we were concerned, the city came to a standstill completely, the snow that had fallen for days was up to the level of the bedroom windows in our street. You opened up your front door to a wall of snow and we were trapped in the houses. Dad hadn't gone to work obviously, so we fetched the tin bath which fortunately was in the kitchen, and not in its usual place hanging on the wall in the yard, and began to shovel the snow into it, and tunnel our way out of the front door, then chucking it out of the back door as best we could. We made a tunnel about 4ft high and just wide enough to squeeze through heading straight out into the middle of the road as we could hear voices and machines going. What evidently was happening was that the services, I am not quite sure whether it was the fire brigade or the council that had cleared a tunnel right up the centre of the street, and were then starting to tunnel in towards the houses one by one, well by this time we had managed to dig our way out to them, and most people were doing the same thing, it was all great fun, and of course no school!.We then widened our tunnel so that you could walk through it. The whole street was like a maze of rabbit warrens, and there wasn't a thaw happening so the snow froze hard, so it was around for quite, some time, Even though they were tunnels it was quite light inside them. You passed your friends and neighbours either on the way to the shops or work or to school, which sadly had opened again. The snow must have been 17 to 20ft deep all the way down the street onto the main road at the bottom.

Can you imagine a wall of snow at the end of the street with tunnels in it, and people coming and going in and out like rabbits in a warren, We didn't go to school at first, and we helped with the tunnelling to the houses where probably older people lived, and we would go and do their shopping for them, which of course earned us a few bob!. So it was great fun whilst it lasted.

Anyway back to our clever kid, he went to work as usual as it was only a street away, but evidently most of the other workers hadn't come in, so there was nothing doing, so our kid asked his boss if he could make a sledge out of all the scrap metal that was lying around, he was nearly 17 by this time, and I think the boss just wanted to keep the workshop open to stop every freezing up, so he said yes. Now our kid produced the sledge of all sledges, we were the envy of all the kids from miles around, it was huge, about 10ft long and 2ft wide, the frame was made of steel with beautiful shiny runners, and it had pivot steering front runners, and wooden seating all along, at the back were two pushing bars where the biggest kid would be the start runner, and then jump on. If he was quick enough! You could get 6 or 7 kids on at a time, all sitting in each others laps, clutching the one in front of you around the neck or waist, it was truly awesome!,

Now our street was a long hill, which went down the hill to a T junction at the bottom, which was also a hill coming from the right down to the left, so our sledge path would be straight down our hill, a sharp turn to the left, which continued downhill but at the end of that hill was another T junction, but that was a main road! The run was great for sledging and trolleys and prams. It was about a 1 in 7 slope so hair blowing speeds were reached quite easily. The trouble was stopping, now the idea was that if you reached the end of the last hill onto the main road, without any accidents, and not losing too many bodies flying off, you had to try your hardest to turn left as the main rd slopped upwards at that point, and that would help to slow you down, and hopefully stop you before you all got hit by a bus or lorry! I would imagine that all the turns we made would be around about 3 to 4 G.

Now by the time our kid had finished the monster sledge, the snow had compacted down and frozen, so it was ideal for sledging. The complete run was about a hundred yards or more. The Christening run of the sledge had to be kept secret, as none of our parents would let anyone on that sledge if they saw it, so it was arranged for after school one afternoon, Dads would still be at work, and Mums would be busy in the kitchens getting tea. I picked the 6 kids we would start with, The biggest lad would be the pusher, starter, he was a bit dim, but big and strong, I had to keep reminding him not to forget to jump on when we got going!. Anyway our kid pulled the sledge from his works and up the hill to the start, he would be too tall to get on it, so he said cheerfully he would go to the end of the run to pick up the pieces afterwards. The word had gotten around and loads of other kids turned up to watch. I had told the kids on the sledge, and as instructed, had turned up and padded their coats, and wrapped scarves around their knees and elbows, and also balaclavas on their heads. We all sat in our places, me at the front as I was going to do the steering, I shouted o.k. and the big lump at the back started pushing, and our kid decided to help him, not that it needed any help as it started to move quite quickly right from the start. I didn't know until afterwards that our kid had rubbed some wax onto the runners, because he thought that that was what you did, so within a few yards we were already going quite fast. Big un at the back only just managed to get on, with a hefty shove from our kid, even then he was only kneeling on the back. By the time we reached the first left hand turn we were going really fast, I had pulled over to the right going down so that I didn't have to turn too sharply, but even then

I thought the sledge was going to turn over. it would not have been very pleasant at that speed to land on frozen ice. Never the less as we slewed around the corner the sledge felt a little lighter, and I saw why, as big lump from the back came sliding came sliding past us on his backside, and into the gutter!, Ah! well, he'll perhaps learn next time to jump on properly, and there was a next time for him, and the next and the next, he said afterwards he loved it, even though it tore a great hole in the arse of his trousers. We were now approaching the main road and to turn left and hoping the upward slope would eventually slow us down before we hit any buses or trucks coming down, so that we could all jump off and make a run for it back. I pulled over to the right again so as to get a broader sweep around the corner, and the Gods were with us, as the roads were so icy there wasn't much traffic, the turn was a bit sharp, as we deposited a couple of the younger ones across the road. I did tell them to hang on tight, after about 20yrds we slowed down and stopped, mind you we were nearly in the middle of a main road, and traffic was coming the hill on the other side. One lorry driver was shaking his fist at us as he went past us only a couple of yards away. We quickly grabbed the sledge and ran back around the corner, and back up to our starting point, after scraping big un of the ice!

It's funny but no one wanted a second go at that time, mind you I don't blame them really, must get some sort of brake system fitted, or we are going to kill ourselves!. Of course our kid sorted that out, he fitted a cantilever arm on each side of the frame, and when you pulled them up. They dug into the snow, but you had to pull them up at the same time, because if only one dug in, it would slew you around sharply, and tip you and the sledge over, as one kid with a broken wrist found out!

We had some tremendous fun with that sledge, and when the snow had gone. Our kid converted it into a trolley with 8 pram wheels on it. Then when the snow came back again, back it went into a sledge. We did some daft things with that sledge/trolley, and the speeds we used to achieve in it were frightening. It lasted a couple of years, until one winter we took it to a local park and smashed it up going down a massive slope that nobody else dare go down, we did, but a large tree stopped us near the bottom, only a couple of broken bones though !. But we won the admiration of all the kids for miles around. A real hero was our kid, and everyone from then on called our gang. the Villiers St Vipers, Our kid at that time was about seventeen and a half, and 6 months after that he would be due to be called up for his National Service stint. But he wanted to go in the Navy,so to make sure he did, he and his best mate Alan, who lived opposite us, who was also due to be called up,as they were both the same age, only a few days apart, to ensure they both went into the Navy. and not wait to be called up, and shoved into any of the services, they both decided to enrol in the Navy, and for 7yrs years !!!. Mum and Dad thought they were both mad, but it's what they wanted, The trades they Wanted to go into were Stoker Mechanics, which basically meant engine mechanics, well after their basic training, they both loved the life, and strangely they both went through the whole 7 yrs without being separated, both went together if they changed ships and also abroad,. They both finished up on Motor Torpedo boats out in the Far East. When they were both demobbed and came home, their one regret was that due to the fact that the Navy were selling off some of the Motor Torpedo boats, that they never bought one as some did, because as they were the fastest things on water, some were being used for gun running in and around the Middle East!, and making a fortune doing it, so they regretted not buying one. One thing that always stuck in my mind was that when he used to come home on leave, I was the one who used to press his Bell bottom trousers. I was quite good at it actually, Mum taught me. On the trousers there had to be 7 creases on each trouser leg, spaced out sideways down the leg, it represented the 7 seas, a Navy tradition. Another tradition he told me about was the daily Rum ration when at sea, called 'Grog'. A bell would ring on ship, I think it was twice a day, 11am & 6pm, I think?. When the sun sets over the yard arm, as they say, then the cry of 'Spirits Up,' would go out, then you queued up on the deck, and a Tot of Rum was poured into your mug, very strong stuff, but it was watered down, simply to keep you sober, also in case you tried to save it as it didn't keep if it was mixed with water!, there was also Nutmeg and Lime mixed in with it, and that's where you get the saying 'Limeys' for British people, because of the lime, which in the old sailing days prevented Scurvy.

Well I think it's now about time to fill you in with regard to my School days as I remember them... For a start, I hated school!!! Right from the very first day I used to lead my Mum a hell of a dance with regard to schooling. So when I reached the tender age of 4, I was informed that I would be starting school, I know my Brother went off somewhere every morning but I didn't realize where, until Mum said he goes to school, the same as I will have to do, but I still didn't think it actually referred to me as I was quite content with life at home, and in the street, and garden. The year would be 1938, about 18 months before the beginning of World War 11

Now I suppose I should have been aware of something going on, because I was beginning to be fitted with some of our kids hand me down clothes that obviously needed altering as he was now 9. I know the shorts were a bit baggy, and his shirts and jumpers came down to my knees, and also his boots had paper stuffed up them, not only because they were a bit big, but because there was a hole in them as well1. I always seemed to have a permanent wet right sock, until finally my Dad found an old car tyre and cut it up, and stuck a piece of it over the hole on the right boot, the rubber was a bit thick as it made me walk with a bit of a limp, and it used to make a 'clod clod' sound as I walked, but woe betide anyone who laughed at me. Now whilst this was going on I was sort of brain washed about going to school, 'it'll be exciting with all the other kids, and all the games you can play, and you can have your dinner there as well', even our kid joined in as well, telling me how good it will be. Mind you when I did start school, 'our kid' completely blanked me as he didn't want anyone to know that I was his little brother, especially a brother like me, and truthfully on reflection. You couldn't blame him. It wasn't until I went up into the seniors that he finally acknowledged me, The school that I was to attend was about 15 minutes walk away, it was called Britten Road School, there was the Infants part, mixed, then the girls junior and senior part, and then the boys junior and senior section, they were all in the same ground but separated by walls and fencing. It was a large School, the boys section had about 12 classrooms placed around a huge playground, and a large assembly hall, plus carpentry and metal workshops.

Well my first day of starting school finally arrived, but I didn't feel like going so I said No, I say my first day of starting, but I didn't actually start, and saying No was the wrong thing to say evidently, "You're going to school whether you like it or not" Mum shouted. Now my Mum was quite a big woman, so when she grabbed you, you were grabbed!, she half carried and dragged me along the street with me screaming and yelling. I don't know what the neighbours thought, one or two came out to see what all the noise was about, but when they saw me and Mum they just smiled, another ones first day at school!!, a bit noisy that one. Well I was dragged all the way right into the Infants School hall, where I was confronted by the headmistress of the Infants. I took an instant dislike to her, she seemed about 9ft tall, dressed all in black with her hair tied up into a bun, and her mouth went up in one corner as if she was sneering, she probably was when she saw me. (It's amazing how I can still remember these things in such detail). Poor old Mum was trying to explain to her that I was just a little bit frightened being away from home, and coming to somewhere strange, and that I would settle down in a little while, whilst at the same time hold ing my arms pinned behind my back, and me trying to bite her other hand which was firmly clasped over my mouth. Not on your life I thought, because I firmly thought that at that time, Mum was trying to give me away to this monster woman, mind you, giving me away to any one had probably crossed her mind many times before!. Especially as her grip on me relaxed a little bit, and I saw my chance as the woman in black was within striking distance, so I planted the toe of my big boot into the shin of the woman who I thought was going to take me away, During the ensuing screams and profuse apologies from my Mother, I struggled free and was up and out of that hall, and up the street like a dose of salts!, but alas, 2 hours later, when Mum came home and found me hiding in the back garden in the privet hedge, she knew all of my hiding places Mum did.

So I was dragged back once again, and by this time all of the other kids had been allocated their teachers and classrooms. I didn't actually see the Headmistress the second time, I know the next time I did I noticed she had a large plaster on her shin, and I never did have any further contact with her again. Then I was taken, or rather dragged to my allotted classroom and teacher. My teachers name was Miss Minns. To me she looked even older than my Grandmother. She was. I must admit a was very kind old lady, and I didn't quite mind her so much, but she still represented an alien authority which I was not used to. Well I was at the tender age of 4, and having only known any form of discipline administered by either Mum or Dad, and the occasional thump from our kid, suddenly being subject to the quite frequent clip of the ear from this very old and tiny woman, it's a wonder it didn't turn me for life!!.

Life I suppose in the infant school was bearable at times, although Mum still had to either chase or drag me to school brandishing a copper stick if I decided I didn't fancy going that particular day. We used to have some marvellous chases through the streets and alleyways, I thought I knew them all, but Mum knew more than I, she could ambush me sometimes when I had done a bunk, she would catch me and drag me back to school, into the classroom, and bang me down on my chair" "now stay there" apologise to Miss Minn, and then leave, but more often than not I would be hiding behind the shed when she got back home, as I had just left the classroom when she left, and gotten back home before her by using back alleys, and side streets, and off we would go again on the same routine, Mum shouting after me" just you wait until your Dad gets home" my God I used to think, is it all worth it, but I still hated school, and a good smack on the head from Dad didn't alter that fact. Many, many years later when Mum and Dad were still alive and I used to go over and visit them, on one visit I went down to the shops on the main rd, Ball Hill, when this old lady came up to me, a complete stranger, and she said "I recognise your face" and that she could remember that when I was a little lad, I used to run past her house sometimes with your Mother chasing you in hot pursuit waving a copper stick and trying to get you to school she guessed, and she used to laugh at our antics. I thought that was amazing after all those years she could remember me, recognise me, still, once seen, never forgotten I suppose! I told Mum and Dad and they both laughed.

The other kids in the class were a mixed bunch, most of the them coming from working class families in the district, one or two from the more better residential areas. You could always pick them out from the clothes that they wore, the posh kids in their clean smart clothes, and the girls in pretty dresses, us common kids in thick flannel shirts and holy jumpers, big boots, sometimes no socks, grey shorts, more often than not, with the arse hanging out, and I finally got rid of my boots with the 'clod clod,' right boot, somebody in our street must have felt sorry for me, either that or they couldn't stand the 'clod clod' as I walked past their house, anyway they gave Mum a nice pair of boots that their son had worn but were too small for him now, and they fitted perfectly, I had to get used to them though, they felt so light, and also I had to get used to not limping and no noise. The other kids in the class were o.k. though, there was never any of the Them & Us thing, the other kids thought it was hilarious the antics I used to get up to with my Mum, there were about 11 girls in the class, but I never had time for girls, they interested me though, I suppose it was because they were different, and I would rather be seen dead than play with them. I used to get invited to girls birthday parties, but I would never go, I didn't want to be classed as a sissy, anyway who played about with girls, besides I was nearly 5 by then so getting grown up.!

After about a year in the infants, the year was 1939 and war broke out, it never really affected us to start with as nothing seemed to change, I think that period was called the phoney war, as nothing seemed to be happening, with the exception that all the kids were issued with gas masks in little cardboard boxes with a string strap which you slung over your shoulder and which you had to carry at all times, supposedly! They were funny little things and they looked like monkey masks. I hated the dam things. We used to have air drill every so often. When the bell sounded we all had to put on our gas masks, and file out of class into the main hall and sit on the floor, God knows why we had to congregate and sit on the floor for, but there were no air raid shelters at that time, but if we had had an air raid, one hit on the school and we would have all been sitting ducks with about 250 kids just sitting on the floor all wearing gas masks with nowhere else to go. It was quite a long time before any shelters were built in the school grounds. But by that time the bombings had begun., so there wasn't a lot of schooling taking place. Which obviously pleased me!

Around December 39' and in the early months of 1940 the raids were few and far between, you could hear the bombs going off, and see the fires in the distance. As our house was on the top of a hill and you could look out and see all the centre of Coventry with the 3 spires, one of the cathedral and the two churches either side, Coventry was known as the 3 spires city. Also in early 1940 it was decided that all children should be evacuated, now me and our kid didn't know what that meant, so Mum and Dad explained that because of the increase in the bombings they didn't want us to get hurt, so it would be best if we went away somewhere where it would be safer, it would mean a nice holiday somewhere in the countryside where there are no air raids, and we would be staying with some nice people, and get to see lots of farm animals, and also perhaps help on the farms and make lots of new friends. Mum and Dad wouldn't be able to go as they would have to stay and look after the house, but they will come and see us regularly, and it shouldn't be for long anyway. It all seemed very strange, and our kid and I mulled it over for a few days, and also all the other kids at school, also my gang, had been told also, so it was quite a big talking point. Now I didn't want to go, and our kid I would say that, but he said it would be fun. He tried to talk me around by saying 'Yippee' no more school, and going on holiday which was something we hadn't had for a long time. So then initially I began to warm to the idea of a short break from school which was the best part as I still hated school, so we thought we would just wait and see what happens, Talking about air raids, one incident that I remember happening before we were evacuated was when Mum and Aunt Nell went to the cinema in town to see a film called 'Gone with the wind' at the Rex, They went to an afternoon matinee, but that evening there was an air raid and the cinema got a direct hit before people could get out to the shelters. The cinema was destroyed, and a lot of people were killed, and Mum and Aunt Nell had only been in there a few hours before, so, soon things began to happen a little bit more quickly now.

Of course Coventry obviously was going to be a prime target for the German bombs, as it was a large manufacturing city with companies such as Daimler, Dunlop, G.E.C, Humber- Roots, plus Armstrong Whitworth, which all had turned to making machines and aircraft, and all the lots of Engineering companies that manufactured munitions. The factory where Dad worked was the called' Rudge', they made motor cycles for the forces, and half of the factory made bombs, The trouble was the factory was right in the middle of the town centre near the cathedral, it was a huge building, and it had a maze of deep underground cellars which were converted into air raid shelters for the families of the people who worked there, but more about that later, Well the day finally came for our evacuation, we said goodbye to Dad when he went to work, then picked up our little cardboard suitcases, tied up with string, which had been packed by our Mum, plus a bag of sandwiches, and off we went to the school playground. Outside the school in the road were a line of chara-bangs(coaches). Mum gave someone holding a clipboard, our names, and he pinned a big label on to our coats. I must say that by this time I was beginning to feel a little bit apprehensive about going and started playing up a bit, and 'our kid' said that did he have to go with me as he knew I would probably be a nightmare!, but

Mum said he'd got to look after me. He seemed quite happy about going away to the countryside. Anyway we were sorted into groups as to where we were going, and which coach to get onto. Mum got on and sorted our seats out, then gave us both a big hug, and said they would come and see us next weekend, she got off the bus, and I started crying and tried to get off the bus as well, so Mum had to get back on, and drag me back to my seat, and told 'our kid' to sit on me if necessary, but he said he didn't want to sit next to me, but Mum threatened him, quietly, so he shut up. Our bus, so we were told was heading for a place called Bishop Itchington, which I later learnt was about 20 or 30 miles from Coventry in the middle of the countryside. I thought at that time that it was at the other ends of the earth. I hated bus rides anyway as i was always sock, our kid' knew that too, so he tried to sit as far away from me as possible, but he was pulled back and forced to sit next to me, and I started to cry again. I mean try to imagine, what it was like for us kids, to suddenly be uprooted from home life and sent off to somewhere for reasons you didn't quite understand at the time. Farmed out to a strange family in another part the big world or so it seemed. The mass exodus of children from the big cities must have been a mammoth task to organise and undertake.

So the engine started up on the bus, and all the kids started shouting and waving to their parents, 'our kid' had hold of my leg because I was trying to climb out of the window. I could see Mum waving, but she was also crying, which didn't make me feel any better. The bus started to move off so I ran to the back window just to look back at all the people standing in the middle of the road waving at us until we turned the corner and they were gone. So here we were on the way to a new life of no one knew what.!!!. but only temporary I hoped, well maybe I could make it so, we'll see.

We had only been going for about half an hour, and I was sick, I hate buses, it must be the smell of oil or the fumes that do it, bit Mum had prepared 'our kid' for that eventuality and given him some brown paper bags, knowing me as she did. After a while we decided to eat our sandwiches, but I was sick again, and had also 'weed' myself. I think if the door had been open, our kid' would have thrown me through it. It must have been one of those frequent when 'our kid' wished that he didn't have a brother.

After what seemed like hours of travelling we finally arrived at the little village of Bishop Itchington, we drove along the narrow lanes with cottages on either side with some farm buildings, and finally to the village green where the bus stopped. Now the village green was about half the size of a football field with cottages on two sides and the church on the other, next to the church was the village hall, and on the other side was the school. All the cottages had nicely well kept gardens at the front and little gates, There were two lanes leading of from the green, down one of them there were 4 council type houses, and the other lane led to the fields, and the country side, just along this lane were 3 cottages at right angles to the lane with a path along the front of them, and then long gardens in front. The population of the village was about 400, I think.

We all trundled off the bus, about 39 of us in all, I must have looked a pretty sight to anyone prepared to take me into their homes, having thrown up onto my jacket, plus wet steaming trousers!, I wondered why 'our kid' wasn't standing near me, still I didn't care, as they can send me back home as soon as they wish, no such luck though, we were all bundled into the church rooms where were told to sit on the rows of chairs, then we were given a glass of milk each and a cake, and there we all sat looking lost and lonely I suppose, a few tears coming from some who were frightened and wondering what happens next.

Then suddenly lots of adults began to arrive in the hall, and they were walking up and down the isles between the rows of chairs looking at us kids, then one of them would grab a kid, or a pair of them if they were together, like me and 'our kid', who by the way was sitting as far away from me as possible, then 'sign' them out and then take them,presumably, home with them. And as the room began to empty, ' our kid' was told to go and sit with his younger Brother, as these bizarre proceedings continued I began to realize that it was first come first served, get there early and pick the best of the bunch, it was like a cattle auction, Well, after about an hour all the kids and adults Had gone, and guess who we're the only two left! yes, me and 'our kid'. Well he did have a chance earlier on, a woman looked at him when he was sitting on his own, and said "I will take this one" but 'our kid' said "my little brother has to come as well" That blew that one didn't it, and he lost his chance to get rid of me, as she took one look at me, and walked out, plus the fact that if I was the only one left, and nobody wanted me, maybe I could probably be sent back home. Another lost opportunity, After a while with no one else coming in, the organizers sat in a huddle in the corner, wondering what to do with us two lads sitting in the middle of the hall on their own, they kept muttering and glancing over at us. 'Our kid' was now sitting a few chairs away from me by this time, because I was smelling he said! Then the door opened, and in came this old couple, an old lady with grey hair, and an old man wearing a tweed jacket, and flat cap,. They went over to the organizers, and some mutterings went on, and finally the couple came over to us, and said" come along boys you're coming along with us". So we picked up our cardboard suitcases, tied up with string, and off we went, probably to a huge sigh of relief from the organizers.

They led us over the green, and down one of the lanes about 50 yards to one of the thatched roof cottages, theirs was the end one. The side of the cottage faced onto the fields, and then a wall down the side of the garden ending at another wall, but this was a very high one, the cottages looked very quaint, and the long garden at the front was very neatly laid out with flower beds and a vegetable patch, and all sorts of fruit trees and bushes, gooseberry, strawberry, raspberry, we had never seen such fruit because of the rationing back home, at least one thing was a bonus!. I could hear pigs grunting on the other side of the high wall, and there was a well up against the wall with a large wooden cover on it, I will have a look over that wall at some time, and see what's over there. Inside the cottage it was very warm and cosy, an open wood fire, with a range, comfortable furniture, with the usual brick- a -brack on the shelves, and of course a picture of 'a Stag at bay' on the wall, also a mounted Foxes head and tail. It was a two up and two down, very small rooms though, there was an outside loo, we had a jerry at nights which had to be emptied in the mornings, there was running water in the kitchen, only cold, and a large stone sink, and stone floors throughout. A narrow flight of stairs to the bedrooms with very low ceilings, and a window which looks out onto the front garden, but I couldn't quite see over the high wall at the end, but you still heard pigs grunting and sometimes squealing, but I will investigate that at a later date.

Our newly adopted parents, as I said, were quite old, and kind I suppose and willing to please and make us feel welcome in their home, and after I had a wash and changed clothes I didn't look too bad to them also,. I cannot quite picture their faces now after all these years as it turned out, as we were only with them for apparently for a short time owing to me, as I later found out, but they were a typical pair of country folk, quiet and homely, so what a situation to put me into knowing how I behaved in those days!. I remember the food was good, and she baked lovely cakes, and plenty of homemade jam. The gooseberry was my favourite also real butter and fresh cream, there always seemed to be plenty of things that back home were becoming scarcer and scarcer. The only things that were too plentiful l were the vegetables. I hated vegetables! And my plate at mealtimes was always piled high with them, and I was always being told off if I didn't eat them, and if I didn't eat them, I wouldn't get any pudding or jam and cake afterwards. I tried to devise a way of sneaking vegetables into it, but I missed the bag, and it went all over my shirt and trousers, and onto the floor. So I tried my best my best, but it put me off vegetables for years to come!

The first night there I know I cried myself to sleep, and kept calling out for Mum, and the old lady tried her best to comfort me, and reassure me that everything would be alright, that I wouldn't be away from home for long, also we would be seeing Mum and Dad at weekends, but weekends seemed so far away, and I had to get through the week days first.

The next morning 'our kid' and I awoke very early to the unusual sounds of the countryside, the birds seemed really noisy, and I could hear cows mooing, and pigs grunting from over the high wall, (must try and have a look over that wall sometime). Also somewhere in the distance the sound of a tractor I guess, all strange sounds for us city lads. So I was up and dressed and down stairs to the kitchen, where the old lady was busying herself lighting the fire in the range, 'our kid' was still upstairs getting dressed and sorting out our clothes from the suitcases, and putting them away in the drawers of a very antique dresser, on top of which was a very large bowl and jug of water, where we were supposed to wash in the mornings. I couldn't be bothered with that today as there was far too much to see and explore on the first day, also we didn't have to go to school on our first day here, so I had the whole day to do it in! So before breakfast was ready I went out to see what the garden was all about, and also what was bugging my curiosity was again, what was behind that wall at the end of the garden? As I have described before, there was a path outside the front door, then a fence and a gate which led into the garden, then a path which led through the garden right up to the high wall and well at the end. I described earlier about the contents of the garden, but now I could see things in more detail, there were vegetables of all sorts all in neat rows, and obviously very carefully tended, also there were the wonderful fruits of all varieties, which I had only ever seen in shop windows before, Raspberries, Strawberries, Black and Red currants, Gooseberries, Apples and Pear trees against the wall, all carefully wired and tied into the wall, espalier, I think they are called, now I know I hadn't had my breakfast as yet, but the things were so tempting I couldn't resist sampling one or two, and proceeded to do so. Which is when I received my first telling off, not knowing that these particular Raspberries, and Strawberries, and indeed most of the garden fruits, and produce, were being carefully nurtured to enter into some country show, and were the old couples pride and joy as they had won many prises before. Well how was I to know!!

So having worked my way along the garden, sampling as I went, I came up to the stone wall, as I did so, I remember that above the grunting of the pigs came this sickening scream which made the hairs on the back of my neck stand up. I ran back into the cottage quite smartly. I wanted to ask what the scream was, but the old dears face had a look of horror, or anger, I don't know which, when she first saw me, there was I, all colours of the rainbow, and all over my face and shirt front. She called to her husband who was out the back, he came in, took one look at me and rushed out the front door. I guess it was to check on any damage I had done to his prize fruit and vegetables. ' our kid' came downstairs wondering what all the fuss was about, he saw me and just said "Oh no!!", just then the old boy came back in muttering and spluttering, and went straight out the back, then came back in carrying some garden tools, still muttering and spluttering and back out the front obviously not very happy!, he didn't speak to me for a few days after that! Also I got a smack on the head from 'our kid'. So that was my first telling off, but being used to being told off, water off a ducks back, as they say !, Anyway, evidently the old boy managed to salvage most of the stuff in the garden, I don't Know what all the fuss was about, you grow stuff to eat don't you?. Also, I was determined to find out what that squealing was.

So as 'our kid' and I had the day to our selves, and he knew anyway that he would be stuck with me, we decided to have a look around the village, all the village kids were in school of course. The lane we were in led down to a gate, and then the fields beyond that with the usual sheep and horses, and a tractor working away somewhere. It wasn't as if 'our kid ' and I weren't used to country life being 'Townies' because we had an Uncle Walter, who at that time had a small farm on the edge of Coventry, it was called '7 fields farm' because you had to cross 7 fields to get to it. It only had a single track leading to it, but that went out the other side of the farm to god knows where! So if ever we went visiting, we had to catch a bus to where the 7 fields began, and then walk the rest of the way, I know we didn't go all that often because of this, but when we did I used to enjoy mucking about around the farm. As we grew older I remember Uncle Walter sold the farm, and bought a small holding nearer to Coventry, near Whitley Abbey to be exact,but more about that later.

So we went just walking around the village, taking it all in, we met some of the other evacuees, and exchanged stories about our first night away from home, some were quite happy, others not, and 'our kid' just had to tell everyone that I cried in bed last night, but we all agreed that us 'Townies' should stick together as we hadn't as yet met any of the village kids, also we had some curious looks from some of the adults as well, some smiled at us, some just stared as if we were from another planet, but I suppose it was strange for them also, suddenly their village life interrupted by a gang of kids from nowhere. They probably didn't know there was a war going on anyway.

As we were talking to the other 'Townies', the village kids started to come out of school, first the little ones whose parents had come to meet them out, then the older ones. I would say the school held about 40 kids in all, out of that, the older ones numbered around 15, aged around 10 and up. Just then a tractor came down the road and a boy jumped on it, and off down the lane, a novel way for a lift home. The others just stood and looked at us Townies, then one of them shouted "cry babies", I think one of lot had been billeted with a family, and had cried when they were in bed last night, the same as I did I suppose. ' Our kid' who was 10 yrs old now, and quite big for his age, and another lad from our lot, went over to the village lot, and told them to 'shut it, or else,' this sort of shocked them a bit, they obviously had never had anything to do with outsiders before, but one of them, a girl, I think it was a girl, about 13, big, horses teeth, and built like the side of a barn, probably the village kids leader, came over and said to 'our kid', "and who said so" well he looked her straight in the eye close up, and said "I do". Well that set the pattern for the rest of our stay there, a good thing that it turned to just a short stay for me and our kid, So from then on it was them and us, There were fights and rumbles on the village green, but we were street kids, and were street wise, o.k. they threw stones at us, but we threw bottles, and we had catapults, also we made mud balls and put a stone in the middle, stuck it on the end of a flexible stick off a tree or a bush, swish it back and whip it forward and the ball of mud would fly off the end like bullet, the younger ones of our lot used to run up and keep us at the front supplied with the ammo. I know I was only 6 then, but I had been street wise for some time, you grew up quickly in those days! The street rumbles used to take place at night mostly, they didn't last long though before the old village Bobby would come tearing down on his bike, the 'Swedes' as we used to call the village kids would scarper And then the Bobby would just say to us, "oh, it's you lot again is it, just clear off." Mind you not all the village 'Swedes' were hostile, I know, because I got friendly with a girl at the school, who was the same age as me, her name was Rosie, and sometimes,after school we would down the lane, and out onto the fields, and she used to keep asking me what life was like in the big cities, she was an only child, and her parents were quite nice also, sometimes I was asked to stay to tea, and sometimes she would come back with me to our cottage for tea, and the old lady would put on a lovely spread foe us, and make quite a fuss of her. Sometime we would catch a bus up to the next village, called Long Itchington, where she had an Aunt, it was about 8 or 10 miles away, where we would spend the day, and stay for tea, so it wasn't all grief and war. I often wondered how she faired later on in life, Now let me tell you about an incident that scared me for life. One Saturday morning I got up fairly early, dressed,and went down for breakfast, a lovely breakfast on Saturday mornings, a glass of warm full cream milk, a boiled egg, and bread and butter soldiers, real butter, then toast and home made marmalade, 'our kid' and I used to love it, anyway after breakfast he said that he was going off somewhere with one of his mates and that I couldn't come, so I reminded him that Mum said that he was to look after me, so he said "so tell her when she comes next time !!, charming,! And off he went. So I thought that I would have a look around the front garden and perhaps nick a Strawberry or two for desert, but right from the back of the bush so that no one would notice. Then a plan began to formulate in my tiny mind. Going down the garden I could hear the pigs grunting again, and again I thought, one day I will climb onto that wall and I will find out what was going on over the other side, and then just at that moment there was that awful terrible screaming that I had heard before, it just seemed so much louder this time, and again the hairs on the back of my head stood up as before.

That's when my little plan emerged from the recesses of my tiny mind. I thought, right, this time I am definitely going to find out what's over the wall, and there's no time like the present, so I went down to the wall, and climbed onto the board that covered the well, this gave me a launch platform so that I could grab onto the apple tree with a little jump, this I accomplished unfortunately I tore my shirt a little and got it a bit dirty, but never mind, those were only incidentals, which were small in my obsession to see over the wall. The squealing by this time had died down a little, and was sort of muted, I scrambled up the tree and grabbed the top of the wall, and hauled myself up onto my elbows. The sight that I behold before my eyes was one of the most vivid memories I had as a child!. Below me was a small holding of about an acre, with several big sheds and pig sty's, and an open piece of ground with trees on it. The ground was barren of grass, just mud and more mud where the pigs had been. There must have been 30 or 40 of them wandering around digging into the mud with their noses. About ten yards away from where I was perched, was a large tree with a thick forked branch about 6 ft from the ground, and tied onto this fork with its head wedged and tied down into the fork, and facing down, was this enormous pig. It couldn't move as its legs were wrapped around the branch and tied together underneath. Its head was sticking out from the fork, and the horrifying aspect was that its throat had been cut, and the blood was pouring down into a hole which had a tin bath in it. it was like water running from a tap. I was absolutely transfixed with horror, as I had never thought of cruelty to animals before, having at home a dog and a cat and a rabbit called Dinky.

Plus the usual few chickens in the back yard. I could not tear my eyes away from the scene before me. There was a man standing next to the pig with a long thin knife in his hand, a big rough looking man with a cloth cap on and wearing a dirty smock, smoking a long bent pipe. I was suddenly shocked back to reality as he must have heard me. And shouted at me in no uncertain terms to clear off, so beating a hasty retreat, and still shocked and stunned at what I had witnessed, I jumped from the tree and landed on the board covering the well, in the process breaking it, before falling sideways onto the Strawberry beds. I picked myself up and ran into the cottage where the old man was sitting and putting on his boots. I must have looked in a bit of a state for so early in the morning, a torn shirt, and filthy, with fruit stains on my face and shirt and hands! Plus a cut on my knee, which was now dripping blood onto the carpet where I had landed on top of the well.

I blurted out what I had just seen, but the old man just casually said that that was the usual way to slaughter a pig, so that it was bled dry for bloodless meat, and that it was done whilst the pig was still alive so that the heart was still pumping the blood out and as much as possible., also the blood was saved to make pigs pudding, what a way for an animal to die. It was there and then that I made my mind up to do something about it later on, if I could. But the memory of that scene kept me awake at nights for ages. When 'our kid' found out, he completely disowned me. When I also explained about the broken board covering the well, the old man took me up to see for himself, and when he saw the state of the garden, plus the greatly diminished stock of fruit, and especially his prise Strawberry's, which were looking rather flattened where I had landed in the middle of them, he sort of blew his top at me whilst I just stared sheepishly at the ground, the damage that I had incurred was after all purely an accident, and to me that seemed far less important than the fate of those poor pigs. When the normal colour had returned to his face, he went to inspect the well, and took the remains of the wooden cover off, he then pointed out to me what would have happened if I had fallen down into the well, he took a stone and dropped it down into the well, god knows how deep that well was, because it took ages and ages before you heard the echo of a splash, evidently it was the deepest well in the village, plus know one knows just how deep the water is at the bottom, I swallowed hard, and promised not to go near it again, but for my pains I had to go without tea that day, mind you it seemed that I went without a lot of teas whilst staying there for some reason or other!!

Having said to myself that I was going to do something about the fate of those pigs, I didn't actually fancy climbing upon the well again, so I had to reconnoitre the surrounding area for an alternative entry of access into the small holding, already a plan was formulating in my small mind, I found out that the small holding where the pigs were kept was on a corner on the edge of the village, and backed onto the countryside, and open fields, having sized everything up, so there and then I made up my plan of action.

O ne evening a couple of days later, we had had supper, and it was time for us to go to bed. I kept yawning and saying that I was tired, 'our kid' looked at me a bit strangely, but off we went up the little wooden stairs to our bedroom. I changed into my Jim jams and had a pee in the Jerry, and 'our kid' told me off, because I should have had one downstairs before I came up, as it was his turn to empty it in the morning. I jumped into bed and pretended to go to sleep, a little while later when he was obviously asleep, I heard the old couple come up to bed. I lay there waited for all noise and movement to cease, and when I was sure that everyone was asleep, I quietly grabbed my clothes which I had put ready, Plimsolls, dark jumper and woolly hat, carefully I made my way downstairs, dressed and gingerly opened the front door and out into the night, It was quite moonlit so I could see where I was going, so down the lane to the fields, through the gate, turn right, and make my way around to the back of the small holding. The house itself was a little way off from the sheds and the barns, the only worry was the dogs, but it seemed o.k. at the moment.

I climbed over the back gate, but left it open on purpose. I then squelched through the mud, which was ankle deep, and over to the to the first two huts, I wasn't sure what was in them at the time, but it didn't really matter, anyway I opened the doors as far as I could, then over to the two big barns, and opened those two as far as I could also. Then I ran, or rather squelched my way back to the gate, losing one of my Plimsolls on the way, sucked in by the mud! I then sat on the fence waiting.

What I was actually expecting next was a stampede of pigs to come charging out of the sheds to their new found freedom, but nothing, I sat there for ages, "come on you stupid pigs" muttered, still nothing, just deadly silence which seemed to last for ages. Then I heard a 'click click' noise from one of the sheds, then a couple of Cockerels came out, strutting carefully, probably wondering what the hell was going on as it wasn't dawn yet!, Christ, I thought, chickens, not pigs, slowly more and more emerged from both sheds, and began to spread all over the place, to me there seemed to be hundreds of them, I am really in for it now I thought, they were supposed to be pigs, not bloody chickens!!, I bet all the pigs have gone to market, I thought, When I heard the first curiosity grunt from one of the bigger sheds, and there appeared the first pig, I must have mixed the sheds up.

It was bright moonlight by now so I could see everything that was going on, then came a few more grunts and more pigs came out and started to make their way over to the open gate, followed by herds of chickens and cockerels, and off they went into the fields, I bet if any foxes were about,they would think it was Xmas!!, So delighted and excited at what I had done for them, or so I believed. I thought now would be a good time to beat a hasty retreat, minus one Plimsoll, I hoped that nobody would find that as it would probably give the game away, I often wonder if anyone ever did, or is it still there! On the way back to the cottage I washed the mud of my feet in the little stream, wondering how I was going to explain one missing Plimsoll and wet socks!. I gingerly opened the front door and crept upstairs, nothing stirred, not even ',our kid', so I hung my wet socks on the window sill, and climbed, exhausted into bed, I lay there for a while quite chuffed actually because I thought, that in my own small way, was getting back at that horrible chap in the brown smock and gumboots I listened carefully to see if I could hear anything from over the wall, but all was quiet, so I assumed that perhaps some of the animals had gone back into their sheds and barns, WRONG!!

Next morning apparently all hell had broken out in the village, evidently one of the farm workers on his way to work on his bike, early through the village, turned a corner and ran smack into a pig wandering along the street, when he picked himself up, he couldn't believe his eyes,as there were pigs and chickens all over the place, in peoples gardens, and sitting on fences and gates, the chickens that is!, the whole village had been invaded by them. He gathered himself together, got back on his bike and rode furiously up to the local Bobbies house as fast as he could to tell him what had happened. I don't think as much panic could have ensued even if the Germans had invaded in force.

What I didn't know was that the chap in the small holding had received only that day a delivery of more pigs, and apparently there was about 50 pigs in total, plus the chickens which numbered about 80. Quite an invasion force! Anyway the Bobby proceeded to go around the village commandeering help from the sleepy villagers to assist in the roundup of the invaders, the pigs had gotten into people's gardens and were eating everything in sight, chickens were flying around and roosting on gates and fences all over the place, mind you I think a few of those chickens found their way into some people's pantries, not voluntary either!

The first thing 'our kid ' and I were aware of what was happening and going on, was when there was a banging on the cottage door to get the old man out to help with the roundup, we of course got quickly dressed and went along to see what all the fuss was about, but when I saw all the chaos that was going on, I swallowed hard, and thought if they ever found out who was responsible for all this, there would be a Public Hanging on the village green, or a beheading!. Nobody ever did find out, but believe me I lived in fear for quite a while after that, especially if someone happened to find a plimsoll stuck in the mud, i only hoped that maybe one of the pigs might find it and eat it, as they will eat anything. Some of the pigs had also wandered for miles over the open countryside, and it took a long time to round them all up, and also many a garden was ruined by them in the village, luckily where we lived there was a strong gate so they couldn't get in.

Of course at that tender age I wasn't to realize the seriousness of what I had done, but in my defence I only hope the pigs and the chickens enjoyed their brief moments of freedom, before they were subject to a horrible end. I never went near the small holding again or near the high wall at the end of the garden. After it was all over, the only reference to that night was when 'our kin' asked why my socks were hanging out of the window, and why I was missing a plimsoll !!

Our stay with the old couple came to a sudden end for some reason or other, I can only guess we were a handful for them, and the scrapes I used to get into didn't help either, plus of course the fights we 'Townies used to get into with the local Swedes, yokels, or spud bashers, as we called them, and we were always doing battle with them at the slightest provocation, but they would always come of worse as us 'City kids' were quite experienced at gang warfare, as they could only resort to stone throwing and name calling, of course us kids would always have to take the blame for these 'set twos ' and at school we would be hauled in front of the Headmaster at assembly and read the riot act, and saying even if we came from different backgrounds, we all must learn to co-exist with each other, baloney, anyway we couldn't understand what that meant at the time, so we just carried on as normal until the next lecture. I don't remember a great deal about our time being evacuated, but as I said we became a little bit too much for the old couple, and I was sorry to have to go, as we were quite comfortable there. So 'our kid' and I were packed off to go and live with another family in the village, which was down the other lane with the 4 council houses in it. Ours was to be the one at the end, and when the door opened, who was it, none other than the big girl with horses teeth, and built like the side of a barn, the one that 'our kid' had first confronted when had arrived in the village, whoops, this would turn out interest I thought, so did 'our kid'. Evidently the family didn't volunteer to take us, but were told they had to, a good start. The family Consisted of the big girl, who was 13, and her little sister who about my age, she wasn't too bad, a bit hick, I don't know whether there was a father or not, maybe gone off to the war. The council house was fairly modern I suppose, 3 bedrooms, one for the woman,the other for the two girls, and the 3rd for me and 'our kid', which was quite small, but they did have a bathroom with a flush toilet inside the house which we thought was luxury, back home out toilet was a flush one but it was out in the yard, so we had to use a jerry upstairs.

We called our new family. 'The Nit family' because they all had them, and eventually us too, it was horrible, we used to have to kneel in front of the fire with one of those nit combs, and comb our hair so that the nits would fall onto a sheet of paper, then shake the nits into the fire, and you could hear the nits, snap, crackle, and pop in the fire. I know that when Mum came to see us that weekend, she was horrified, and did her nut, and when she went to catch the bus back home, she promised that she would be back very soon, and as the bus drove away with me running after it crying, as I usually did, i was saying to myself, please, please make it soon. Sure enough, 2 days later back she came, packed our things, didn't say anything to the woman, just to us to come on we have a bus to catch, and 'our kid' and I, to our great joy we came back home to our beloved street and home, all amidst the air raids, and bombings, and the shortages, but it was heaven compared to evacuation. We thought that we had been away for months, or so it seemed, but it was only 5 weeks!

Back home now I did wonder what the real reason was to bring us back home, I know our last digs were a bit crabby, and we didn't get on with the other two kids and their mother, but really I think Mum and Dad wanted us to be a family again, despite what was going on all around us, and if we were destined to go, we would all go together, and they didn't want us to be perhaps told at some time that our parents had been lost in the bombings whilst we were still evacuees. I don't know if this was a general thought by some of the other parents in our street but, the amazing thing was that all of our mates in the street were all back home also!!! So 'our kid' could get his gang going again, and I could do the same also, The time now was getting to late Autumn 1940, and the bombings were beginning to escalate, so far our street had been spared, We were back at our old school, and I am now in the Juniors, but life has changed, as we became 'shelter Kids', If the sirens went when we were in school, and they did quite regular, we had to dash across the playground into another building which was a bit more substantial than our classrooms. Our classes were much thinner now owing to the evacuations. After school we had to go straight home as it was getting dark now in the afternoons. In the street opposite our house they had built in the road a shelter, I think they called them 'blast shelters', it was just a small brick built place with two rooms, but nothing in them, and the entrance door had a wall built in front of it. I think they were there in case anyone was caught out in the open if any bombs fell nearby, mind you if any bombs did fall within a hundred yards of it, it would probably blown away anyway! But it came in useful as our gang hut.

In our house, Dad had put some steel mesh grating around the dining room table which we were supposed to dive under if the sirens went, and if any bombing was getting near. It was then that the daylight bombing became more intense, so Mum would meet us out of school with our teas packed, and we would make our way to some larger shelters which had been dug underground in a loca about 15 minutes walk away along the Walsgrave Rd near the Forum cinema, the shelters had long twisting passages, with large rooms off to the left and right with tables and chairs, and cubicles where you could buy food and drink, but Mum used to bring flasks, everything was a bit basic and no heating to start with, but things improved as time went on. There were rooms with bunks in, I suppose for us kids, also piles of blankets, but Mum wasn't keen on us using them, as she would say "you don't know who's been using them!! Good old Mum. We would stay in the shelter until about 9 p.m. when Dad would come to fetch us. But if there was an air raid on, Dad would still be on duty, so sometimes we would have to sleep down there. When Dad finished work at night, he would have his dinner, and then he would become an AIR RAID WARDEN, funny as our family name was Warden!, he would put on his blue uniform and tin hat, he looked very smart, he also carried a stick, what for we didn't know, and a whistle on a string, and a big torch, There was an empty house opposite our house and that was used as the Wardens operational base, there were about ten of them in all Their job was to patrol the streets at night, and as there was a complete blackout at nights at that time, so every house had to have their windows blacked out, usually with thick heavy curtains, and not a chink of light was allowed to show, you could be fined heavily if you did, and the Air raid wardens used to patrol the streets, and if they saw a house with any light showing they would bang on the doors, and shout "put that bloody light out" if they didn't they were reported, a note was pushed through the door with a fine which had to be paid at the Wardens H,Q, in our street the next day, I can't remember how much the fine was. Then if you didn't pay you could expect a visit from the police. The Blackout was taken very seriously, as any lights showing could be seen by the bombers flying overhead and they became a target to aim at. I often wondered what happened to all the money that was collected, but the Wardens H,Q, always seemed to have plenty of food and bottles of beer in the cupboards !!! The house that they were using was empty, probably whoever lived there had left because of the bombings, as lots of people did, so most of the furniture and things were still in there, so that's why it was commandeered for use as a A,R.P. H,Q, (air raid police) For the Wardens it was like home from home for them, and if it was quiet, there were beds so that they could have a kip. I used to go over sometimes to take Dads tea if he had missed it at home, you opened the front door and were met by a wall of cigarette smoke, and some of the chaps would be sitting around a table playing cards, and they would quickly hide the bottles of beer under the table. Some would be playing darts, and you could smell the smell of cooking, it was like a private club, no wonder there were never any vacancies ! they worked a shift system, 2 hrs on duty, and 4 hrs off, 4 at a time in pairs patrolling the streets.

One evening whilst we were down the underground shelter in the park, and when Dad was due to come and collect us, he came down and said that the sirens had just gone off, and some bombs were dropping nearby, so we would have to stay until the all clear sounded, (I forgot to mention the sirens, when an air raid was imminent, the sirens would sound all over the town, an undulating wail, so people would then make a beeline to the nearest shelter, the sirens could go off at any time of the day, then when any raid was finished, the all clear would sound, one long blast of the sirens.) Dad was in his uniform and had to get back on patrol with his mate. Another they had to do was that if any bombs exploded in their vicinity, they had to dash back to the H,Q, or a telephone booth if it was nearer to inform the services where and what had happened and what had been hit, houses or factories. I believe a little later on in the war they were issued with 'walk and talkies phones, anyway when the all clear had sounded, Dad came back to collect us, but as he was walking down the stairs in the shelter a bomb exploded in the road behind him, it must have been one of those delayed action bombs they used so that any rescuers could be killed by the delayed explosion, and it blew him down the stairs, the big heavy doors at the entrance blew open and the place was filled with dust and debris, choking everyone as it penetrated through the shelter. We had been sitting there I think doing home work or drawing, and Mum was doing some knitting, when all of a sudden this huge thud, and everything started to rattle, the door flew open on the room we were in, then a roaring sound and clouds of dust started to blow in, some women started screaming and kids also, it was chaos for a while, you couldn't see much, we covered mouths, then the dust began to clear a little, and of 'our kid' and I wanted to see what was going on so we went out the door into the corridor, and there were people running around like mad, Mum was still inside the room looking after some woman who had hysterics and then fainted, so she didn't notice we had gone, just then out of the dust cloud came this grey figure, grey because of the dust, and lo and behold there stood Dad!! Two eyes peeping and blinking through a grey dust plastered face, and his nice blue uniform now grey. He could see we were o.k. although also covered in dust. He pointed to his ears, and waved that he was completely deaf from the bomb blast, but mouthed, where is your Mum, just then she came out, having calmed the hysterical woman down, and just stared at Dad, at first not recognising him, then gave him a hug and proceeded to wipe and dust him off, dad was relevantly o.k. just a bit shook up, he twisted his ankle as he was blown down the stairs "arse upwards" as he described it. Come on he said, "let's get you all home". We went up the big stairs of the shelter, the large doors had been blown off, and we found Dads helmet, but his big torch was smashed.

The bomb had landed in the road, and all the shops had all their windows blown in and the flats above them, a bit of a mess, but it was all quiet now, except you could hear the sirens and the bells ringing on the ambulances and fire engines, The police and Wardens were checking on the people who lived in the flats, one chap was standing outside covered in blood, probably from flying glass. We made our way home as dad had to try and clean up a bit, and get some sleep as he still had shifts to do. When he talked he was shouting, so I guess he was still a bit deaf. On the way home we passed a few houses that had been bombed or fire bombed with incendiaries, and were smoking, and people were digging in the ruins. I suppose for survivors, as I still couldn't comprehend what war was all about. But it certainly didn't take me long to find out!

At home we had the dining room table for an emergency shelter, not adequate I know, but our next door neighbour, who was a spinster, had now had an Anderson shelter put in her back garden, and we were told that we had to share it with her, it was good because that meant that we didn't have to go down to the shelter in the park if there was a raid on. Just pop next door. But that arrangement only lasted for a short period of time because of the intensity of the bombings. An Anderson shelter was dug about 6 ft into the ground, then lined with corrugated steel sheets, then a domed roof of the same steel, then all the earth that had been dug out was piled on top of the roof. Then some steps dug out to the entrance, it measured about 6ft by 6ft, Dad fitted some bunk beds along the inside and some duck boards on the floor, as in time water seeped in, and had to be bailed out, there was a table and some stools, a paraffin heater, and a methyl spirit stove, so all In all it was quite cosy, but damp in the winter months, also as long as nobody had too much wind, which unfortunately our neighbour had, bless her.

At that particular time our part of the city was comparatively spared any major bombings, mainly as I suppose, because it was a residential area, but by the months leading up to November they became more and more concentrated with lots of daytime bombings, and at nights virtually carpet bombing of the whole city, with hundreds of homes being destroyed, you could stand at the top of our street, I know we shouldn't, but if Mum had taken some supper over to Dad in the Wardens house, 'our kid' and I would sneak out to see what was going on, and you could see all over the city as we were on a hill, and it was as if the whole of Coventry was under floodlights with the masses of fires that were burning, also you could actually hear the pulsating drone of the bombers overhead, a very distinctive sound, also at the bottom of our street was a railway line behind a row of houses, it was only a single track, it was used to carry coal from the pits at the Binley colliery to Bedworth and Nuneaton, but when an air raid was on a train engine would be going back and forth towing two flat open wagons, and on one would be an Ack Ack gun, and on the other a long barrelled gun, and these would be firing continuously, so the noise was quite something. It was very impressionable to a young mind as you can imagine.

As I have said before, Dad worked at the Rudge factory, which was actually near the town centre, and only about a hundred yards from the Cathedral, St' Johns, the factory was a large Victorian building about 4 floors, underneath the building were some very deep cellars they had now been converted into 24hr air raid shelters for the employees and their families, and because it was a munitions and motor cycles for the forces, it was operating 24hrs a day, with many women and families working there, so the cellars provided cover at any time. I suppose the shelter was like a town underground, there was a nursery, a large shop that sold almost anything, a medical centre, large kitchen, school rooms and play areas, rooms with bunk beds and camp beds, a lot of things were run by the Salvation Army, Families were allotted their spots in the tunnels, and their chairs and tables, and when the kids were in bed, the adults would sit around listening to the radio, or playing cards or darts. It must have been very hard on parents to exist this way for such a long time. It was also the time that Mum and Dad decided that it wasn't very safe staying at home, so they decided that we would use the Rudge shelter until perhaps the worst was over, so when school was over, we were still going to school, but not for long, Mum would meet us out, and we would catch a bus, that was if they were still running, or walk to the shelter, which would take a good hour, and then be prepared to spend the night there, sometimes if the bombing had been particular bad, and perhaps the roads were blocked by debris, we just stayed there, sometimes we wouldn't see Dad for days, which of course worried Mum. For us kids it wasn't too bad, there was plenty to do, and there were kids of all ages there, sometimes we had to have lessons as there were teachers down there as well, but not too serious, perhaps that's why I'm so backwards !!!

At nights if people were asleep, and it was pretty quiet and there was a raid going on upstairs you could hear the thud. thud, of the bombs, and if one was fairly close, everything would shake. Sometimes, if no one was looking, 'our kid' and I would sneak up the stairs, which were wide marble stairs which went up one flight, round a corner, up another flight, around another corner, and up one more flight up to some large steel doors, which had a small door in them that led out

On to the main road to the city centre, we would sneak along to the left where there was a low wall, and we would sit on it, and watch what was going on. it was amazing that no one stopped us or missed us, mind you there was nobody about as a raid was going on and people would be occupied on other things. You could see the fires and the flashes, and the brilliant white fluorescent flares dropping slowly by parachute, and the search lights sweeping back and forth. It was quite exciting to us, you could hear bombs dropping in the distance, but they seemed to be getting nearer so we did a hasty retreat in case we were missed. We must come up here again another time.

In the mornings we would get ready for school after breakfast in the canteen, then Mum would attempt to get us to school. Depending on the conditions on the roads outside, it usually took about an hour, longer if we came across roads that were blocked by bombed buildings or houses that were spread over the streets, some still burning and men digging in the ruins for perhaps survivors or bodies and tractors trying to clear the roads of debris. Once we were climbing over some rubble when someone shouted "quiet" then all engines would be switched off, and everyone would listen as perhaps someone had heard a cry or a shout from somewhere in a building, and then frantic digging would begin to try to get to them.

What 'our kid' and I were interested in on the way, was the collecting of 'shrapnel ' as amongst us kids now a days, it was nearly as good as currency, you could swap a good pieces of 'shrapnel' for almost anything, I know as that's how I got a decent saddle for my bike at last. All kids collected it during the war, there was always swapping and bargaining going on as to who had the biggest and shiniest bit, once on our way back from the shelter I found the empty shell of a flare, which was I believe was very rare I was told, as the phosphorous usually burnt away the shell casing as it was falling, of course 'our kid' tried to bribe it away from me, but I already knew exactly what I wanted for my pot of gold! A kid in the next street had a couple of bicycle wheels and a saddle up for grabs, just what I wanted, and he was over the moon, even through in a bicycle pump!!

When we would finally get to our street, we would nervously look around the corner to see if our house was still standing, and you could hear Mum breathe a sigh of relieve. It must have been awful for parents in those days. Mum would do a quick check in the house to see if everything was o.k. Then down to our School, mind you hoping that the school had caught it!! Even if it hadn't, more often than not before we got there the sirens would go again, as daylight raids were on the increase. So we would make a quick dash to the nearest shelter. Education was a bit of a hit and miss during the early years of the war in Coventry. NOT THAT I MINDED!!!

As I have said it must have been hard to have to exist in that way for such a long time for parents in those times. To have to leave your home every evening, just leave everything behind, and then spend the next 14 or 16 hrs or so down in the bowels of the earth, and listening to the dull thud of bombs dropping and shaking when one was near. And wondering which part of the city was getting it tonight, and wondering if your house would still be standing the next morning as you made your way amongst the bomb damage and the streets littered with debris, sometimes climbing over mountains of rubbish, and it taking 2 or 3 hrs to get home. To us though it was better than being evacuated!!!

The days went by during late November and into December, and the bombing was gettingheavier and heavier, most times all day and all night. The 'Jerries 'were really after Coventry, and on the night of February 14th was the 'holocaust' as far as we were concerned, and of course the thousands of people of Coventry. We had been in the Rudge shelter all day because of the daylight raids, but it eased off a little around tea time, so 'our kid' and I decided to go upstairs and see what was happening, so we crept up the stairs and out onto the street, we went and sat on the low wall again, but as we did we heard this very heavy low droning noise, bombers, it was in the distance but getting louder and louder,. Just then a Warden came pelting down the street, saw us sitting there, and shouted at us "get down that bloody shelter NOW, we did, as he sounded a bit frightened about something, and he also ran down the steps into the shelter with us. He started running through the corridors shouting "Collect your children and keep them by you". Then all of a sudden the ground started shaking, and there was a loud thud, thud, continuously. The lamps were shaking, and dust was coming down the stairs, There were some heavy curtains at the bottom of the stairs, and they were pulled across which made it better. The noise and the rumbling carried on for hours, in fact all night. A Warden came by us and Mum asked him what was going on, and he said "Were really getting it tonight" of course Mum was worried about Dad, there was one slight pause around midnight, but it started again soon after. This night was to be known as 'The Blitz' The night the whole centre of the city was destroyed above us, it's a good thing this shelter is so deep underground, as we are more or less in the centre! Also a new word was coined ' Coventration, ' because of the concentration of bombing on one city. The November 'Blitz' is still very vivid in my mind, also what happened later that evening.

Also a funny thought entered my mind at that time which I couldn't quite understand. Why the hell were we in a shelter underneath a munitions factory situated right in the centre of the City! I can only assume that it was because they were so deep, plus the fact that no one could guess how intense the bombing would be. One other thing that I forgot to mention was the fact that down in the shelter behind one of the walls ran a river!

An underground river which ran from one side of the town to the other, If you put your ear to the wall you could actually hear running water! If the factory had been hit with one of those 'land mines' which burrow deep into the ground before exploding, if we hadn't all been killed by the blast, we would have all drowned anyway. Anyway back to the Blitz.

At the bottom of the stairs the curtains were suddenly opened and people rushed in carrying stretchers, police, firemen, all sorts rushing through to the medical centre, and first aid rooms, some on stretchers, some being carried, one bloke was being piggy backed and I could see that he only had one leg. The stretchers were being laid out in rows now in and outside of the medical centre and first aid room, and they were being treated where they lay. I know I probably shouldn't have been there, so of course that's why I was. Everybody was dashing around trying to help the best they could. I was walking up and down the rows of stretchers but nobody was taking any notice of me. Some people were moaning and crying out, some heavily bandaged, some lying very still with staring eyes, others covered over with blankets. My wanderings bought me to the bottom of the stairs, so I decided to go up and see what was going on. At that moment 'our kid' grabbed me by the neck, and wanted to know where the hell I had been. I said nowhere, but I wanted to go upstairs and see if anything was happening. Now I quite expected him to drag me back inside, but curiosity got the better of him, and he said o.k. let's go, we started up the stairs, keeping ducked under the hand rail as much as possible. I noticed there was a lot blood all over the stairs. Nobody took any notice of us as everyone was rushing up and down the stairs. The time must have gone midnight as we climbed the last flight of stairs. The huge steel doors were open with people running in and out. Outside it looked as if it was daylight, plus the noise was terrific, seizing a quiet moment we slid around the entrance and out. There were two policemen standing in the road but they had their backs to us so we crouched down and crept along the wall to the left where we stood before, and sat on the wall, and we both just sat staring at the scene before us. it was as I said just like daylight, but the light was bright pink, red, and orange, it was real spooky. It seemed as if every building in the city was ablaze, up and down the road out of every building window smoke and flames bellowed, buildings were collapsing out into the road with terrific roars, flames were reaching high into the sky illuminating everywhere around, strangely there wasn't any dust or smoke blowing around, which was probably because of the heat, it was going straight up. The heat was terrific and blowing with gale force, but a very hot gale. I think they called them 'fire storms'. Our faces and legs were burning, the noise, the roar were terrific, I could see above the flames and the Cathedral tower stood out against the skyline, although most of the cathedral building and the roof had gone. The tower stood out amongst the smoke and flames as if defying to be destroyed.

The acrid smoke was now beginning to get down our throats so we pulled our jumpers over our heads, nose and mouths and continued to stare, wide eyed and trembling with excitement, and every terrifying explosion and roar made the hairs stand up on the back of my neck, as blast after blast roared out, and the hot wind was nearly blowing us over the wall. We then noticed that some people who came out of the entrance of the shelter were pointing up at the blood red sky, we looked up, and there illuminated against the dark sky was a parachute drifting slowly down, you could even make out the figure hanging underneath. It appeared to be motionless before plunging down into the masses of flames underneath it. We wondered at that time whether he was one of ours or one of theirs, and it went quiet all of a sudden..

Suddenly the people who had been looking upwards Turned and noticed me and 'our kid' sitting on the wall, and they yelled to the two policemen who ran over to us (it was too late to do a bunk) and they shouted at us "what the bloody hell are you doing out here" they picked us up and proceeded to carry us down the stairs and into the first aid post, where we were checked out to see if we were o.k. Our faces and legs were bright red from the heat, so the nurse dabbed some cream on them, she told us to stay where we were until she found out who we belonged to, but as soon as she was gone, we quickly made our way back along the corridors to where mum and dad were. Dad had been working that night in the factory on the 2nd floor, but a bomb had landed onto the top floor and destroyed half of it, so they were all told to get to the shelters below as the raid was getting bigger. When Mum and Dad saw us they wanted to know what the hell we had been doing, as we were red and smelled of smoke. We said that we had been sitting around the big stove in the canteen because we felt cold, I don't somehow think that they believed us, as we both got a good smack around the ears! Told to go and have a good wash, get into our bunks, and get straight to sleep, we couldn't of course as the bombing was still going on upstairs, and I just kept recalling what we had just witnessed upstairs. as I have said, a night of vivid memories that remain with me to this day. I don't think many people managed to get much sleep that night, as the bombing carried on all night, but finally started to ease off around 5-30 am, and then after a while the all clear sirens sounded, we had some breakfast, and around 8-30 Mum and Dad decided that we would try and make our way back home.

It wasn't until we came up and out of the shelter that we realized the true extent of the damage that the City had received. Almost every building had been raised to the ground, the few that were still standing were just shells, a couple of walls, no windows. The whole of the City was shrouded in smoke and drizzle, as people wandered around in a daze trying to take in all the destruction around them. A FEW STATISTICS AT THIS TIME.

There were 4,330 homes destroyed and, and three quarters of the Cities factories damaged. Amongst the rubble lay the human remains of some who were never identified, 534 men, women, and children lay dead, 865 and injured. it's amazing and perhaps a miracle that the figures were not much, much higher, as the city had been hit with 30,000 incendiaries, 500 tons of high explosives, 50 land mines, all nonstop for 11 hrs. The world had never previously witnessed this sort of airborne destruction before, and the Germans coined a new word for it 'Coventration'. The City's tram system was destroyed with tram lines ripped from the ground, or left arched up in the air, and twisted with the heat. Also out of a fleet of 181 buses, only 73 remained. Practically all of the water and gas supplies were smashed, and people were even advised to boil emergency supplies as well.

Hundreds of troops were drafted in to help and to try and bring some sort of order to the city. also machinery to start and try to clear the roads so as the rescue parties could get around, also troops and the general public worked day and night trying to dig out those who lay buried in the rubble. Vans toured the streets where possible advising people where to obtain food and shelter, food canteens were set up in various parts. Within 3 days the Royal Engineers had restored the electricity and water, and soon after the gas supplies, On the 20ᵗʰ November the first mass burial took place at the London Road cemetery, and the second a week after. Also it was said another took place at the Memorial park.

Another statistic not officially recorded, but was told to my Dad by a Fireman friend of his, was that a large department store in the centre of the city, I think it was Owen and Owen, had some underground shelters in the basements for the staff and shoppers if there was a raid, On that night it was hit by several bombs and incendiaries, and was totally ablaze with no hope of rescuing anyone as the bombs dropped were oil bombs, so they just turned the hoses on and flooded the basements, they reckoned there were around 200 people down there, so any that were perhaps still alive, were drowned.

That was not the end of the raids, although generally they were not quite so heavy, Two however were, the Easter week raids of the 8th and 10th of April 1941 which were between 8 and 10hrs long. The last bombing raid on Coventry was in August 1942, by that time the city had suffered 41 actual raids, and 373 siren alerts. Official figures say 1,236 people were killed, and 808 of them rest in the 2 mass graves at London Road cemetery.

Now back to the story. Anyway when we came up from the shelter and decided to try and find our way back home, the usual road was completely blocked by masses of rubble, as were most of the roads, in fact you couldn't tell where the road was. Dad decided we would try and find our way back via Pool Meadow, as there were more open spaces that way so less rubble, although it meant going by the Cathedral. The Spire was still standing, but the roof had gone and all the stained glass windows, but the walls were still there, and as we picked our way past, the maim doors were missing and you could see all the way up the inside right up to the Alter. The whole floor inside was piled up with huge blocks of stone and timber, still smouldering, and up on the Alter was a huge wooden cross which was blacked and still smouldering, but still standing, as if in defiance, At the back of the Alter, where there used to be large windows, you could see through and over the City, and also the other two Church spires, That's where the City gets one of its names from, the city of 'The Three Spires ' .Dad said that he wished that he'd had his camera with him, as that would have been a picture to remember for all time, Well I can still remember it Dad. we all just stood there for a while, just looking, and I am sure Mum had tears in her eyes.

Picking our way carefully, and me and 'our kid' looking for bits of shrapnel at the same time, there were also some streets we couldn't go down, stopped by the army, unexploded bombs. after about an hour and a half, we finally got to the start of the Walsgrave Road, and Ball Hill, still a bit to go though, In all I reckon it took about 3 hrs. The devastation was unbelievable. We couldn't turn left to get to our street, so we had to go up Ball Hill. Now on the left hand side of Ball Hill were rows of houses, which were higher up on a bank, their back gardens backed onto our back gardens, so our street was behind those houses which runs parallel with Ball Hill. The reason I explained this was because as we made our way up the hill we could see in front of us loads of rubble out into the road, and as we got nearer there was a gap in the houses, so obviously some of the houses had caught it in the bombing, and sure enough 4 or 5 had been bombed and were flattened,. Now Dad was quite a way in front of us, but we could see him standing with his hands on his hips just staring at the missing houses, which of course weren't there any longer. Now just before we got to him, he turned to us, and said quite quietly "Our bloody house has gone" I'll never forget him saying that. Sure enough when we got to him you could see straight across to our street now, but oddly enough not the back of our house, only the front of the houses that were opposite us, our house and the three houses to the left of us were gone also, to the right of our house all of the houses were gone right down to the corner were flattened. We just stood there transfixed, and Mum said "Oh God no" and hung on to Dad crying, After what seemed ages, Dad finally said we might as well go and see what's what. So we went up the hill, then turned left and left again into our street, Villiers St, The whole side of the street where our house had been was flattened, we could see that one wall was still standing but only because a floor beam of the bedroom had fallen down one side and that end was resting on the remains of the piano in the front room, when we got to our house there were firemen tying a rope to the end of the beam resting on the piano and shouting to everybody to get back. They pulled on the rope from the middle of the road and the beam slid of the piano and the only wall of the house standing came crashing down with dust billowing all over the place. When it finally cleared, the piano was gone, and Dad said "My bloody piano" he loved that piano, so I think the things that were happening today had put him in a swearing mood.

I have tried very often since those days to try to and visualise the feelings of not only my parents but the thousands of victims of the bombings when they are faced with the sight of their homes and houses, just lying there, just a pile of smouldering debris, where they have lived probably for years and years, and most probably past generations as well, brought up children and seen them grow up and leave home probably, then all of a sudden in the flash of a pan, It is all gone, everything, just everything, and you are left with just the clothes you are standing up in as we were. It just doesn't bear thinking about.

The houses opposite us were all still standing, but most had had their windows blown in, and some, the doors as well! A lot of the neighbours were about but probably a lot were still in shelters somewhere. We didn't hear of anyone being killed at that moment, but later it emerged that a young lad and his family further down the street had just left their house to make their way to a shelter when the young lad said he wanted to go to the toilet. So his Mother took him back to the toilet in their back yard when the bomb landed, they say the blast blew the lad through the wall and then the house collapsed killing the Mother also. I didn't actually know the lad as they were fairly new comers, the lad wasn't in my gang also.

Being young at that time It's hard to imagine the enormity of the situation and the shock that my parents must have been feeling at that time, or indeed any person who had felt the effect- of the bombing, to suddenly lose in one single blow a house, a home, everything that you owned, a place where your children were born and bought up in. To see it all gone and just a pile of smouldering rubbish left where lives were once lived, and there you are standing there every gone and all you have left are the clothes that you are standing up in, as I've said it's hard to imagine.

Dad said to us" Let's go and look and see is anything is worth trying to save" but the Firemen would only let him have a quick look on his own, I know we did hear Mum say "It's a shame about the coal" everybody looked at her puzzled "Well she said "we've only just had a delivery" everybody laughed. Evidently the bomb that had landed and done all the damage was a 'land mine' yes, just one bomb. It had landed in a back garden of a house just a couple of doors from us, the hole it made was about 25 yards wide and about 20 yards deep, and was already beginning to fill with water. When Dad came back he just said that most things were gone, but we might be able to salvage a few clothes and such, providing the Fire brigade stop spraying everything with bloody water! One amazing thing was that they eventually found my bedstead, an old iron framed one, a hundred yards down the street! it certainly must have been some sort of a blast. Dad was really upset about his piano. But he did manage to salvage something that was really special to him, although it was in many pieces. A pendulum clock, it was about 2 feet high and it sat on the mantelpiece in the front room. He was very proud of that clock as he had built it from scratch when he was younger, so sometime later he went back and spent hours digging in the rubble and debris where the front room was sorting bit by bit to try and find any remains of the clock which fortunately was found underneath the upturned settee which had saved it from the falling bricks to a certain extent. It was in bits though, and the case was squashed, but he collected every bit and months later in his shed in our new home, which incidentally was nearly opposite where our old home had been, but more about that later. He then proceeded to re-assemble his beloved clock, which he restored to full working order. I think it kept his mind occupied as to what was going on around him.

From the time of finding our house demolished, I'm afraid things are a bit hazy, perhaps its something I tried to blank out, I don't know. I remember that night we were transported to an Aunts house in another part of the city, she had an Anderson shelter in her garden so that's where we spent the nights during the bombing, until Dads factory started up production again, so we went back to the old routine, school whenever it was open, closed more often than open, then up to the factory shelter. We couldn't go back to our Aunts house anymore as that had also been bombed, luckily it was a daylight raid.

As I have said, because of the daylight bombings the school was closed more than open so we lived full time down in the air raid shelter where we did our schooling, it wasn't too bad really as me and 'our kid' if we didn't feel like any schooling, we would sneak out and go exploring around the town if it was quiet, also adding to our shrapnel collection. I remember one day we were around by the Cathedral so we decided to have a look inside, a lot of the rubble had been cleared and a path made up to the Alter. The burnt cross was still there, and remained there for years afterwards, as we had thought when we last saw it burning. ' A symbol of defiance'. Whist we were there a lot of people came in and walking at the front of them was none other than Winston Churchill himself. He was doing a moral boosting tour of the City. It was great seeing him, as he was a hero to all the people in those difficult days. Also just after that King George gave them to Mum. She said you can eat them as they are just like chicken eggs only smaller. Mum did fry them for us, and they were o.k. as eggs were on ration, so we thought it was quite a treat. She also owned several houses in our street of which our old house was one of them which, we rented from her. When she heard that one of her houses had been bombed, our house. She got in touch with Mum and offered us a house just opposite as it had become vacant as the tenants had moved away because of the bombings in Coventry. We could move in as soon as the front door and one of the windows had been replaced because of the bomb blast. It was a stroke of good fortune which I think Mum and Dad deserved, also we prayed that we would not get hit again. The house was exactly the same as our old one. Two up and two down, 'our kid ' and I slept in the back bedroom which had an open fire in it, which we did light in the bad winters, There was a flush toilet tacked onto the end of the kitchen, very posh. The kitchen had a big stone sink and in the corner was a big water copper which was heated by a fire underneath. We did have a gas fire but no electricity at that time as I remember, because we had gas lamps on the walls and it was my job to change the little gas mantles in them which were very fragile. In the pantry was a large marble slab where you placed things on to keep them cool, no fridges in those days. Also hanging on a nail outside on the wall was the inevitable tin bath. Friday nights were bath nights for everyone. My job was bailing the hot water out of the copper into the tin bath in the kitchen, but why was I always the last one to have a bath, especially as our grubby kid had been in before me.

The copper was where Mum boiled the clothes washing, and also the Xmas puddings!! In the other corner was the mangle, which when folded down turned into a table. Also it had this shed in the back garden which just suited our Dad! Mum said as it was handy to our old house, so me and 'our kid' now had the job of digging through the rubble of our old house to find the coal hole, and transport the coal, which she said had only just been delivered, over to the new house!! 'Waste not, want not' she said, that was a back breaking job but we did manage to save quite a lot of things by digging through the debris. A lot of Dads tools and things from out of his shed, also clothes which were in wardrobes but squashed, but once washed they were o.k. The house was furnished fairly well, but if you needed anything you got in touch with the WVS I think, and they would try and get it for you, as you had been bombed out.

Before we had electricity installed, which was done a few months after we had moved in, Dad used to be able to make crystal radio sets, they were called 'cats whisker' radios. I'm not sure whether or not you had to wear headphones though. You huddled around this 'cats whisker' to hear any news about the war, It was run by a accumulator, a type of battery which when it ran low,it was my job to take it to the garage, and they would recharge it up for 6 pence. Dad made quite a few of those sets as it was the only way to get any news, as there were no radios, only newspapers, and they were rationed as well. Out in the garden we kept a few chickens on one side and vegetables on the other side which also had a gate and a passage that ran along the back of the houses for about 3 houses then in between the houses and onto the street, where it went in between the houses it was covered. it was called an entry. We used to put our backs onto the wall, and our feet onto the opposite wall, then ease our way up bit by bit until we reached the ceiling, then with a nail scratch our names into the brick work. I often wonder if they are still there.

Now a little bit about rationing. How our parents managed to feed us during the war years I don't know. Basically everything was rationed, you had a family ration book, inside it were coupons for such things as, eggs, bacon, butter, meats, and so on, for each weekly period, which was then marked or cut out when you bought it, that's also only if it was in the shop that week, sometimes they ran out so you would have to wait another week. As I've said, just about everything was on ration. When you see what one person was allowed per week, nowadays it would only last about one day! about the only thing that wasn't rationed were Vegetables, if you could get them that is, we used to try and grow some in the garden. It's funny, the word used to go around that so and so shop on Ball Hill has just had a delivery in of something or other, the next minute there was a queue outside the shop. Sometimes a queue would form outside a shop even if it was only rumoured that a delivery was due! Sometimes our Mum would say to me or 'our kid' quick," run down to so and so shop and get in the queue and save me a place whilst I get myself ready". Sometimes you were lucky, sometimes not. Fruit was quite scarce, apples and pears not so bad as we kids had become quite expert 'scrumpers' by now, but after a while that became a serious offence, and wo betide you if you got caught, but we were very careful. Some things you could get on the 'black market' if you knew the right contacts, after all, it was the survival of the fittest. There used to be a bloke who came around the streets pushing a barrow with vegetables on it, and he used to ration people to what he had on his barrow, and he always knocked on Mums door because he knew he always Mum had a cup of tea waiting for him, I think he fancied her actually, sometimes he would say "I got something for you here Maud," and he might produce a rabbit or even a chicken. Mum would quickly stuff it under her pinafore and whip it indoors in case anyone saw. great Rabbit pie or chicken for a few days, and not a bit was wasted, the rabbit skin was washed and dried and cut into insoles to keep your feet warm in the winter, the bones, or bones of anything, were put into a stock pot and boiled down to make soup. Under the counter stuff used to happen with Bill the Coalman, a huge chap, I think he fancied Mum also, He would carry on his back a couple of bags of coal around to the back and dump them in the coalhole, rationed of course, Mum would have his cup of tea waiting for him, and perhaps a piece of cake, Bill would then say" I've got a bag of slack for you, but don't tell anyone will you "canny our Mum! If you had a fire on at night in the winter, before when you went to bed, if you threw some slack on the fire, or 'Banked it up' as they say, the fire would only burn very slowly throughout the night, then in the morning you just poked the fire and it would burn up again, you used a bit more coal by doing that, but handy when you knew someone like 'Bill'. Talking about coal, I also remember when me and 'our kid' used to walk miles along the railway track that ran along the bottom of our street, looking for any pieces of coal or coke that had fallen of the coal wagons on their way to Bedworth or Nuneaton, sometimes if a train went by the engine driver would throw some lumps of coal from the train for us, and we would wave our thanks to him.

You hardly ever saw Bananas perhaps once a month or maybe even longer, you were lucky if you got even 4. Mum would cut one into 3 pieces, and save 2 of them for as long as possible, then slice the one piece wafer thin for a pudding for us kids, she made some sort of custard out of corn flour and some sort of essence. Pineapples I don't think we saw one during the whole war. Dripping was also a luxury, it was my job early on a Saturday morning, to get down to the butchers, with a basin, and wait outside in the queue with a 6 pence in my pocket, yes, there was already a queue at that time in the morning! I wouldn't be surprised if some of them had been there all night! The butcher only did this Dripping thing once a week on Saturdays, it was first come, first served. I would stand there in the freezing cold or rain for ages, but if I was there for a long time Mum would send 'our kid' down to relieve me. all for a bowl of dripping. It makes you realize just how hard times were in those days. Sweets were also hard to come by, the usual rumour would fly around that a certain shop had had a delivery in of sweets, so again it was post haste down to that shop and get in the queue, and wait and see what you were allowed on your ration book. Very occasionally you might be lucky and get a Mars bar, and 2 or 3 sweets. Mum would slice the Mars bar again into wafer thin slices, and we could have one slice a day if we behaved ourselves, then she would hide the rest, I never ever did find out where she hid it, and believe me I searched !. Mum also made toffee, out of what I don't know! and also lovely bread and butter pudding, the ingredients probably came from the black market! well you had to be on your toes those days.

I was now 7 yrs old, us Blitz Kids grew up quickly in those days. Some days if there wasn't any school, and the weather was lousy, Mum tried to keep me, especially, amused, so as to keep me out of trouble. Our 'kid was 12 then and he would be out with his mates as he was considered grown up by then, so if Mum was doing some cooking or ironing or sowing, she would teach me how to do it as well. I quite enjoyed it actually, and I know some of the things she taught me stood me well in later years, and still do.

By this time I was starting to get my gang organised again, there were about 6 of us Blitz kids, my second I.C. was Johnny Gardener, treasurer was Roy Howkins, their real names by the way, I wonder if they are still around? As a gang by today's standards I suppose we were mini gangsters, but that's what life was all about them, survival, there was no T.V. and electrical gadgets, mobile phones. you had to amuse yourselves the best that you could. we did the usual things, football, cricket, swimming, in the canal, until they eventually re -opened the baths around 1944. we played the games in the street until they eventually cleared and flattened the whole of the bomb site. The bomb crater which filled with water was great fun, we used to get the tin bath when Mum wasn't looking and paddle around and try to tip each other out! it was deep but we could all swim, I think. One of our other traits was 'scavenging'. With all the bombed sites around us and empty houses, that's where we would be most of the time if we were off school or after school. We used to meet up in the 'gang' hut (The air raid shelter in the street), and plan what we would do, and where we should go. It would be that some houses had been bombed, so we would go and have a look to see what we could pick up. Now we were not looters, the Police saw to that, they would stand guard over a newly bombed house or whatever until the owners had come and taken anything they could retrieve from the ruins, then we would go in and have a look to see if there was anything useful or could be worth a few pennies. We used to dig around in the rubble, especially where perhaps a shed had been, or a kitchen. The things we treasured most were bicycle parts, and tools, because we were all trying to build bikes for ourselves so that we could become a mobile gang. Jam jars and bottles were another good thing to collect. You could get a half penny a jam jar from the Co-Op, and a penny for a beer bottle from the outdoor beer shop, also magazines, books, and old newspapers were like gold dust, because of the shortage of paper. We stacked all of our ill-gotten gains in one of the lads shed in his garden, his Dad was away in the Army so it didn't matter. The shed looked like Alladins cave!

The magazines, books and papers were useful, so to try and build up a good stock we would go around the streets knocking on doors asking if they had any of those they were done with. When we had collected a good pile of them we would get a few floorboards from a bomb site and a few bricks, or anything flat. take them onto Ball Hill, the main road, then make a bench up and put all the magazines, books, newspapers on to it and sell them to shoppers and passer bys, you would surprised at the interest from people as they went by, everything would sell like hot cakes, even the Coppers would come and look to see what we were up to, and probably want to buy something they had seen, but being diplomatic we usually let them have it for nothing, unless it was one we didn't particular like, it was one of our better enterprises. but one of more naughtier schemes was beer bottles. On the corner of Ball Hill was a Hardware shop, now it sold just about everything, including bottles of beer, now the back yard of the shop ran along the side of the pavement of the side street next to it, it had a high wall and a big gate where deliveries were taken in. now we did notice once that when a delivery was being taken in, you could into the yard and in the corner of the yard were some crates with empty beer bottles in them, so that gave our devious minds something to think about, we could if we were very careful and not too greedy, use the hardware shop as some sort of withdrawal bank! Where we could guarantee some cash in an emergency! So when it was dark and no one was about, we put the lookouts on station, 3 of us would go to the gate, two would help the third to bunk up and over the wall, there were some boxes up against the wall so it would be easy to get back over again, of course it was me as the 3rd one! anyway I went over to the crates and quietly put a dozen empty bottles in a bag which \I had with me, then climbed up onto the boxes and handed the bag down to the other two, then dropped back into the street, job done! The next day one of the lads took 6 of the bottles back into the shop as returns, we got 1d for a small bottle and 2p for a big one, a whole shilling! a bit more pocket money for us all, we didn't over do it, only when needed, and the shop owner never did twig onto us, we did it for ages and ages. Naughty I know, but, Survival !

As far as the gang were concerned, we decided that to be true gang members we should all have to complete some sort of initiation ceremony or test, and we decided that the test should be as follows. The whole street was terraced houses with gardens at the rear, then an entry, then the gardens of the next street, now the gardens on the hillside end of the street went from the road at the end, up the hill to where the bombed out houses had been at the top, about thirty houses in all. So the task set was to climb into the garden at the end house, it was dark at nights now, then try to make your way by stealth across all the gardens and fences, walls, hedges or whatever, up to the last house where the bombed site was ! There was always the alley at the end of each garden for a quick escape if needed, myself and my no 2 were of course exempt! Well somebody had to watch and make sure nobody cheated, Adjudicators we were, I asked 'our kid' to watch at the top of the street in case anyone came down the alley, he thought we were stark raving mad, but he said yes, as he wanted to watch us being caught!.

We fixed a night, and we all met at the bottom of the street when it got dark, everyone had on dark clothing and balaclavas and gloves even I was having second thoughts, but 'our kid' kept jibing us on, and I now know why, It had been decided by a majority vote, edged on of course by, guess who, that the heads of a gang should set a precedence by example, so that meant that myself and Johnny should go first! so as not to lose faith I said of course. I will get 'our kid' for this! Johnny and I decided to go first, so we climbed over the wall at the first garden and dropped down onto a lawn which went across to a small fence to the next garden, all was quiet at the moment so far, so over the fence onto a vegetable patch, past a chicken coop, they squawked a bit so we lay low for a minute, then pushed through a hedge into the next garden, just at that moment the back door of the house opened and the light lit up the garden, we flattened ourselves onto the ground and thought that was it, but someone had only come out to go to the outside loo, we froze onto the ground until they had finished and went back inside, then onto the next garden over another fence, all was quiet in the house, must be out. 'Our kid' of course was in the alley keeping up with us, laughing to himself I bet. All in all we made pretty good progress, and evidently the others behind us were doing o.k. as well. We came to one garden that had a long greenhouse in it, also a shed on the end of it, so there was no way through. I crept over to 'our kid' in the alley and told him we couldn't get through, so we would come out into the alley and go around the next garden and then back into the next. He said, if you can't go through then go over the top!! If we didn't he was going to make some noises and we would get caught. The swine!, So we decided to climb over the shed, very quietly, there was a chair handy, so I climbed up on it and hauled myself up onto the shed roof, with a little bunk up from Johnny, then proceeded to haul him up after me, not knowing of course that there was a dog asleep inside the shed!, and just as I had gotten Johnny onto the roof my foot went straight through the roof, of course the dog started barking and growling. I extricated my foot rapidly in case the dog got hold of it, and we both jumped down into the garden next door and flattened ourselves against the backside of the shed. The back door of the house opened and we heard someone walk up the garden and shout at the dog to be quiet, luckily it was too dark to see the hole in the roof. The chap who had come out of the house stood there for ages until the dog was quiet before he went back inside. 'Our kid' had done a bunk when the dog started barking but he was back now, I'm sure I heard him laughing!

After that things weren't too bad except when Johnny put his foot through a glass frame that was on the floor, and also trampled flat some things that were growing with netting over them, it took ages to untangle him, At last we reached the end garden and onto the bomb site, the others followed shortly, one had to pack up halfway as he had twisted his ankle jumping off a shed roof that had a hole in it and a dog growling inside! So mission completed and we were now true gang members. ' Even ' Our kid' said he wouldn't subject his gang members to what we had just done. we must have seemed to be like the S.A.S. on a mission. Anyway from then on we called ourselves 'The Black Hand Gang' and I asked Mum if she would knit me a black left hand glove, and so did the other kids Mums, and we wore these whenever we met up. It took one and a half hours to complete the course, and I tore my trousers in the process, but I didn't tell Mum until she found she saw the tear later, and I said they must have been caught in the mangle when she washed them!

As most of the streets had gangs there were of course gang fights, as you guarded your own territory jealously. Also say if a member of your gang had been ambushed and beaten up by another gang, then a gang fight would be arranged, so two mediators from each gang would meet to arrange a time and a place where the altercation should take place, usually on a bomb site somewhere. When a site was chosen we would go to the site early in the day, pick a good spot and try and build some sort of barricade, and also make a stock pile of ammo, stones, bottles and so on, one very effective weapon was a bottle with a screw top, fill it half way with water, so when you were ready to throw it, put some Carbide pellets in it, screw the top on, shake it well, leave it a few seconds, and then lob it at the opposition, like a hand grenade, when it landed it would explode like a bomb with the build up of pressure from the carbide gas. so a few of those lobbed over followed by catapults and bricks, and the other gangs would flee like hell, I know we were mad! and it is a wonder that nobody got seriously hurt. I know I got caught once from a thrown bottle, it smashed next to me and a piece of glass went into my thigh, a long pointed piece, I had shorts on so I pulled it out and the blood spurted out just like a tap. I stuck my finger over it and it stopped, I took it off again and it spurted out about a foot away. We were on our bomb site in our street at the time only a few yards from home and 'our kid' was with us at the time, he said keep your finger on it and he ran over to tell our Mum what had happened, she came running over, still with her pinafore on, she had a tea towel in her hand so when I took my finger off to show her what it did, she gave me a smack and made the tea towel into a pad and put it over the hole and then bound it with her pinafore then picked me up and started to carry me back home. There was a dust cart in the street and the two dustmen had seen what had happened, in fact they chased the other gang off that we had been scrapping with, and I think they were on their way over to chase us away too, but when they saw Mum carrying me they came over to see what's what. When she told them that a piece of glass had probably punctured a vein, they said that she had better jump into the dust cart with me, and they would take us to the nearest hospital, which was Gulson Road hospital, which wasn't too far away.

So there we were, riding in a dust cart with two dust men, Mum pressing hard on my leg with the tea towel. The cart was travelling pretty fast and the driver was blowing his horn like mad, and people were scattering out of the way, the two dust men were laughing and joking and trying to make Mum feel better. Me? I thought it was great fun. The Gulson Road hospital wasn't really a A&E Hospital, I think it was a T.B. hospital, but they took me to treatment room, and said the bleeding was slowing down, so they made sure there wasn't any glass in there, put a pad on it and bound it up tightly and said I could go. when Mum and I got back outside the two dust men were still waiting for us, so they took us home and Mum made them come in and she gave them tea and cakes and thanked them for what they did. They said they enjoyed doing it. "beats sweeping the streets" they said.

When the workmen finally came to remove all the debris from the whole of the street, where all of the houses had been, and to fill in our boating lake, shame, we used to follow the diggers with their big shovels just in case we saw anything useful exposed from underneath the rubble, I know that's where I got some more parts for my future bike. plus an assortment of cooking pans which I gave to Mum. After all the debris had been cleared and flattened by big rollers, it looked a huge area in size. We could play football or anything on it. It was great to build huge bonfires on, but only after the war of course, As the bombing began to ease a little bit towards the end of 1941, so school became a bit more regular, and I was going on to nearly 8 yrs of age, and perhaps a little bit more responsible and grown up. We didn't need to go down the Anderson shelter so much as our area of the city was comparatively quiet at nights. there were still the daylight raids over the city and now we could stand on our nice level bomb site and watch the bombing over the city in the distance. I suppose we became a bit bla'se, but we were shaken out of that feeling rather sharply one evening as we stood watching things happening over the city. It was still light and you could actually see in the distance 'dog 'fights in the air between the R.A.F. And obviously the German fighters that were escorting their bombers, when suddenly, someone said there's one of them coming our way, and sure enough one of the fighter planes had broken off from the melee and was heading our way, and getting lower and lower, We kids were hoping that it would come low enough so that we could wave to it, when all of a sudden two Air raid wardens came charging over shouting "it's a jerry, run over to the institute now ". St, Margarets, institute was just across the open bomb site, down onto the main road, and on the other side of the road, it was where they held the cub and scout meetings, and luckily the doors were open at that time. We all ran like hell, about a dozen kids, and a couple of adults and just threw ourselves through the doors because as we ran, believe it or believe it not, bullets were splattering the ground behind us. One of the big thick wooden doors was open and one of the air raid wardens slammed it shut just as we heard 'splat, splat' on the brickwork outside. After everybody had been checked, and it went quiet, we cautiously ventured outside and you could see on the facade of the building chips and holes made obviously by the bullets, We all went back over the road and up onto our bomb site and there were a lot of people about who had heard all the noise and wondered what was going on, and when the Wardens told them, Mum gave me and 'our kid' a big hug, then she gave me a smack on the ear and told me not to do that again!! What!! But it was a great story to tell all the other kids, and to prove it really happened we would take the kids and show them the marks on the wall of the institute, I don't know if the institute is still there today, if it is, go and have a look.

At one time during the war there was a big drive on for scrap metal to aid the war effort, even the railings around Gosford Park had been removed, and all the gangs used to compete with each other to see who could collect the most scrap, it was piled up in the corner of the bomb site and jealously guarded, mind you that didn't stop us raiding other gangs stores. anyway off we went scrounging whatever we could find that was metal, we knocked on doors, dug down into bomb sites, went around the garages and factories, we pinched a couple of gates and some metal dustbins from behind some shops, we even sacrificed our collections of shrapnel pieces! We even found up an entry a kids tricycle with no wheels on it so we had that away, I don't know if it belonged to any body. My gang and 'our kids' gang worked together on this project, and we actually won for our area, and the mayor came and congratulated us and the outcome was that they said that all the scrap metal that was collected in Coventry went towards building a Spitfire fighter, which would be named 'The City Of Coventry'. We all felt mighty chuffed that we had done our bit.

Rationing was still a problem and most things were becoming shorter and shorter, and the queues getting longer and longer, as soon as the word went around that a shop had had a delivery of what ever, it didn't really matter what it was, there would appear an instant queue. In fact when you saw a queue you just got onto the end of it just to see what was going, Dad smoked and getting cigs was difficult, there was a lot of black market going on, it was always the case of not what you know, but who you know. At the bottom of our street was a little shop, well I say shop, it was actually just a terraced house but the front room had been turned into a shop, it was run by an old dear called Granny Kent, it was a sort of generally anything. if she had it you were lucky, if not, tough. Now Mum and Dad used to get on well with her, they had known her for years, so that if anything came in that was short supply, she would keep things by under the counter for her favourite or regular customers, jam, vinegar, perhaps some tinned things, she even had a barrel of beer behind the counter, but she didn't sell anything that needed a ration book, although sometimes she would quietly say "would you like a bag of sugar, or a jar of honey, nod, nod, wink, wink, cigarettes were the same, if Dad was short, he'd say "pop down to Mother Kents and ask if she has any cigs, but make sure the shop is empty before you ask her, which I did, if she had any she would get a little white paper bag, bend down behind the counter and put 3 cigarettes in it and tell me to put it my pocket quickly and tell no one. The cost would go on Dads 'tab,' inflated probably. Sometime's she would give me a couple of mints, oh yes, she also sold small bottles of stout, which when it was winter Mum would have one, pour it into a thick glass, then put the poker into the fire, them when it was red hot she would stick it into the glass of stout, a winter warmer she would say.

Dad smoked of course, but Mum didn't, and shock horror so did we kids, yes at our age! anything we could get our hands on, herbal cigs from the chemists, something called Pasha, we think they were made from camel dung, dried tea leaves, sometimes real cigarettes, perhaps ones that I or the other kids had pinched from their parents, most times one cigarette went round the 6 of us, one puff each, Schooling was now getting much better, I didn't hate it quite so much, as being in the juniors was in the same area as the senior lads. So I used to knock about with them at break times, and also I began to get into sports. Our school was only a cricket and rugby school, we weren't allowed to play football, but we did have gymnastic classes in the assembly hall, I myself got pretty good at it actually on the ropes and the horse and parallel bars, in fact on Parents day we had to put on a display inside the hall, also outside in the playground where you could get a better run up. We would take all the padded mats outside and do exercises, plus I was the first one in the school to do a running somersault and then another one, it had never been done before as it was considered too dangerous, my claim to fame, I felt good and I know Mum and Dad were proud of me.

The rugby and cricket was sometimes played in the playground if we couldn't get down to the playing fields, in case there was a raid. The playground was very big which was good for cricket, plus we played rugby on it as well. It wasn't grass by the way, it was concrete, and the rugby wasn't touch rugby, as they teach kids nowadays, it was full on contact rugby, there were always scrapes, knocks, bruises, and bloody noses going around. They would never allow those things to happen nowadays, especially to 8 yr olds, we grew up tough in those days!

A couple of the lads in my gang had joined the Cubs at St Margarets, in the institute, (where we were shot at), so I thought I would give it a go, so I joined as well, it was called the 12th cub/scout group. It was quite good really, we learned quite a few things, tying knots, nature, semaphore, and we used to go on trips, and as I kept it up, and not just a flash in the pan, Mum and Dad bought me the uniform, green jumper, socks, shorts, sock tabs, and neckerchief. You could do all sorts of tests and if you passed you got a little badge to sow on the sleeve of your jumper. I wasn't so much interested in the indoor stuff, I liked the outdoor much better, surprisingly enough I kept it up and progressed into the scouts as I got older, and when I was about 15 or 16 I became a Senior Scout and used to help out with the cubs and young scouts when we went to summer camp. One year there was a big cub and scout jubilee held at the Memorial Park, for all cubs and scouts from Coventry. Princess Margaret was to take the salute, then she walked through the ranks afterwards, and she actually stopped by me, she shook my hand, left hand of course, and asked me how long I had been a cub and a scout, I told her, she smiled and walked on. From then on she was always my favourite Royal! I thought she was lovely.

Now going back a bit, It was now 1942 and the bombings had practically ceased in Coventry. The actual last air raid was in August 1942. of course no one knew it would the last one, so precautions carried on as usual, but there were no more sirens, so people began to feel a little easier, I was 8 yrs old, quite grown up actually, my gang was still going strong, still had the occasional fight with other gangs, and still scheming to make a penny or two. the bottle and jam jars were still a source of revenue, I did try a paper round but you had to get up too early for my liking, besides there was still a paper shortage so you didn't have many to deliver, no, definitely not worth it. The gang needed a sort of regular income because the Saturday morning cinema had started up again for the kids.' The Tuppenny Rush ' as it was called, and after I had done my stint with the basin for the dripping at the butchers, the gang would meet up and off we'd go to the pictures. I can't remember the name of the cinema, something like 'The Picturedrome' anyway we called it the 'flea pit', it was in lower Gosford Street. We were of course still doing the old beer bottle routine, out of the back and into the front!! so it raised a few pence for us all to get into the pictures. We became little kids again for a while, cowboys and Indian films, Dan Dare, Flash Gordon, it was great fun. We used to act out the films on the way home.

On school mornings the gang used to call for me. Even though we didn't all go to the same school, and especially on Monday mornings because they all knew they would all get a slice of cold Yorkshire pudding with jam on it, the left over from Sunday lunch. Mum used to ask them if anyone would like a glass of cabbage water, which was unanimously declined, surprise, surprise. Well, 'our kid' and I had to have it, so why not them! It was a rich source of vitamins Mum would say, yeah, Of course cooking the Sunday lunch with Brusell sprouts and cabbage, the water was saved for that purpose, we were supposed to drink some every day until it was all gone, we used to try and tip it down the sink when she wasn't looking, plus if I was helping to dish up the Sunday lunch and volunteered to strain the vegetables, I would do it straight into the sink, and then say sorry that I'd forgotten to strain it into a bowl! another clip around the ear. I wish they would clip 'our kid' a bit more often around the ears, he could do with it the way his ears stick out!

When we were in school I would always try to get the job of milk monitor, as a half an hour before break in the mornings, I was allowed to go and sort out the milk delivery, which meant sorting a crate of milk for each classroom and how many were in each class, then leave a crate outside each classroom with a straw stuck in each bottle through the silver foil top, then after break collect up all the empty crates and bottles and stack them up near the school gates for the milkman to collect, it wasted a bit of time. One trick I used to play was that if I had to go into a classroom to collect a bottle, (I always kept a tiny piece of Carbide in my pocket,) and as I walked past some ones desk I would drop the piece of Carbide into the ink well, and then quickly disappear. For about a minute nothing would happen, then all of a sudden the ink well would erupt like a volcano, and ink would boil out of the inkwell and run everywhere, but of course I was gone !!

Now as for my relations who lived in Coventry, we didn't actually see a lot of each other in the early years as it meant public transport and walking miles as most of them lived quite some distance, plus the fact that the war restricted a lot of visiting obviously, but after the war we did catch up with each other occasionally. My Uncle Walter and Auntie Alice (Dads sister) had sold their small farm in the sticks, and now had a small holding and a cottage over in the Whitley area, which in the old days was on the outskirts of Coventry, which meant catching 3 buses, but there was a short cut if you fancied walking for about an hour, so if the weather was nice we would walk. you went down by Gosford park and along the Ryton road until you came to the Folley Lane tunnels, now these tunnels went under the railway line and you finished up on the London road near the common and cemetery, which saved you miles, then down between the common to Whitley Abbey, where they lived. The small holding was about 3 acres with a wood behind it. There were pig stiles and goats and chickens, ferrets, which were used for catching rabbits and a donkey, Uncle Walter used the donkey and small cart to deliver stuff from the small holding to the shops and neighbours, he also had a small van, which I used to sit in when no one was around, and pretend I was driving it. I think he only ever used it to go to market because of petrol rationing, but he did give us all a lift up to the Folley Lane tunnels when we went home. Also up on the London road was a pub called 'The oak' I believe, and a row of cottages, Abbey cottages. and in one of them lived Dads sister and Mother, Auntie Nell and Uncle Jack and Grandma. They were an interesting family. Grandma sat in an enormous arm chair all day just knitting. Aunty Nell could make wine from just about anything that grows! nettles, berries of all sorts, plants, she used to walk over the common with a bag collecting all sorts of things for the ingredients for wine making, she made the wine, and then store it and then at Xmas time if there was a family party, most times at Aunty Alice's and Uncle Walters, out would come the bottles of wine Nellie had made, very potent stuff as well, as everyone seemed to get very merry. Some years we would stay for Xmas lunch or Boxing Day, as there was no shortage of food at Uncle Walter's small holding. Goose, chicken, ham, forget rationing for a while! With the wine flowing and also the home brewed beer, courtesy of Uncle Walter, things went very merrily along, they had a piano which Dad would play and every one would be singing, and it seemed to get louder as time went on, and every one would be jigging around, courtesy of the wine and beer I suppose!!! then aunt Alice would lay on a cold supper in the kitchen, again cold goose, chicken,ham, cheeses, pickles. Then back to the singing and dancing. It would go on to the early hours, then everyone would crash out where they could until the next morning. They were great Xmas do's. It helped to forget for a while that there was a war on.

Now Auntie Nelly's husband Uncle Jack, was in my opinion a remarkable person, I told you they were an interesting family, he was very tall and strongly built, swarthy, with big hands, he came from a Romany background, and he once said that at one time he was elected as king of the gypsy's for a certain term. He actually knew a lot about folk law, nature, the country side, and wild animals, I know that this may seem hard to believe, but he could go into the garden with me and 'our kid', tell us to sit still and be quiet, then he would hold his arm out and start whistling a birds song, and incredibly birds would fly down and land on his arm, sparrow to start with, then change his tune, and other birds would fly down, blackbirds, a robin, even sit on his head. He could also do all sorts of tricks with playing cards, and magic, making things vanish. He was quite an entertainer at parties. Also if any of the livestock on Uncle Walters small holding were off colour, he would send for Uncle Jack, he would take a look at them whilst talking quietly to them, then he would take a walk over to the common and come back with some weeds or leaves, wild flowers, either give it to eat, or tell Uncle Walter to boil them up and feed it to them, next thing they were as right as rain. He did like his beer though and as there was a pub next door he spent a lot of time in there. He had also at the bottom of his garden, covered over with a tarpaulin a 3 wheel open top car, but the wheels were 2 at the front and 1 at the rear, and the engine was mounted right on the front in a 'V' shape which had on it a plate with J.A,P, on it. I have an idea the car was called a Morgan. I never saw it being driven as you couldn't get the petrol at that time.

Talking about transport, sometime in 1942 Dad suddenly came home one afternoon riding a motor bike and sidecar, now I don't know if he had had it in storage somewhere when the war started, or he decided to get it out now as things had quietened down a little now with regard to the bombings but I couldn't remember it being around before the war, probably too young, I think the bike was a Rudge or an A.J.S. probably a Rudge as that's where Dad worked. It was a lovely looking bike. I remember the gear change lever was on the side of the petrol tank, a lever with a knob on the end. The sidecar was enormous, longer than the bike I think, shining black with a huge see through canopy that lifted sideways so that you could get in, and it had sliding windows, it had two seats in it as well, I don't think Dad had just gone out and bought it as he had all

59

the riding gear on to go with it, a long black leather coat with big collars, big leather gauntlets, leather knee high leather boots, leather helmet and goggles, he really looked the part!.

Evidently he knew someone in the next street who lived in an end house, and on the side of the house was a large shed with a large door out onto the street, and that's where Dad would put his bike at nights, as he didn't use it during the week, he only fetched it out at weekends. Sometimes we would all go fishing, which he loved, and he taught me and 'our kid' to fish also. Anyway Mum would pack a picnic, and off we would go, Mum in the sidecar and me on the' Dicky' seat in between her legs, 'our kid' on the back of the bike behind Dad, all wrapped up. Dad liked fishing in the canals, so we would either go to Ansty, or somewhere on the road to Lemington., we used to love it out in the countryside. Mum would lay out the picnic and Dad would light the primus stove by putting a drop of Methylated spirits in the dish, lighting it and pumping up the gas, on with the kettle for a nice cuppa. We would be fishing and Mum took the opportunity to have 40 winks or read a book. They were good days out.

Dad was a quiet person as I've already said, he never raised his voice, quite a withdrawn sort of person, so he never really say much about his side of the family, except I found out that his father was a Freeman of the City of Coventry. I only found that out years later when 'our kid' turned up the scroll or certificate when he was going through some papers. We think it was to do with some his Engineering services to the city. Mum filled us in a bit about his younger days as she said that he had always had motor bikes. After the first world war where he was an aircraft engineer, he worked for a motor cycle company, it may have been Rudge where he works now. Anyway he evidently worked on the Technical Development' side where he actually used to go to the old Brooklands racing circuit to do testing on the banked track and also to watch the racing, I wished that he had had some photo's taken. Probably that's where he met Mum, as she used to go there as well, it was the in thing in those days. But Mum came from Surrey at that time. but hoe they got together I never knew.

As for Mums side of the family, as I've said, originate from Surrey, Staines, and Egham to be precise, she came from a rather well off family, she had one sister and a brother, Tom, Aunty Bessie and uncle William. He owned a very large Engineering company, W, Try & co, ltd. It was a huge Victorian building about 4 stories in height. They had a large house on the side of the Thames just down from the Staines Bridge. I know Uncle Willy had a chauffeur driven Rolls. Mum took me down there occasionally on the train, and once after I had had pneumonia, I was 9 at the time, I spent a month with Aunty Bessie re cooperating. I used to sit on the terrace overlooking the river if the weather was fair, with a board and easel, drawing the boats that were moored on the other side of the river, also with a blanket wrapped around me, or when I could, walk up to the weir, and watch the men salmon fishing, oh yes, they had salmon in the river those days, or at least that's what they told me. Aunty Bessie had 3 sons, my uncles, but they were grown up, well they were to me, probably in their late 30s. But they were always nice to me, Arthur used to call me ' poochalaley'. Where he got that from I don't know!. Rob had an engineering company and Gordon a furniture company, he also had a band, he played the drums, and in aunties house there was a small ballroom with a stage and on the stage was a set of drums, which of course belonged to Gordon, and of course I used to mess around with them, and he used to tell me off and aunty would say it's all right he's not doing them any harm!, I loved that house, It was called 'The Old Bridge Cottage' in 'The Hythe' I wonder if it's still there.

Around 1943-44 cinemas started to open up again, and about once a fortnight Mum and Dad would walk down to the Forum cinema on the Walsgrave road, and take me with them. In those days the programme would probably start with a cartoon, or short film, documentary type. Then Pathe News, If anything came on about the war, there would be boo's, and cheers if it was either about the jerries or the British, if Hitler was shown everyone hissed! And if Churchill came on everyone cheered. Then the main Feature film would play, All of that for 1shilling and 9 pennies. At the end of the show, the National Anthem would play and everyone stood until it had finished. That was true British loyalty and spirit, something that is sadly lacking these days. Then if it wasn't quite yet 10 pm, there was a pub just up the road and Mum and Dad would pop in for a quick one, and I would stand in the passage with a bottle of pop. Either that or I would go straight home to see if any of the gang were still around. if not I could still get into the house as the door key would be on a length of string hanging inside the letter box! Everyone did it.

Talking about letter boxes! There was a trick we used to play on some of the neighbours, the ones we didn't particular like, we would get a cotton reel of black cotton, then at night we would quietly tie one end onto a door knocker, then reel it across the road onto the bomb site, hide in the rubble and then pull on the cotton a couple of times and wait, you could hear the knocker knocking, someone would come to the door, see no one there, look up and down the street, then go back inside. Then we would tug on it again then let it go loose, again they would come to the door, see no one there again, step out into the street and look up and down again, go back inside scratching their heads. we would do it once more, they couldn't see the cotton as it was pitch black because of the black-out, this time a couple would probable come out. We just hoped they didn't step on the cotton, if they did, and realized what was going on. We would be gone sharpish!! if not we just snapped the cotton. It was great fun.

We now get to 1944, and of course the D'Day landings in France, everyone was listening to the news more closely, We had a real radio by this time, not run off the electric but off the usual battery, or Accumulator as it was called, which still had to be charged at the garage. I think that I have said that it was my job to take it to the garage every so often to get it charged up. They charged 6 pennies to do it.

Of course D.Day was in June, and Dad said the war will be over by Xmas as everyone seemed to think so as well. But of course it wasn't, although people began to relax more, although rationing was still a bug bear. the Black market was thriving in those days, I believe it was all due to the Americans being stationed in the U.K. as a lot of stuff being traded was American, cigarettes, alcohol, sweets, bully beef as they called it, we used to love it, I often wondered how Dad got his petrol for his bike!, and Mum was still doing well with all the under the counter stuff. We always had a full table, so I suppose we were lucky in many ways. And as I've said before all the kids still called for me in the mornings to go to school, because they always knew there would be a slice of this or that waiting for them !

By this time with what the gang had collected from bomb sites around the town, swaps, and the occasional pilfering. We all had bikes of some size, shape or whatever, The frame of mine was a little big, but it didn't matter as I could still pedal by wobbling side to side, oh, and I didn't have a saddle! so I tied a cushion onto the crossbar. We were now a mobile gang, so now our activities of search, find, and reclaim, became a little bit more widespread. Point being, you couldn't keep on scrumping the same places over and over again. So fresh fields were now required. We also went on bike rides into the countryside to woods, or find a river to swim in. I had learned to swim from quite an early age. I had to because my lovely Brother pushed me into the canal once. "swim" he shouted, and I did. We would swim in our underpants, until our Gran found out and decided to knit us both some trunks out of wool. The trouble was that when they got wet they would hang around your ankles, so you had to tie a piece of string around the waist and put it around your neck! What did we look like, who cares, we were only kids, street kids.

Once we all decided to go cycling for a whole weekend. We all had a few shillings each, so we each had a blanket, a few sandwiches and bottles of pop or water, so we set off early one Saturday morning to make a weekend of it. I mean, who would allow a gang of 10.11.12yr olds to go off for a weekend on bikes, to god knows where, these days. Perhaps it's because we were allowed to have, and nurture, the spirit of adventure. Our parents didn't seem to mind us going, probably looking forward to a weekend without us around! But of course things were different in those days. We decided to head for Kenilworth first, as we wanted to see the castle, it was about 7 miles away, we got there o.k. but was my arse sore sitting on that cushion, instead of a saddle, that was tied onto the crossbar! I must get a saddle somehow. Around the castle were some steep grass banks which was the moat I suppose, but we found a sheet of corrugated iron which made a great sledge and it shot down the bank at crazy speeds, we then decided to head towards Stratford-on Avon, about 20 miles away so we set off again. We were about halfway there when it started to get dark, so we decide to find somewhere to spend the night, as we hadn't got any lights on our bikes. We never thought about getting lights back home. We rode around without them as we didn't want anyone to see us. Anyway we were near a village called Wavely, I think. It was all countryside and we had noticed that in the middle of a field was a large dome shaped metal barn type place. It was open at one end and we noticed bales of straw or hay piled up inside, so we headed over to it. There weren't any other buildings around so it was isolated which suited us as it was the ideal place to spend the night. So we hid the bikes and then stacked the bales of hay and made a den, it was lovely cosy and warm, so that's where we kipped down for the night. Next morning we were up early, and we straightened everything up and set off for Stratford. We had a great day there, we had a boat out on the river. then strolled around the town and saw the famous theatre. It was lunchtime so we decided to head home, and stop at Warwick for some tea.

On the way back we came to the place where we had spent the night, and as there wasn't anyone about we decided to go and climb on the roof of the barn as it would be fun to slide down the sloping roof, which it was, only I went down once and there was a bolt sticking up which we hadn't noticed, and it caught in my shorts and tore them from top to bottom. I shouted to the others to warn them but Roy was on his way down and he suddenly cried out that he had caught his leg on something, sure enough it was another bolt, and when he got to the bottom you could see that a piece of flesh had been gouged out of his thigh, not too bad but it was bleeding quite badly, so we bound it up tightly, one of the lads tore the sleeve of his shirt to bind it up with. my shorts were hanging in half so I couldn't really cycle in them, but I had a polo neck sweater in my bag so I put my legs down through the sleeves, tucked the neck under and it looked as if I was wearing a pair of leggings, job done, I couldn't cycle around in my under pants could I! we got to Warwick and found a cafe where we all had some cake and a glass of milk. The girl behind the counter noticed that Roy's leg was wrapped in some cloth but the blood was showing through it, so she took him around the back and dressed it properly, which was very good of her. After a short rest we cracked on as we wanted to get home before dark. Mind you from Warwick it was a hard slog, especially with my improvised saddle, we rode in single file and kept changing the front man who would go to the back for a rest, like they do in the 'tour de France' so that we could make up some time, as we had no lights. But oh my arse! I think I walked bow legged for at least a couple of days! Mum said we shall have to get you a proper saddle when we can afford it, but luckily one of the gang had been sorting through some rubble on a bomb site and unearthed a smashed up bike, he salvaged a wheel and also the saddle, another problem solved.

Now just down the road and across the main road and up a lane was a swimming pool which ran alongside the railway, Gosford Park pool, it was called, it had been closed at the beginning of the war, but was now re-opened, we couldn't afford to use before it closed, but now with our little schemes going we could. It was a smashing pool shaped like a letter T, with slides and a terrific set of diving boards, in an A shape, there was a ground level spring board and a static one, then up, and another spring board and static one, then up and two more statics and up again to the top board which must have been at least 30 ft high. If you jumped of the second static one down on to the lower spring board, you would shoot way up in the air, but you had to be a bit careful because if you went too high you could miss the water all together and land on the side of the pool ! So you had to make sure there were no attendants around. There was a sun bathing area which went up in large steps, showers, changing rooms and a cafe. The pool was open from May until October. it was cheap to get in, and in the end our parents bought us all season tickets, as we were down there so much, also because they knew where we were most of the summer time.

I was 13 by now, and to try and get a bit more pocket money, I went for an after school job at the Co-Op on Ball Hill, it was a delivering job, taking out orders to customers. I had a typical delivery bike, a small basket on the back, a small front wheel and an enormous basket on the front. When you had a big delivery to do it was hard to get on the bike, so you had to run with the bike and get enough speed and then jump on quickly, trying of course not to squash your 'what its', When there were no orders to take out I used to help out in the shop or out in the back, perhaps cutting up and weighing pats of butter or cheese, or lard into rationed sizes from large slabs, or sugar into paper bags, sometimes I even served in the shop. I used to like it and the women in the shop used to make a fuss of me. In fact when I left school I went to work there full time for about a year, for the after school work I was paid £1, 50 pennies, but that included Saturday mornings. Then full time £3, 10s. Three pounds and ten shillings.

My last year at school was o.k. I was in the Seniors so I could boss the younger kids about, especially as you were a school prefect. I still hated Maths, I could never see any practical use in learning Algebra or Logarithms. I was good at mental arithmetic though, probably because I was mental. I liked English as well, I know, you are probably saying not after reading this!! I know, but I am a phonetic writer, that is, as I am writing one sentence I am thinking of the next sentence in my mind. So perhaps I make a few mistakes here and there, maybe if this manuscript ever gets into print someone can sort out the mistakes. I also liked acting in the school plays. My best subject, apart from sport was Metal work. I disliked woodwork. You could choose which subject to do in your last year. I could read drawings, Dad taught me that. I loved using the machinery. In my last year I made a teapot stand out of brass, and an ornate fire poker out of steel and brass, the teapot stand had some quite intricate fretwork pattern work in the brass. the poker looked like a miniature trident. They must have been o.k. as both of them were sent down to London to be in an exhibition. I was allowed to keep them and they stood in the hearth at home for years. I wonder what ever happened to them, perhaps some distant relation has them.

I now at last left school. 14yrs of age, and now a young man. As I've said I went to work at the Co-op grocery store, and working 6 days a week full time came as a bit of a shock, and for only £3, 10 shillings a week. Now all of my mates all left school around about the same time, but some were earning a lot more than me for just 5 days a week, plus the fact that I was now contributing to the family budget, paying a bit of bed and board as they say. A pound a week doesn't sound much, but it was a lot from what I was earning.

Around this time a new sport started up in the country, and that was Speedway racing, and it became, and still is, a national sport. Coventry started up a team called the Brandon Bees, The track was at Brandon on the outskirts of Coventry, just past Binley, Myself and the gang used to catch a train there on a Saturday night to watch them and we had great times. The train was only on a side line and only took about 20 minutes, but it used to be full of speedway supporters, and when they got off everybody walked up to the stadium singing and chanting, and on the way back, louder if the Bees had won. The speedway craze gave birth to 'Cycle Speedway' for all the kids in the streets, and it really took off in Coventry. I know it did in our street. We all converted our bikes into speedway bikes

You stripped them right down, no mudguards no brakes straight handle bars and a low ratio gear, only one gear actually, and all the parents got involved in it as well. The bomb site in our street had been flattened so it was the ideal place to make a speedway track, we marked out the oval circuit and raked it. took out all the stones and used garden rollers to flatten it even more, some of the parents got interested in it too as I've said. We lined the track on the inside and the outside with house bricks and painted them white. At each end of the track we made servicing pits for both home and away teams. One of the kids Dad who was an electrician rigged some spot lights on poles, about 6 of them, they were on stands so that you could take them away, they ran on car batteries, plus Johny's Dad and my Dad rigged up some starter gates with thick bungy elastic bands and high poles, one each side of the start line and some ropes stretch across from one pole to the other, and when you pulled a lever the start gate would shoot up and of you'd race. it was just like the real thing, lots other tracks copied the idea. On race nights the women had a stall selling tea and cakes, it really was an organised thing in Coventry, with teams from all over, and proper leagues and race officials with loud hailers, music would be playing, it really took off. Teams and leagues were divided into age groups, 6 to 10 yrs 11 to 14,yrs 15 to 18yrs, Teams had their own colours and names, we retained our gang name, the 'Villiers Street Vipers'. Everything was really organised. on race nights, which were advertised, you could get a hundred plus come to watch.

Most areas in Coventry turned out teams. I think though that we had one of the best tracks to start with. But then it expanded rapidly with lots and lots of teams, so some official body was set up to control it all, and then you had to register your team for a fee, then leagues made up, and even some riders had transfers to other teams. Some of the teams had riders in their 20s in them. It became really competitive, some teams even travelled to other towns to race. We were quite happy just sitting in the lower Leagues, and just racing for fun. I think we lasted about a year or eighteen months but it was great whilst it lasted.

I seem to have skipped forward a couple of years, as I have missed out on one of the most important times of our lives during the war, and of course that was the end of it. Yes, the war was finally over. After 6 years, I can't imagine how Mum and Dad felt at that time, after losing a home and everything lost in it, the constant worry during the air raids, back and forth from shelter to shelter. Worrying whether your children would be safe going to school. When will the next air raid begin. Will Dad be safe out on his 'Air raid Duties' Will our sons, husbands, wives, sisters, brothers, any family member return home safely? It's hard to imagine for us, then children, on how people managed to cope with the emotions that that time had created.

The end of the war as far as we were concerned was a bit confusing, a rumour had started to go around that someone had heard that an announcement was to be made on the radio about the state of the conflict in Europe, so of course everyone sat listening to the Radio, waiting for any news, evidently Mr Churchill was to speak to the nation around lunchtime, which came and went, then it would be later, then in the evening. The date was the 7th of May 1945. Then finally after apologies for the delays due to technical difficulties, Mr Churchill came on and announced that hostilities in Europe had ceased, Hitler was dead, and that Germany had unconditionally surrendered. Well, there was silence for a few seconds. Then Mum started crying, Dad sat staring at the floor for a while then hugged Mum, Our kid and I just went' bananas', jumping around and punching each other. We all went to the front door and looked down the street. It looked as if everyone else had the same idea. People were out in the road shaking hands and hugging each other, women were crying, kids were running wild, although it was getting dark everyone had their doors wide open and people were opening the blackout curtains after all these years, mugs of tea were going around and bottles of beer if you had any, one of the neighbours had a bottle of whisky which he said he had been saving it for just this occasion and he gave Mum and Dad a tot! It was as if the cork had blown of a champagne bottle!! It was also broadcast that tomorrow, May 8th would be declared. V.E. day, Victory in Europe day, and also that the next two days are a ' National Holiday,' great no school, What also seemed strange was that the Church bells began ringing all over the City, strange because we hadn't heard a Church bell ring for 6 years!. The street celebrations lasted well into the night, any cars or buses that were around were blowing their horns also, so it was a pretty sleepless night for everyone. The next morning all the women got together to organise a street party for all the kids on the following day, everyone got involved, So when things were arranged, they started cooking and baking things. So the next morning people bought out tables and chairs, put them all together with table cloths on, then they all set about furiously cooking and baking things again for the party which was to take place later in the day, I think that most things that were on ration were used up in that one day, plus the black market flourished also!. Of course rationing didn't finish at the end of the war, as it carried on for a few years yet. Slowly getting better and better as the years went by as the shops were able to obtain more and more items. I think the final item to come of rationing didn't actually happen until 1957!! 12 yrs after the end of the war!!!

The war in Europe was over but it was still going on in the Far East against the Japanese where the Americans were heavily involved, and of course the British and Commonwealth countries, That was until the advent of the Atom bomb developed by the Americans, so after Japan refused to surrender one was dropped on Hiroshima in the August and then a couple of days later, one on Nagasaki. which, thankfully brought an abrupt end to that war, so at last world peace reigned. They say it was the war to end all wars, perhaps hopefully yes, a world war, but obviously not all wars!

Now it's time to get back to where I left off. By this time I was about 15 yrs old, and getting a bit fed up with working for such a low wage at the Co-op, so decided I needed to earn more, the same as my mates were earning. Now one of them worked at A.W.A. at Bagington airport works, it was called Armstrong Whitworth Aircraft. He said he would ask about trying to get me a job there, which he did, and I went for an interview, and low and behold I got a job as an airframe fitter. I turned my bike back into a normal one again as I would be biking to work with my mate. It was about 6 miles, but if the weather was really bad you could catch a couple of buses to get there, and at home time the company laid on special buses for the workers. The only trouble was that when the hooter sounded to go home and the gates were opened there was a stampede to get on the first bus which filled straight away and was gone! then you would wait for the other buses to fill up, But I was pretty fit and usually managed to get on the first one with a bit of push and shove!

In the huge hanger workshops there were rows of benches, and you worked in gangs of about 8 with a ganger in charge. In our gang we were all young chaps but good workers and our ganger was a smashing bloke. He used to say "do the work well, with no rejects, and I'll make sure your all o.k." which he did. The work was all assembly stuff, riveting, drilling, bolting things together which were parts of an aircraft. It was piece work so the harder you worked and the more work you turned out, the more you got paid, and that was the same for the ganger as we all worked as a group, the ganger always managed to get us the better paying work, At that time the company were building a new type of airliner, a short haul plane, similar in size I think to the American Dakota, it was to be called the Apollo. I fell into the work straight away as I was good with my hands and worked quickly, and if anyone left it was left to me to teach the new replacement the job, after a while I was promoted to 2nd in charge and when the jobs came up it was left up to me to allocate them out as I knew by then who could to what, how, and when, the best. If the ganger ever had any time off or was away looking for the best to do, he knew I would keep things running. My mate who worked on another gang managed to wangle a transfer to our gang as we were earning more money than anyone else. I was now earning about £7 to £8 pounds a week for 5 days, for 15 and 16 yr olds that was very good money in 1949, 1950. It was so good that I decided to buy a new bike on the never, never (finance). Now four of us lads had become interested in cycling, as one of the lads father usedto do track racing up at the Butts cycle stadium. where there was a proper banked cycle circuit, and sometimes we would go and watch the racing. A couple of the lads had touring bikes already so it was up to me to get one as well, I reckoned that out of my wages, and after I had paid my board and with a bit of spending money I could afford £2 a week on the never never. In Coventry there was a well known cycle shop called Dawes, who made the bikes themselves. So I went up to have a look. I felt very grown up at that time, me a 15 yr old kid going to buy a brand new bike, Oh, my Dad was with me by the way, I needed him to sign all the paperwork as I was under age, also for his advice, I didn't want a bike straight off the shelf, It needed to be one with all the special parts on It that I needed specifically. I wanted a sort of multi- purpose bike. so with the help and knowledge of the chap in the shop I first picked out a frame, a Dawes own make, it was light green in colour, sturdy but light, it would be used for touring, road and track racing. The wheels were thin and light weight, the gears were ones that had just come onto the market called 'Simplex' which gave you a good range of ratio changes. I also bought another wheel with a fixed cog for use on a track, racing dropped handle bars and saddle. A pannier frame and a pannier for touring, alloy pedals and toe clips, water bottle holders and clip on lights, cycling shoes and shorts, Well that little lot came to just over £80 pounds! A lot of money I know, but if you are going to do something, do it properly! I was finished with second hand parts and make do's. Also the saddle I chose was lovely, suede nice and soft. I t was the best because I thought of the time when rode an old made up bike dug up form a bombed site and a cushion tied on the crossbar as a saddle!

The shop was going to assemble the bike and check it out for me, and I could pick it up next week. Dad signed the Hire purchase forms and I paid a £20 deposit, and it was then £2 a week forever and ever! That following week seemed like forever. But Saturday finally arrived and off I went to pick up my brand new Touring, Racing, and Time Trial bike! all rolled into one! I went into the shop and there it stood on a stand. It looked terrific. The shop owner was himself was there to see me take delivery. I sat on the bike and they adjusted the saddle and handle bars to suit me. I was just about to go when the owner came over to me and gave me a race helmet and glasses, and said he hopes that I have many happy hours cycling. That was really nice of him. Riding the bike home was so exhilarating. I couldn't wait to show it to everybody. So now and with my mates we had our own Touring Club. no longer scruffy, snotty nosed street urchins, pirates, or gangster street lids, we were now respectable, well nearly! We even joined the Y.H.A. youth hostels association, so that if we went touring over a weekend, we could stay overnight in one of their hostels. we also joined the Butts cycle club 'Coventry Godiva's so that we could use the butts track for some training, hence the wheel with the fixed cog, we then decided to try road racing or Time Trials, 25 and 50 miles, the 50 miles were a bit too ambitious so we stuck to the 25 mile trials. and we clocked up some respectable times too.

Cycling to work now took on a different meaning, as I have said it was around 6 miles from our street to Bagington, airport works, so my mate and I would ride one behind the other then keep changing places. We would time ourselves to see how quickly we could get to work, and then every day, try to beat that time, it was good fun dodging in and out of traffic, something you couldn't do nowadays. At work, the new airliner was apparently ready for its maiden flight, so the whole factory stopped work one lunchtime and went out onto the runway. The' Apollo' stood on the end of the runway engines running, it was a nice looking plane, then it started moving and gathering speed, and then lifted off to a great cheer from the crowds. It's funny, but I never did know what the future of that plane was, as I left there shortly afterwards.

I was now around 16 or over and began to smarten myself up a bit clothes wise, I used to be a bit sloppy I suppose, and kids my age were getting into fashion and courting and all that stuff, but my mates and me were too busy having a good time to bother with all that stuff. o.k. a couple of girls started knocking around with us, one was the sister of one of the gang and her mate, one thing that was a regular must not miss, outing was the Sunday evening picture show at the Gaumont cinema, The afternoon matinee would finish around 6- 30pm, but there was already a big queue outside stretching around the corner and up the street, because all of our gang had been in the queue since around 5pm. It wasn't the fact that a really good film was showing, nobody knew what the film was anyway. no, it was because of the entertainment that would be going on in the queue, everyone was around our age, and everyone started queuing that early because of the entertainment, the queue would build up until it was about a hundred yards long and 3 or 4 deep, and all sorts of antics would be going on, fireworks going off, people singing, and someone blowing a trumpet or playing a mouth organ, whistles blowing, and sometimes fights breaking out, and everybody would be laughing, There was always a Copper walking slowly up and down the queue. It must have been a rotten job, because some of the remarks that came out of the crowd would make everyone laugh, and make him smile as well, it was all in fun as he got offered sweets and chocolate. There was a cafe across the street, and I think they opened purposely on Sunday evenings as they did a roaring trade from the people in the queue. Going to the Gaumont on Sunday evening was the in thing, it became a cult thing. As I've said it didn't matter what film was on, it was what went on in the queue and inside. They wouldn't let anyone inside the place until it was empty from the matinee, When it had emptied, the queue would start to slowly move, it was strictly controlled at the door. 2 doormen and they would only let a few in at a time, and look over everyone in case you were taking in something you shouldn't be taking in, but of course nearly everyone concealed something or other. O.K. someone would probably be stopped from taking in a double base, or a piano! but hey, it was all part of the fun. They would let anyone into the circle by the way, because of throwing things down.!! Now before the lights went out the usherettes would walk up and down the Isles making sure everyone was seated and behaving themselves. Then the lights would go out and everything would be quiet for a few seconds, then someone would start coughing, then someone else, then a few more, and suddenly the whole cinema would start coughing, the usherettes would run up and down flashing their torches, this used to happen every time., in the end the lights would come back on again and they would walk up and down but everyone would be looking ahead all innocent like. The lights would then go back off again and the film would start, then suddenly an alarm clock would go off over one side, again the usherettes would flash their torches over the audience. Then from the other side a whistle would start blowing or a trumpet would sound, it was hilarious. If during the film there was a quiet moment, a whoopy cushion would sound, and some of the comments shouted out during the film would have everyone in hysterics, Whilst all this was happening, and before they closed it off, a constant shower of peanuts and crisps and cardboard cups would be coming down from the balcony. But as I've said if you wanted the perfect end to a weekend and laughing until you wet yourself, it had to be a Sunday night at the Gaumont!!

On Ball Hill, the main road, there was a pub named appropriately 'The Old Ball Hotel' and on Saturday nights we would all go in there for a drink, we were still only about 16 or 17 I know, but 2 or 3 of the gang looked older, I've told you we grew up quick in those days, the bigger ones would order the beers, and gin and orange for the two girls if they were with us. the landlord didn't seem to mind us. We drank Atkinsons bitter at 11 pennies a pint, which in today's terms would be under 6p! We would play darts until about 9 pm. Then it was off to the dance hall. The dance hall was at the G.E.C. works on the Binley road, about a half hours walk away, it was a great place, big inside with a stage and a bar, with tables and chairs around the outside of the dance floor. You were supposed to be 18 to get in but we always blagged our way in somehow. there were live bands playing, no disco's in those days, strictly come dancing stuff. We would grab a table for the 6 or 8 of us, and put 5 shillings each in the kitty for drinks. We would sit eyeing up the girls or dancing now and then with the girls who came with us, Blokes were fairly shy in those days with regard to asking women to dance, so now and then the band would play a 'Ladies excuse me' dance, so if any girl fancied a fellow it was quite in order for her to go over and ask him to dance, me dance! not likely, I was too busy getting plastered. I remembered once, I'd had a few pints and decided to go outside and get some fresh air, so I put my donkey jacket on, as it was the middle of winter, they were all the rage in those days, and went out into the yard where all of the firms vans and cars were parked, I thought that I had better to sit down, before I fell down! So I went in between two cars and sat on a low wall. I put my arms on my knees and just rested my head on them for a few minutes. the next thing I remember was the shivering that woke me up!, and It was dawn, and I was covered in frost, my jacket was frozen stiff, and I couldn't feel my hands or feet. I reckon I had hyperthermia! Anyway I very stiffly got to my feet and painfully started to walk very slowly and gingerly home. It was a good thing it was a Sunday morning and nobody was about. The feeling started to come back to my feet so I started to jog very slowly to get the rest of my body working again. Got home, had a nice cup of tea, Mum said where was I last night and I said I stayed at a mates house, and she cooked me a lovely breakfast. When I saw the lads that evening they said that they noticed that I had been gone for a while and came out to find me as they were going home, couldn't see me, so they thought that I had already gone home. That's mates for you!!!

I said earlier that I was starting to smarten myself up a bit, so one Saturday I went into town to have a look around some shops. The rage at that time was the Italian look, so I bought myself a 4 button, small collared, hip length jacket in black. A white fly away collared shirt, with big cuffs for cuff links, a bootlace tie. Slim tight slacks, winkle picker shoes, the slacks were Grey. And wait for it, pink socks!!. Everybody seemed to be wearing pink socks, so I thought that I would be the bees knees. I wore everything that I had bought, and put my old clothes in a bag and swaggered along the road, To top it all, on the way home I decided that I might as well go the whole hog so I called in at the barbers and got myself a crew cut! Mind you I wished that I hadn't because that wasn't specifically Italian, but hey, ho, when I got home I was expecting perhaps something like, my you look smart, but Mum giggled, and then said sorry, Dad said I looked like a bloody German, and of course 'our kid' took the piss for ages. My mates all gave me the Nazi salute, and called me Her'Raymond. Was I glad when my hair grew back again.

in the winter of 1951 I was still cycling to work at aircraft factory, but with the snow and ice which seemed to go on and on it was getting a bit treacherous, as I came off a couple of times and also busted a front wheel, and nearly got run over by a bus. you could get to work by catching a couple of buses, it meant getting up at the crack of dawn and it was late when you got home at night, so it was just basically work and sleep, and by the time the weekend came you didn't feel like doing much. Plus the fact that at work they cut out a lot of the piece work, so I wasn't earning such good money any more. So I decide to look around for something a bit nearer home, besides in just about 18 months time I was due to be called up for Nation Service anyway.

One Sunday night on our usual jaunt to the cinema and we were in the queue as usual, over the other side of the road were a row of shops. One of the shops was a Sports Outfitters, Davies it was called. It was well known in the Coventry, they catered for every sport going. this particular shop was an ancillary of the main shop which was in Gosford street. Anyway in the window was a notice, so when I went over to the cafe to get a coffee, I walked past the shop and had a look at the notice in the window, it said that there was a vacancy for a shop assistant, preferably young and smart, interested in sports and willing to learn the trade. so overnight I thought about it and decide to find out what it was all about. on the Monday I took a sicky, dressed as smart as I could and biked up to the shop. There was a man standing outside the shop with his hands on his hips looking at the window, so I guessed that he was something to do with the shop, so asked him if the manager was inside and could I possibly speak to him, and he replied, "I am the manager, and I am not inside, I am standing here looking at the window to see if it needs changing, so why do you need to speak to me" Good start I thought, so I explained that I had come about the vacancy as the position really interested me. Well he then smiled and said "o.k. lad let's have a chat inside, you have a nice bike so bring it inside so that you can keep an eye on it, and we'll have a cup of tea and a chat" I began to feel a bit more at ease now. he asked me lots of questions and I said I liked all sports, and that I was also a senior scout, I was fairly good at Rugby, Cricket, Swimming, and cycling. Ricky was his name, and he ran the shop on his own but it was getting busier and busier so he needed some help. Someone who could learn quickly, deal with customers, work a till and good with money, and who could look after the shop if he had to pop out or go down to the other shop. I said that I was willing to learn all of that, He said "That was the answer I was looking for, just stand in the shop whilst I go and ring the boss, Mr Davies down at the other shop"

I was standing in the shop when a chap came in carrying a football, a flat one, he said could you blow it up and lace it for Saturday, as you usually do. I said "o.k. what name is it" he told me and left, just as Ricky came back "I see you have started already, jokingly, we get a lot of those, and Rugby balls, but I find it difficult doing them and looking after the shop at the same time, that's why it needs two people now" Anyway, He said, I've spoken to Mr Davies Senior, and he would like you to pop down to the other shop and have a chat. So I thanked him and off I went down to the other shop which was only a couple of hundred yards down the road, It was much bigger than the other one, and carried a lot more stock, and a bigger range of sports goods and equipment. I went into the shop, and an elderly gentleman was standing there, and asked me if I was Ray. I said yes, and he said "let's go upstairs for a chat" Upstairs was a large store room and an office with a secretary in it. we sat down and Mr Davies senior, asked me a few questions, and told me all about the company and the shops. He was obviously the owner, but only came in now and again to check that everything was o.k. his Son ran the business normally, he was about 40. there was another chap that worked in the shop, plus a chap upstairs who did all the sports repairs, re-stringing racquets, repairing cricket bats, and such. everyone was nice to me and I felt at ease straight away. Anyway, I got the job, start next Monday.

So having worked my notice at A.W.A. I was really looking forward to Monday. the hours were 9-5pm, 6 days, Thursday afternoons off, that was o.k. as I had done that before at the Co-op, plus dealing with customers was no problem. So on the Monday morning dressed in my best bib and tucker my new career started. It was a bit strange at first I must admit, but also fascinating in one way as there was such a variety of things to learn about, so your mind was continually absorbing knowledge about the products you were selling, also what and how they were used. and also as time went on giving advice on such things. Better than the repetitious, mind blowing, and boring work on a bench. I started by learning how to blow up football and rugby balls, getting the correct pressure by digging in your thumb and by the bounce, lacing it properly, and then hammering the lacing flat for heading the ball, the balls of course were thick leather ones then. Then fitting people up with all sorts of sports gear, taking orders for whole teams, arranging discounts for bulk orders. Putting new handle grips on all sorts of racquets, cricket bats, hockey sticks. Advising people which and what was most suitable for them with regard to the type of equipment or clothing they were looking for. Everyone seemed pleased with the way I was fitting in at the shops. Also Ricky was quite happy to leave me on my own in the shop if he had to go out, Another item we retailed was' Hornby' rail equipment. O and OO, engines carriages, rolling stock, anything to do with model railways, nearly all the model railway enthusiasts in Coventry came to our shop for their things, as there was another shop somewhere, and we used to order whatever they required. they would spend ages looking at whatever we had in stock, I got to know them all quite well, and it gave me an idea, so I said to the boss, that upstairs in the big stock room was a long table in the middle of the floor, so what if we set up a working miniature railway set on it, and kept everything that was to do with' Hornby', lots of brochures and that up there, then the enthusiasts could go up there instead of cluttering up the shop. He thought it might be a good ides, so he left me to organise it. Now I didn't know a great deal about model railways, so I asked the chairman of one of the clubs if he thought it was a good idea and would he be willing to help set it up. He thought it was a marvellous idea, and he said we would no doubt get all the custom from the town. So we let him loose upstairs and he built a layout on the table, only smallish as the equipment was very expensive, well it went down like a bomb, the expenditure more than outweighed what we took in orders. On Saturdays loads of them came in and up they went upstairs like a club meeting, then they would finally come down with all their orders. Even the Rep from Hornby came in, out of curiosity, to see why we were sending in so many orders. He thought it was a good idea, and I do believe we received a bigger discount for so many orders! Even Mr Davies, senior and junior, came and had a look. That was a feather in my cap! and the good thing also was that the chap that helped to set it up would come in on Saturdays and supervise it all upstairs, voluntarily. We would take the orders, let them know when it had arrived, they would come in, pay for it and then take it upstairs and try it out!

After I had been there for a while, Ricky said to me that would I like to have ago at dressing the small front window, there were two window, one large and one smaller, with the entrance door in the middle. So I said I'd love to, as I was quite artistic. (I forgot to mention earlier, that in my last year at school I had day release one day a week at the Coventry College of Art, I specialized in commercial art. advertising and that sort of thing) So I thought about what to do and decided to devote part of the window to Model Railway bits and pieces, engines, coaches, stations, signal boxes, also some boxed sets for children and as Xmas wasn't too far away I thought it would be a good idea to promote them. In the window looked pretty good, also I put in some lighting and a timer so that the window lights would stay on until 9pm. Ricky said it looked good and that I could do the big window next, another job. Also on the strength of the window display we sold a lot of the boxed train sets.

Every now and again I would go and spend a couple of days down at the other shop to get to familiarise myself with some of the sports equipment that we didn't stock at my shop. i.e. sports guns and pistols, shotguns, all types, ammunition, archery equipment, golf equipment and all accessories, also model cars, 'Dinky', all sorts, a huge range of them, and they sold well. Also the chap in the workshop taught me how to restring racquets, tennis, badminton, oil cricket bats. I learned how to record a handle and fit rubber sleeves onto bats and hockey sticks. I used to like the days I spent down there, and I got on well with Mr Davies junior, and the other assistant Eddie. We used to have some fun taking the mickey out of the office girl, and it's surprising the fun you can have with customers. If it was quiet and Eddie and I were on our own in the shop and a woman came in, we would be looking around on the floor and under the cupboards, and Eddie would say "be with you in a moment madam, only there's a big rat running around in the shop", then, "so how can I help you" if she was still there of course!! another time when someone came in you would pretend to be a foreigner and can't understand what they are saying, so you call the other assistant to help out, and he would come over either me or Eddie and say "you will have to excuse him as he's from Barcelona" or whatever ! Naughty I know, but we used to crack up. Eddie was ex R.A.F. handle bar moustache, and could talk very posh if need be, very smart and a great guy. In fact, apart from the influence from my Dad, he was also the reason for me wanting to go in the R.A.F when my National service was due, which would be in about 10 moths time.

After about 6 months I was practically running the top shop on my own as Ricky kept disappearing for some reason or other, or taking 2hr lunch breaks, and he would say "if anyone wants me, say I've gone to the bank, or haircut, or something. After a while questions were being asked and the boss would come up and when he did come back they would go into the back room for a while. Well eventually after a couple of months Ricky left. So there I was, running the shop practically on my own. I was responsible for opening up and locking up, cashing up and taking the takings down to the other shop, all the ordering. Mr Davies Senior would come in for a few hours one day and then Mr Davies junior and then Eddie for a couple of days. He said that they were quite happy with me running the shop on my own, with him, Eddie, helping me out at times, especially on Saturdays, as Mr Davies junior had a 14 yr old son who would go into the bottom shop with his Dad and start learning the trade, and that Eddie would flit between the two, which worked out quite well, plus I got a good rise!

As I was selling lots of different sports gear for different sports, I thought it would be a good idea to try and experience some of the different sports which I had never done and by that I would then know what I would be talking about when handling customers. Now Eddie used to go to archery sometimes, only because he fancied one of the women there!! So he took me along a few times and I was quite surprised just how technical it was. Also on the gun side, when some of the farmers came in for their ammunition, I would ask them what sort of guns they had, 12 bore, 16 bore, single or double barrelled, 12. 10s, and what did they use them for and when. One farmer invited me and Eddie to his farm one Sunday morning, it was only a pigeon shoot as they were getting to be a bit of a nuisance, sometimes it would be foxes, anyway we got to fire different shotguns from a hide in a field, and found out it was important to have your face covered with some sort of camouflage as pigeons have excellent eyesight and can see some ones white face from miles away. I wondered what those little green squares of mesh were for that were in the ammunition drawer, they fitted over your cap and hung down in front of your face. Never managed, by the way, to hit anything though!!

Another sport I had a go at was Fencing, There was quite a big fencing club in Coventry and they used to buy all their gear from us, foil, epee, sabre, and all the clothing, Which, if you were fully equipped did cost quite a lot, anyway I was curious about it, so was invited along one evening to a training session. I didn't have any kit but was lent some, helmet, jacket, one glove, or rather gauntlet, and a foil. Before you actually did any fencing you had to do what they called, 'circuit training 'to warm and to sharpen you up. I don't know about that, because it absolutely knackered me up! and, I thought that I was fit, but a very interesting evening, really enjoyed it.

I also had a go at target shooting with pistols, not ordinary small hand pistols, these were quite big with sights and wrist and shoulder straps, quite complicated really. Anyway with all the things I tried it did give me a little insight to the various sports, so that I was able to be a little bit more knowledgeable as to what I was selling.

For the next few months things seemed to just sail along in a routine manner, I still went along to help out with the cubs and scouts, In the pub a couple of nights in the week, down to the G.E.C. on Saturday nights, and of course the cinema on Sunday nights. it seemed funny standing in the queue opposite the shop where I worked.

Then came the time that every young man had to face up to in those days as he neared the age of 18, National Service! Two months before my 18th birthday, though the post came the formal invitation to join one of his Majesties three armed services, for a period of 2yrs, that is unless I had some form of exemption, i.e. a trade apprenticeship where as you wouldn't be liable for service until another 2 yrs when you had finished your apprenticeship. or if you were employed in an essential service such as coal mining, oil worker, or merchant navy, farmer. also I think what came under that category was being a conscientious objector, they would send you down the mines anyway if you were. The thought did cross my mind about running off to sea, but I knew that I would be sea sick all the time! No, if I was going to go, I wanted to be in the R.A.F. like my Dad

The only problem was that with National Service you didn't have any choice as to which service you wanted to go in. They just stuck you where was a shortage at that time! I then recalled that 3yrs ago when 'our kid' and his mate Alan were due to be called up for Nation Service, they both wanted to get into the Navy, nothing else would do, so as to ensure that they got into the Navy they volunteered just before being called up. Mind you, singing up for 7 yrs!!! was a bit over the top I thought. So the thought began formulate in my mind as to what they had done. Of course everyone one was saying go, on get into the forces it'll do you a power of good and make a man of you! I used to think, hang on, it's me that's going in, not you, anybody like to take my place!! Now about my idea, there was an R.A.F. recruitment place in the town so one Thursday afternoon, half day, I went along to make a few enquiries. I went in and at the desk was a Sergeant. I spoke to him and he asked me go and sit down and he would call me in a minute, also waiting was another lad, and we started chatting, his name was Jim, and blow me, we found out that we had both come up with the same idea about only wanting to get into the R.A.F. Just then the sergeant called Jim up to his desk, and at the same time an officer came out of a room and said who is next. So I went into this room and sat down opposite this officer, a pilot officer by the way, and he said "what can we do for you" so I asked him what was the shortest time that I could sign up for in the R.A,F. he said 3yrs.. I then said if I signed on for 3yrs I wouldn't have to do National Service and that it would guarantee that I would get into the R.A.F. (a stupid question), He smiled and said yes that's what we are here for. he asked me a few more questions and gave m some forms to fill in, and said if I still liked the idea of joining the R.A.F. fill in the forms and let me have them back as soon as possible, then we'll take it from there.

So I went home and talked it over with Mum and Dad, I think Dad was pleased that I had chosen the R.A.F. Then talked I it over with everyone at work. They said that there would always be a place for me when I came out, which was very nice of everyone. I filled in the forms and took them back, they said they would send for me for a formal interview in a few days time, and sure enough 3 days later they wanted to see me in 2 days time. so I went to the recruiting office and saw the same officer that I had seen before, but this time there two of them. they asked me various questions and said had I any idea what sort of trade I would like to follow. I told them of the work I was doing at the moment, but they didn't seem impressed, a store man was mentioned, o.k. for a national serviceman, but not for a 3yr regular so it seemed. I told them about my work as an aircraft detail fitter at A.W.A. Armstrong Whitworth Aircraft Company, and they jumped on that straight away. They said that there were always openings for aircraft fitters, especially experienced ones like myself and that I could go far in that trade. Perhaps once that I had completed my initial training (square bashing) and a refresher trade course, I could possibly be accepted for officer training as there was a shortage of officers in the trades, but of course it would mean signing on for a further 5 yrs or more. Tempting, not bloody likely, 3yrs was bad enough. So I was to be an airframe fitter, and a 3yr regular. Anyway, regulars got more pay than Nation Service people.

So I signed on the dotted line there and then, I still had a month to go before my 18th but as soon as that was here I'd be off. I should hear within the next week through the post, where and when I would be going and how to get there. When I came out of the office who should be sitting there but Jim, the lad I met on the first interview, and he had just been called back for another interview, and he also said he was going to sign on for 3yrs as he wanted to be in the R.A F. also only he wasn't sure which trade to go in for as he had been working in a friends repair shop doing all sorts of repairs on all sorts of things, cars, motorbikes, bikes, cars. so I suggested to him to try for aircraft fitter, airframes or engines, which he thought would be a good idea and worth considering. So I said perhaps we'll be seeing each other as his birthday was in the same week as mine. So now it was just a matter of waiting for further instructions, or should I now say orders to arrive.

The next couple of weeks were a whirl of wrapping up where I worked, going out with my mates quite a few times, saying cheerio to family and all that, but wondering mostly what the next two years had in store for me! I felt as if I was being evacuated again, only a grown up one. At least there were no wars going on, or so I thought.!!

Then finally my orders arrived, they were actually delivered by hand by a RAF bloke in uniform, no excuse to say they were lost in the post!. My instructions were to report to the railway station in 2 days time at 9am, where I would be met by a RAF officer and given further instructions. I was to pack a small suitcase with just a few civilian clothes. At the station I will be given a rail pass to my destination. The rail pass is to Bedford station where I will be met by RAF transport and taken to RAF Cardington, near Bedford, for my initial 6 weeks induction and training,(square bashing) Then(if I was still alive) you will be granted one weeks leave, that's if you have passed your training, You will then receive orders as to where you will be going to do your trade training which will consist of a period of 12 weeks, 10 weeks instructions and 2 weeks exams, if you fail these, you will have the option to retake them, or given other trade options, I didn't like that last bit!. If you pass you will be sent to your permanent stations according to your trades.

So it was to be RAF Cardington, where the hell is that! Actually it's ironic but when I told Dad he said he had spent a short time there as that's where the two largest hangers in the country were, they used to house the airships of the First World War and he worked on them for a short time. I had no idea where Bedford was, but Dad told me and that it was an awkward place to get to as there's no direct route by rail, you have to go to Rugby, out in the sticks, and the most miserable station in the country, and then on a branch line to Cardington. When he was there he went on his motor bike. The last night arrived so all there was to do was go and have a few beers with my mates and say farewell, then off to another mysterious journey in my life. At least this time I won't have a gas mask in a cardboard box hanging around my neck!!

The morning arrived and I said my goodbyes to Mum and Dad, of course Mum had packed some sandwiches for me, and Dad gave me a fiver which was handy as I wasn't exactly flushed as I'd spent a bit on beer this last week!. I caught the bus on ball Hill to the Station, it seemed strange getting on a bus with a suitcase amongst all the other people going to work, doing their day in and day out routine jobs, and here's me not knowing what the hell's around the corner. As I walked into the foyer at the station the first person I saw was, damn me, Jim, standing there with his little suitcase looking a bit lost. His face lit up when he saw me though. Evidently he had received the same marching orders as I had, the same day the same place, everything. I think we both began to feel a little better now that we wouldn't be in a strange place on our own, at least we'd have each other as company. the problem was we couldn't see anyone around to meet us. after about ten minutes an RAF corporal came running in, "sorry I'm late lads, the bus was late" anyway he said lets go and have a coffee and we can sort out all the paperwork, you've plenty of time before your train arrives", so coffee it was, and he paid for it. he was quite a nice chap really, round about our age, or maybe just a little bit older, he was national Service, and had another year to go, but he said he was going to sign on again when it finished as he had such a cushy number here in Coventry. He actually came from Nottingham, but he had an Aunt who lived in Coventry. Anyway when he was called up he asked for a job in administration of some sort as he was an office worker in civvy street., so he was assigned to the Recruitment office in Coventry, right where his Aunt lived, so now he works office hours. He travels around a bit when there's a recruitment drive on somewhere. He is allowed to be in digs, and gets an allowance for it, but his Aunt doesn't charge him anything for bed and board. He can go home to Nottingham more or less when he wants to. He now has a girlfriend in Coventry. They gave him Corporal stripes, and pay, so that he would look more official in the recruitment office, no wonder he wanted to sign on for more, he's got it made, apple to orchards eh!

Right, so we caught the train to Rugby, only a short journey really, we had been given rail passes for the next train trip to Bedford, and when we get there, there will be transport waiting for us to take us onto RAF Cardington we were told. As I've said before, Rugby station was a miserable place, or it was in those days, miles from anywhere and open to the elements, when the wind blew, it really blew!. One little waiting room and tea room, when they were open that is. Still had gas lamps. I spent some miserable hours on that platform in future years, but more about that later. Rugby was only a branch line which served other out in the sticks places, so when we asked when was the next train to Bedford was, he looked about a hundred years old by the way, he said don't worry it'll be along sometime? It was blowing a gale on the platform so we huddled up in the cold waiting room, the tea room wasn't open of course. On all the occasions I have had the misfortune to spend time on that platform, I have only seen the tea room open once, and that's I believe, was because they were cleaning the windows on the inside!! Mind you that was nearly 50 years ago, so I hope things have improved by now.

The train did finally arrive, two carriages, no loo, half expected it to be pulled by horses! We got on and waited and waited, I looked out of the window and the engine driver was standing having a smoke. I would have thought that he had had enough of smoke the way it was bellowing out of the engine, anyway when we had cleaned the chicken and goats shit of the seats, only joking!, we started off, well off? I think I could have run faster.

At last we arrived at Bedford station, and we went through the hallway to look for our transport. We noticed a lot of other blokes standing around with their little suitcases looking lost. In all there must have been around 60, some were in the station but a lot were outside standing on the pavement, I asked a couple of lads if they were waiting for transport to RAF Cardington, and they said yes. So it looked as if all of the lads that were hanging about were all new recruits on their way to Cardington to do their 6 weeks square bashing course, the same as Jim and I. At that moment into the station yard came 4 RAF lorries, I knew they were RAF because they were RAF blue with badges and numbers on, clever sod aren't I !! They stopped and out jump an RAF chap, no stripes or pips, or shoulder flap stripes. Just a badge on his sleeve, we found out later that he was a Warrant Officer, someone to be feared! There were three other corporals with him as well, but he was obviously the boss. He stood there holding a clip board and a polished cane, walking stick, or whatever, looking very much in charge. He suddenly shouted, in no uncertain terms, "line up in ranks of two you lot" which later interpreted meant stand in 2 s in a line one behind the other.! It took a little while for everyone to work out what the hell he was on about, but the corporals herded us into whatever the chap with a badge on his sleeve wanted! "Now," he said, "When I call out your names, pick up your little suitcases and double over to the three tonners, and a score to each three tonner". (Interpreted, go quickly as possible over to the lorries),and only 20 on each one. Must try and get used to all this Military jargon! The journey wasn't very long as the camp was only a few miles from Bedford. As we got nearer to the camp you could see the two huge hangers that Dad had told me about, they were enormous.

We went through the camp gates and on the side was a building, (called a Guardroom) and on each side of the entrance door were two large and long mirrors,(so that when you leave the camp you have to check to see that your dress (uniform) is correct. Then down the road past an enormous car park, (The Parade Ground) on to rows of wooden huts with numbers on them. (they looked like rows of huts you saw during the war in concentration camps, (ominous). the lorries stopped and a shout of 'all out' came from the Warrant officer,(from now on, W.O.) "When I call out your name and hut number the first 15 will fall out (go) into that hut and sort yourselves out a bed and a locker" Then the next 15 and so on, there were 4 huts and in the end of each hut is a room which is the corporals room, opposite that a storage room. At the back of each hut is a long hut which contains the toilets (ablutions) and showers. Each hut has a corporal assigned to it, he is in charge of you for the next 6 weeks, and is also your drill instructor, his word is law, remember that. Jim and I sorted out our beds and lockers, we had grabbed the two beds furthest away from the corporals room and nearest to the ablutions, getting canny already! the beds were just camp beds the mattress consisted of three biscuit shaped squares made of horse hair, a pillow, two sheets, and three blankets, a steel locker 6ft tall and under the bed a wooden chest to put your civvy clothes in.

We put some of our things away and we all sat on the beds chatting. The chaps in our billet(hut) were from all over the country so it seemed, mostly National Service but a few regulars, and also from all walks of life, and all shapes and sizes, a couple of Welsh,a couple of Scots, mostly Southerners, and Londoners, so quite a mixed bunch really, 20 in all.

Just then the corporal came in, stood at the end of the room hands on hips looking at everyone, and in a very authoritative voice said "Right you lot, I don't have a name, so you will refer to me as corporal, only speak to me when spoken to, also when I come into the billet you will all stand up and shut up. The gentleman with a badge on his sleeve is the Warrant officer, in charge of us all. and when he comes into the room someone must shout 'officer in the room' then you quickly stand at attention at the end of your beds, get it. Also opposite my room at the end is a store room so put your suitcases and jackets in there tidily. It is now 16.30, (4,30pm) at 1700 (5pm) I will shout 'fall in outside' and you line up in two ranks standing at attention, then we will march over to the mess (Dining room) for dinner, as you go in the door there will be a table there with your weapons on it (cutlery) pick up a knife fork spoon and mug, they will be yours for the rest of your stay here, so look after them as you won't get any more! So you'll eat with your fingers!, charming! So he shouts, we go outside, two ranks, he shouts attention, left turn, quick march. I don't know what he actually expected with those commands, but we turned left and started walking and when we had only gone a few yards he shouted 'Halt' Get back into the billet now and sit down." Which we did, after a few moments he came in and Jim and I stood up and then everyone else did, I'm sure I saw the crack of a smile on his face, he said "I'm glad you remembered something I said, right, now let me put you all in the picture right from the start, just then outside, you looked like a shower of s—t, there are 4 billets in this intake(group) 60 men in total, each billet has a corporal in charge, and the 6 weeks that you are here each billet competes against each other in everything, dress, drill, marching, sports, cleanliness, rifle range, etc, etc and the W.O. awards points, so as far as us corporals are concerned we strive to turn out the best billet and if we do, at the end of your course, the billet with the most points, that corporal gets two weeks leave. If not, nothing. So it is very competitive between us. More so as I have won it the last few times and I aim to carry that winning streak on. Loose, no, over my dead body, or yours, so can you all see where I'm coming from, you do your best to help me win again, and I see that you are, I'll try and make your stay here as easy as possible, if not, you have just stepped into the jaws of hell !! on the other hand, scratch my back ?? I may shout and bawl at you at times, and you will sometimes s—t your selves, but it's all part of the process to turn you into military men. Now what I have just said stays in this room o.k. Now get outside and try and look as if you are RAF men!

So, still trying to digest what he had just said, we assembled outside again, this time the corporal showed us how to turn left and right correctly and how to march, figuratively speaking, in some sort of fashion, left foot first, and then counting to yourself left, right, and so on. Actually we didn't look too bad with the 'Corp' marching along side of us. as the rest of the billets just ambled along, so there endeth the first lesson! In themes we grabbed our weapons and joined the queue for food (nosh). The food didn't look too bad actually with two choices, take it or leave it. Our billet sat together on an allocated bench with our hut number on it, all the corps sat at a table at the end of the mess. We had 20 minutes to eat then the Corp came over and told us to put our plates at the end of the table and then on the way out swill your weapons at the sinks provided and line up outside, which we did. The Corp came out and said attention, left turn, quick march, left, right, left, as he had showed us, keep together you idiots he said, but we were already learning. When we got back to the billet the Corp came in, we all stood up, he said 'stand easy' (relax). He said that that was a good start as he thought we were the best squad out there just now, and was pleased that he had seen the W.O. watching, but there are one or two idiots in here who don't know there bloody left feet from there right, but I will sort you out don't you worry, even if it means painting L and R on your boots! Now all of you relax now and get to know one another as you are all going to spendthe next 6 weeks living in each others shoes so relax, as you are not allowed outside for the first week, except to go to the ablutions, lights out at 21,oo hrs (9pm) reveille at 0-600 (6 am), There is a N.A.A.F.I. on the camp, (Navy, Army, Air Forces Institutes) but again you can't use it for the first two weeks. Tomorrow will be a long day as you will after breakfast go for a medical, then get kitted out (get uniform), try everything on to see that it fits reasonably well, if it doesn't tough s—t. so see you all in the morning at 6 am, and welcome to the RAF, I am off to the NAAFI, now, so when I come back later, after 9 pm, I will expect all the lights out and complete silence, upon pain of death.

When he had gone there was complete silence for a moment, I think everyone was trying to digest what had happened to them since waking up this morning, then someone called out "I want to go home", then "I want my Mum" Of course everyone burst out laughing which broke the ice, then everyone started chatting and getting to know each other, one or two were a little bit toffee nosed, but the majority were o.k. The London lad's and a couple from Liverpool and Portsmouth were obviously ' street kids ' who had gone through the war and the Blitz. a couple worked on farms, they were a bit peeved when we said you could get exemption from National Service if you worked on the land!! Thick or what? A couple were air cadets, they might come in handy. We all sat around chatting and laughing. One thing the Corp said before he went was that he wanted us all to appoint from amongst us a 'Spokesman ' for the hut, as he would be the only one he would confer with if anyone had anything to say regarding anything in the billet. Well the first thing to say is, are there any volunteers, silence, o.k. any proposals, so I said I would like to propose a chap called Max. I had chatted to him earlier, and he worked in a bank, but not on an apprenticeship. He spoke well, and seemed to have his feet on the ground, He seemed slightly embarrassed as he was the only candidate but agreed when everyone said yes.

As the time was getting on by now, we made up our pits (beds) and went over to the ablutions. it was a long hut with rows of sinks and mirrors on one side and rows of traps (urinals) on the other. And at the end about 5 showers, all open, you get no privacy in the forces. I quite liked the idea of having showers, better than a tin bath in the kitchen although I didn't tell anyone that. Then at the other end a row of 'Thunder boxes' (toilets.) Some of the lads had dressing gowns, very posh, me, I had a big towel. It was the middle of summer so it was quite pleasant in the billet. I don't know what it would be like in the winter? There were two large cast iron stoves in the middle of the hut with the chimneys going out of the roof. Promptly at 21-00 the lights went out, but we carried on chatting as we knew the Corp wasn't back as yet. Gradually the silence fell, except for the snoring and farting, and the occasional swearword if someone cracked their toes on something going out to the toilet. Must get a torch from the NAAFI as soon as I can. It had been a long and interesting day so I must have eventually dropped off. although the beds weren't particulary comfortable.

Apocalypse has arrived, or so I thought, there was a banging and a shouting going on, enough to wake the dead, awake, that's what is was !. ", Wakey wakey, you horrible lot, feet on the floor,and into the showers, and outside in one hour, or else. It was of course the Corp deciding it was time that everyone was up in his most charming manner, just because he was. Banging on every ones bed with his yard stick, (a device to measure the exact step when marching, one yard) How can any one look so smart at this unearthly hour, I must admit he did. Also be so bloody annoying! More about the' yard stick' which is owned by drill instructors, and W.O.s, it looks like two polished walking sticks with brass tips, and joined together at top with a brass hinge, and an elaborate brass handle, now when it opens at the top, it measures at the tips, one yard, which is one marching step from the tip of your left boot to the heel of your right boot, a drill instructor would march alongside a column of men, put one tip of the yard stick on the ground, then swivel it around until the other tip touches the ground, and so on and so on, all done as you are marching along, but its bloody loud, and noisy when its banged on a metal bed !!!, so that's a 'yard stick'. I just know that you wanted to know all of that !. Also its surprising just how quickly you can get showed and dressed when you have to. Before we went out on' Parade' as its now called, the Corp came in and said "I suppose when you were all at home your Mummy would make your little beds for you,"" he could be a sarcastic bastard when he wanted to be, "but now you have to make your own, and it's done in a special way, which I will show you" so you put your three biscuits on top of each other at the head of your bed, then two of the sheets and two of the blankets you fold all the same size in a square, then you put sheet, blanket, sheet blanket on top of each other,all nicely squared off and all the same, then the last blanket, fold it into a strip and then wrap it around the sheets and blankets like a sandwich, place the lot at the head of the bed," mind you it did look neat and tidy the way he had done it, "Right" he said "I'll give you ten minutes to practise that, then I will come and inspect your efforts, those who get it right will go for breakfast, those who don't, well !!!. So start practising. Now it looked easy when he did it, but it was difficult getting the edges square and straight. He did it in about 90 seconds, some were still struggling after ten minutes. Then he came back in, "right you lot, stand by your beds and I will inspect your efforts" He then walked along the beds, some he said needed more practice, some, he just picked up the blankets and threw them on the floor. no comment, and about 5 or 6 were good efforts, but try harder, practise he said, and we'll see again tomorrow. Overall, not too bad, now let's all go and get some breakfast.

We fell in outside and marched to breakfast carrying our weapons, getting the hang of this marching business, must be from when I was in the scouts. Breakfast wasn't too bad really, you could have some sort of porridge, either beans on toast or scrambled egg on toast, tea was in a large urn at the end of the table, but the tea had a funny taste, and I later found out why. after breakfast we marched back to the billet, even the Corp said we were shaping up better on the marching, but still a long way to go, wait until I get you all on the square!(parade ground). a few minutes later we were off again for our medicals, we went into a large hut, all 20 of us, and told to strip down to our underpants, and then go into another room 5 at a time, there were 4or 5 medics in this room and presumably a doctor, who looked into your eyes, mouth, and ears, asked if we had any medical conditions, I was sorely tempted to say Leprosy, but thought better of it as it didn't look as if he had a sense of humour. He then said drop your pants and lifted my do-dar up with a ruler. Then grabbed my whatsits and said cough, again, I was tempted to say, are you going to change my nappy too, again had second thoughts. Whilst all this was going on, a medic sneaked up behind me and stuck a needle into my arm, I said you could have warned me, he said we used to but too many fainted! No wonder I thought when I saw the size of the needle. Evidently someone did pass out, I don't know whether it was the needle or when he grabbed his whatsits. Plus a thought struck me that when he was doing all the grabbing of you know what, he never washed his hands once! Outside the Corp told us that at 19-00hrs tonight there is a film on in the gymnasium, and we will all be going, I hope I haven't seen it.

Assembled outside the medical centre the Corp said that we are now going to get you kitted out (collect uniforms) but to get there we will have to go through the centre of the camp, so I want you lot to try and look a bit like airmen, and march in step, shoulders back and swing your arms and look straight ahead, he gave a little demonstration, and if I see anyone put his hand in his pocket, I personally will tear his arm off! You never walk around camp with your hands in your pockets at any time. Plus swinging yours will help with the pain of your injections later on! Something to look forward to I must say.

I noticed as we were marching,(a loose terminology) around, there were other squads also marching all over the place, all in uniform, some squads carrying rifles, and as we passed each other they were all smiling at us, now was it a, good luck chaps, or a leer, as. we feel sorry for you ha ha, smile or leer?. I later learnt that every two weeks an intake like ours finish their 6 weeks square bashing course, and have a 'Passing out Parade' on the square, usually on a Friday, Parents and relatives can come and watch it if they want to. Then on the Saturday that intake go home on a weeks leave before they are assigned to their permanent stations or on to a trade training station, so after we have been here for two weeks, another intake will come in behind us, So every two weeks as one intake leaves another intake arrives.

We arrived at the clothing store which was a long building and inside was an anti-room where all your measurements were taken by a half a dozen chaps who were obviously civilians, they had there clipboards out and were asking everyone their sizes, shoes, hats, waists, if you didn't know they would measure you, I would have thought that everyone knew their shoe size, but other sizes would be a guess in most cases. I mean how many know their hat size or inside leg measurement. When all that was done they gave you your sheet to take with you through another door into the warehouse where there was a long counter and behind the counter rack after rack of clothing. The counter was manned by lots of staff, so you started at one end, handed your sheet in and the first thing they gave you was a large canvas bag for you to put all your kit in, hence a kit bag, plus a pair of boots and shoes, they gave you you're sheet back and then on to the next bloke, hand your sheet over, 2 pr of trousers, belt, socks, lumber jacket, best dress jacket, beret, forage cap, 2 shirts, ties, 3 pr underpants and vests, 3 shirt collars, collar studs, jumpers and a housewife(sewing kit) a small cloth bag with all sorts of stuff in it, brushes, polish, boot and brass, button plate, and finally an overcoat. It was a good job the kitbag was big, but you had to wear the overcoat as it wouldn't go in. It was all a bit fast and furious like an assembly line. So there we stood outside wearing our overcoats and our kitbags over our shoulders and then trundled our way back to our billets

By this time it was 3pm, 15-00 hrs, and we had missed lunch. Never mind said the Corp, you will enjoy your dinner more, now put your kit away in your lockers as shown in the photo's that are on the bulletin board, and I will come and inspect everything later. There were three large photo's on the board one showing what went into the locker and where, each locker had 3 compartments in the lower half. Another on how to lay your kit out on your bed for when there is a kit inspection, which is every two weeks, and is inspected by either an officer or the Warrant officer, added to that, there could be a snap inspection if your billet had done something wrong. Or it was deemed that a particular billet squad wasn't pulling its weight either in dress or on the parade ground, The Corp warned us that if ever our billet gets a snap inspection for any reason at all, it would mean a black mark against him, and then our lives wouldn't be worth living!! Fortunately that never happened, thank god! As it also showed that everyone seemed keen to pull their weight.

And the last, a photo of two airmen, one in every day clothes, and the other in best dress. Another article that we collected also, was a load of webbing, there was a belt with brass buckles, ankle spats, they wrapped around your ankles and covered the top of your boots and the bottom of your trousers pulled together with a couple of straps and buckles, lots of straps that held back packs and chest pouches, all of this was canvas webbing which had to be cleaned with 'blanco' like a grey coloured paste and then buffed up with a brush.

As we still had an hour before we went for dinner. Mac, the billet spokesman, decided to call a little meeting for the whole billet, and he wisely pointed out that if we all pulled together and did our best at everything that was thrown at us, and also helped each other, it would obviously please the Corp, which would then make our lives less miserable, especially if he saw that we were trying our hardest. I knew when I proposed Mac that he had a logical head on his shoulders.

After dinner we marched over to the gym to watch the film, our marching was getting better and better, you could tell because we weren't yelled at so much. FILM, did I say, it was all about sex! Not knowing how to do it, how to do it, what you can catch from doing it, another part about V.D. and some of the pictures they showed, it was a good job that we had had our dinners, and it was enough to put you off sex for life. Anyway when we got back to the billet the Corp said that now that we put our kit in the lockers he would come and have a look to see the results, we quickly tided up a bit, and had a look at each other's lockers to see if we could see anything wrong, which was a good idea. The Corp came in and we all jumped up and stood by our beds, and he slowly inspected each locker in turn, pointing out this and that, do it this way,fold it like this, he was very calm and spoke quite softly to each one. also it was easier to learn that way instead of being bawled at and nearly s----ing yourself, Now when he got around to Mac, he went over his locker and said very good effort, then he stood looking at him, and said "You know my room is on the other side of where your bed is, and these walls are quite thin, I was reading quietly and I actually heard everything you were saying at your little meeting with the other lads in the billet,!!! I think you will go far. No more said. he then turned to us all and said "not a bad effort on the whole, but always keep your lockers tidy, now that you all have your kit I want you to get dressed in your day uniform lumber jacket and shoes, and get used to wearing them for a couple of hours. Now I don't usually do this, and it's something else that stays in this hut. But as you are trying things on I will walk around and tell you on how to what and wear, because I want you all to look smart out there, I have already received a sort of back handed compliment from the W.O. on how my squad is beginning to shape up, and I intend to carry that on" so, I don't intend also to see anyone outside of this hut looking like a bag of s——t tied up in the middle o.k. because again it will reflect on me, and believe me we don't want that do we ? "No Corp" came the unanimous chorus.

Actually there were a lot of laughs that evening, well imagine it, young lads suddenly having to wear uniforms, and quite complicated too, especially trying to put on shirt collars with collar studs, one dumbo nearly chocked himself, there's always one isn't there! We had already given him his nickname 'Cyril' a real nanny's boy he was, but, as we later found out he could play the piano well. Some of the lads had never worn ties in their lives, but I was used to it having worked in a shop. The berets and the forage caps had to worn at a certain angle, the berets were huge, they looked like saucepan lids on your head. The Corp gave us a tip on those, as his looked half the size of ours and very smart. When you get home get your Mum to boil your beret in a saucepan for about 15 minutes, then put it on your head whilst it's still wet, Also cold !!! better emphasize that to Cyril ! then put it into the shape you want and let it dry, after all you don't want to look like an Erk" (new recruit) all of your career. He then showed us how to clean all of the brass bits, cap badges, buttons, lots of them, all the bits of brass on your webbing, you had all the cleaning kit supplied initially, but when you ran out of anything you had to buy it from the NAAFI Now the boots were another thing, when you looked at the Corps boots, the toecaps and heels looked like shiny patent leather, ours were all crinkly and lumpy like leather is. The Corp said yours will look like mine in time, smilingly, but it will take hours and hours of patience to get them to look like mine, but you will, and the sooner the better! and that's not a promise, it's a threat! and he meant it ! but out of the kindness of my heart, sarky, I will tell you how to do it, first you get an iron, not too hot or you'll burn the leather, then gently iron over the toecaps and the heels, it will smooth out the lumps, there are a couple of irons and ironing boards in the store room, then comes the arduous part, you light a candle and put a bit of polish on the bit you want to polish, a small area at a time, take a spoon, heat up the end of the handle, and proceed to rub around and around in little circles on the polish, also spitting on it at the same time,(hence the expression, spit and polish). do it every spare minute you can, when you're sitting, talking, walking, even sitting on the loo, then, perhaps in a couple of weeks, maybe you will start to see a bit of a shine coming!! I will get you some candles from the NAAFI, one between 4 of you. Then once you get a smooth surface you can use a piece of cloth and your finger tip to polish with, just remember around and around slowly, slowly, spit, spit. You must be joking, but, no he wasn't.!!.

He then enlightened us to the fact that of course you'll be wearing your boots on the parade ground, on the assault course, on the rifle range, in fact everywhere you go, so of course they are going to get scratched and scrapped, but you will keep them clean and shining won't you ! Also what I have divulged to you all this evening, stays in this room, o.k. Now tomorrow at reveille 6 am, you will put on your P.T. kits, vests, shorts, pumps, as we are for a little run just to shake off the cobwebs, wash and shower when we get back ---if you can!!! Didn't like the sound of that and it will give you all an appetite for your breakfast, maybe!! Also tomorrow I will be dishing out the cleaning duties and rosters, well, come on, you didn't think you would be living here for 6 weeks and using all this wonderful equipment provided for you without helping to keep it clean did you ? Goodnight.

O.K. the banging on the beds went off again with the usual shouting, also "up up up, you lazy lot and out of your pits, on with your gym kit and outside in 5 minutes or else". so bleary eyed we went and lined up as usual. It was a lovely morning actually. the Corp had his usual kit on and when he went around to the back of the billet we thought he had gone to change into his gym kit, but no he came back pushing a bike! I think he heard a few sniggers and said," you didn't think I was going to run as well did you, now I'll set the pace, so nice and steady to begin with, its only an hour's jog, and the last hundred yards we can race o.k. We can race !! and him on a bike. So off we went on a steady jog, the other 2 billets were out too, "keep together and look as If you are enjoying it, one or two began to lag behind a bit so the Corp slowed us down a little so that the stragglers could catch up so that we looked as if we were one unit. I think the Corp thinks that the W.O. may be watching somewhere and we look good as one unit as some of the other billets were all over the place. The camp was pretty big, as the perimeter must have been 4 or 5 miles long. the two huge hangers and some runways were in the middle. We went around once, which was enough for first time, some lads were gasping and poor old Cyril was struggling, so who would cleaning Corps boots, as the last hundred yards was supposed to be a sprint, we tried the best we could, but we did stick together which seemed to please the Corp, as he said" well done, now quickly shave and shower and get dressed in your uniforms and outside for breakfast parade, but before you do I will come in and inspect each one of you to make sure you are all correctly dressed as I showed you last night, and everything is nicely pressed also as I showed you. As my Mum had taught me how to iron things when I was little, I had to spend time showing some of the lads how to do it last night. Anyway a few minor adjustments here and there then off we marched to breakfast, looking forward to it after that run.

We were really getting into this marching thing now, I think we looked good and the Corp hardly ever had to say a word to us as we were marching which is something I noticed with the other squads, as with the run this morning and the marching, the other Corps seem to be shouting at their squads all the time as it was the first time all of the squads were out at the same time. I wonder why our Corp had a smile on his face sometimes.

As promised, after breakfast, the Corp came in and we all stood. He said sit and listen to the cleaning roster, firstly everyone is responsible for cleaning his own space, that means no dust anywhere, clean windows, floor polished and lockers tidy at all times exactly as the photo shows, in case of a snap inspection by an officer or the W.O. so if one locker or dirt is seen anywhere then the whole billet is penalised, and a black mark for the Corp, and we don't want that do we, !! Next he called 4 names out, "you 4 will be responsible for the toilet areas, the ablutions, that area is to be cleaned every evening when everyone has used it and left tidy in the mornings and I mean everything, showers, thunder boxes, sinks, taps, shower heads, and no dust anywhere". Now another 4 names were called out," you 4 will be responsible for the hut (billet) all ledges to be dust free, the floor centre to be polished, the 2 stoves to be black leaded and polished, the store room to be kept tidy, and an inventory to be kept and any supplies needed, give me the list, all the materials needed for all the cleaning are kept in the store room, all the outside windows to be cleaned weekly" 4 more names were called out, "you 4 will be responsible for the exterior of the building, the grass surrounding the billet is cut by the maintenance staff, civilians, we daren't let you lot loose on motor mowers! but you will keep the edges trimmed, and the stones around the edges to be kept white washed. If I see one blade of grass out of line, I will jump on you hard, now the last 4 names have a special task When the ones inside have finished polishing the floor to the best of their abilities, inside the store room you will notice a stack of thick felt squares about 9 x 12 inches. Now I had them made for a special reason. So as from tomorrow when you have all done your initial clean, All morning you will spend doing it, and if it's not up to my specific standards by lunchtime, you will come back in the evening and do it again, even if it takes all night, clear? "yes Corp" when you have finished, and the centre of the floor has been polished the last 4 will each take two of the felt squares, stand on them and slide up and down the centre of the billet until everyone else has finished their cleaning duties then each one of you will be given two of the felt squares and for all of the 6 weeks you are in the billet, you will walk around, or slide around actually on those pads, every time you leave the billet you will stack them up at the entrance door and when you return you will use them again, so don't let me catch anyone not using them, thus the floor will be kept highly polished all the time, and make cleaning easier. I know it didn't look like it when you first came in, that was because the lot before you had finished the course and done their passing out parade and were going home the following day so why should they worry about the floor, and you lot will probably do the same, Now I know there are 4 names left, well these are the floaters, who will help the others out if things get a bit behind, you have a billet spokesman, so he will decide on that issue. All of the jobs you have will be rotated every week, which will be decided by me.

You will all do the cleaning tasks for one week, then you will all change duties for another week, and so on, is it all clear and any questions, good. As I've already said, play fair with me and do your best and I will play fair with you, so talk amongst yourselves about it all, then outside at 12-30 for lunch, then this afternoon you'll be going to listen to a talk by the camps Commanding Officer o.k. So the billet went into a huddle called by 'Mac'. The cleaning duties seemed pretty reasonable, after all we are in the forces and there are no domestic servants to do it for you!! plus we can't expect to be looked after like we were at home, and if we are living in this space for the next 6 weeks it's only reasonable that we should keep it clean and tidy. are you listening Cyril ! One way of making the cleaning duties easier was that everyone took responsibility for everything they do, e.g. washing and shaving, clean sink afterwards, the same with the showers and thunder boxes, after all the cleaning of the ablutions was going to be the worst job, as it was evening work, so simple, everyone wash shower, or shave as soon as possible after we have finished for the day, it will make things much easier for the evening cleaning crew, if everyone pulls their weight, said Mac, So it was agreed, which was amazing really, as I think we evidently had a billet of sensible guys who were all going to get along together. I wonder if the other billets were the same, I doubt it. There's an old forces saying that my Dad told me,--'Bullshit baffles brains' and it's true.

As far as our billet was concerned, things seemed to tick along quite nicely, and we were all feeling a little bit fitter now with our runs and also we had physical exercises on the parade ground and in the gym. We did a lot of marching, a lot! But we picked it up quite quickly. The Corp shouted at us of course but not so much as the other two squads were being shouted and screamed at. We had by now sorted out our uniforms, we pressed and ironed them so we were beginning to look a lot smarter too. Also we got on top of the Bull s-----g, mind you 'Mac' asked a lot of questions of the Corp and he was very forthcoming with advice and tips, which was making his life a little easier.

We did have our first kit inspection by the W.O. It was one evening after dinner of all times. It was quite a process, you laid a blanket over your pit (bed) tightly, then you laid out various items of your kit according to the photo on the notice board, e. g. socks rolled up a certain way, clothing folded and pressed, personal kit, toothbrush, paste, comb, brushes, your 'housewife' open and the contents showing, a housewife is a cloth bag containing sewing kit, needles, cotton reels, wool rolls, Brasso, polish, spare laces, blanco blocks, shoe brushes, a brass button plate, (something you slip underneath a button or badge when polishing it, so that the polish doesn't get onto the cloth) your shoes and boots under the foot of the bed, all your webbing laid out and blankowed. It covered the whole of the bed and took quite a while to lay it all out. The inspection was due to take place at 20-00hrs, and 'Mac' went and asked the Corp if he wouldn't mind having a quick look to see if everything looked reasonable, and was quite surprised to see that the Corp had also had laid his kit out for inspection as well.! The Corp walked up and down the billet adjusting this and that, spent some time at Cyril,s bed. "Not bad for a first try", he said," But beware the W.O. is a stickler for perfection and it depends what sort of mood he's in, He might be o.k. if he's had a couple of beers in the mess, depends, now check each others to be sure, and be prepared for when he enters.

Sure enough at precisely 20-00 hrs we heard him talking to the Corp outside his room in the corridor, apparently after he had checked his kit. The door opened and 'Mac' jumped up and shouted "Officer in the room, stand by your beds" We all jumped up and stood to attention at the end of our beds, full of anticipation and quite frankly, dread! as we had heard of lots of horror stories about these inspections. The Corp had told us that the W.O. was nearing retirement, and obviously a career man. If there's one rank in all of the forces to be fear full of, it's a W.O. or Staff Sergeant. or Boson, they have seen it all, and done it all. Even Officers of all ranks are wary of them! Anyway he just stood there with the Corp behind him for a minute just looking up and down the billet. He looked extremely smart, grey hair and moustache and peaked cap. He addressed the whole billet. "My name and rank is Warrant Officer Wainwright and I run this camp, and it's my duty to turn you civilians into military personnel, with the help of your Corporal, in the short space of 6 weeks. I have been in the RAF all of my adult life and I'm still learning, so don't get the idea you will know it all in 6 weeks, l have heard some good things about this squad already, and also seen it, so do not disappoint me and your Corporal, now let's see if the things I've heard are true, you may stand at ease now, but if I approach your bed you will come to attention, If I speak to you, you will address me as Sir, but I'm sure the Corporal has told you all this.", I'm sure you could hear the sound of knees knocking all around the billet!"

He first went to 'Mac' and the Corp pointed out that he was the billet spokesman." I see that you have signed up for 5 years as Technical support and Administration" said the W.O. (he had certainly done his homework) "if it suits you, go for a commission and sign on for a few more years, I think you will find its worth it" Mac said, "Thank you Sir, it will be worth thinking about." he then walked slowly down the line, pointing out things to the Corp who was taking notes, then he got to Cyrils bed! Now no one knows what he had done to his bed, as the Corp said it looked alright when he had seen it and checked it out, But the W.O. stopped and looked at

Cyril and asked him his name, and he said Cyril ! in a squeaky voice. The W.O. said "Full name airman, and call me Sir" I thought that Cyril was going to pass out!. The W.O. walked down one side of his bed, looked at his locker, walked back and down the other side. Looked at the Corp and said "Does he belong to you", then he actually said "There's always one" then he grabbed the corner of the bed blanket and tipped everything onto the floor, then said to the Corp "This man will re-do this, then I will return to inspect it at midnight" he then went out to inspect the ablutions and then left. Poor old Cyril, everybody started throwing things at him and calling him everything. Just then the Corp walked back in and it went silent. He walked up to Cyril, put his face right up to his face and shouted" What the bloody hell did you do to warrant that" I think Cyril p----d himself "Sorry Corp, I only adjusted a few things, I think" the Corps face went purple," What the hell did you do that for when it looked passable when I looked at it, now lay it all out again, I will check it again, and if you touch anything after I say its passable, your feet won't touch the ground for the next 6 weeks, understand, you have 15 minutes to do it and get it right, then I'll come and check it again, and do you realize that as the W.O. is coming back at midnight, that all the lights will have to stay on, so that means that myself and all of the rest of the billet won't be getting any sleep until well after midnight, so you balls it up for everyone, now get on with it" with that he strode down the billet looking at the floor and shaking his head, he paused when he got to 'Mac' and said "you had better tell the rest of them to carry on cleaning their kit for the next couple of hours, but be ready to jump to it when the W.O. comes back, I'm going for a drink to try and calm down a bit!!

A couple of the lads and Mac must have felt sorry for Cyril, as when they had put all their own kit away, they went and helped him to relay his stuff out again, exactly as the photo showed it. The Corp came back after a while and looked at it again, didn't say anything, and just walked out. Well that was it, our first kit inspection, which seemed to be going o.k. then suddenly, blew up, The Corp did say that on the next one the W.O. would be accompanied by an Officer, and that they would be both wearing white cotton gloves, so if there was any dust or dirt about, watch out for the repercussions, something to look forward to!! Poor old Cyril, I think that every time someone walked by his bed they called him something or other.

He was sitting on the floor near his locker as he daren't go anywhere near his bed in case he disturbed something. so everyone got on with cleaning their kit and bulling their boots, cleaning brasses, and trying to figure out where all this webbing went without strangling yourself, by 11-30 everyone was now tired, it had been a long and event full day and night. We were all in our jim-jams, except Cyril who was still in his uniform of course. Just before midnight the Corp came in from his room, he said to Mac that he had just had a call from the W.O. to the effect that he wouldn't be coming down as he is otherwise engaged (probably p----d in his mess) and that he will leave it up to the Corp to instigate some form of punishment for the offence committed! Blimey, it was only a kit inspection, Cyril didn't shoot anyone, Yet! We were all standing by our beds of course, The Corp walked up to Cyril, didn't look at him, just said softly" you will change into your P.T. kit, go to the store cupboard in the ablutions, get a mop and bucket and mop the ablution floor, when you have done, come back in, make not a sound, the lights will be out, leave your bed as it is now, you have spare blankets, sleep on the floor", he then turned and walked out without another word. There was silence for a minute, and then I think everyone began to realise this 6 weeks was going to be no picnic, especially if the Corp is upset for any reason, as obviously he has had a black mark put against him, and I think the punishment he gave to Cyril came from the W.O. after all, it did seem to be a little O.T.T. but all in all we are on a training camp doing our square bashing, and an introduction to military life may be a bit of a culture shock to some.

I myself felt that something should be done, so I went and had a word with Mac, and we both agreed that we thought our squad was getting on o.k. with our Corp, and that he seemed pleased with the way we were progressing, until now. Especially when you witnessed how the other Corps treated their squads. So Mac called a 'huddle' with everyone, whilst Cyril was mopping, and we all agreed that we were going to try and right a wrong as to try and make life a little easier. We will all try our hardest to do things to the best of our abilities. Also to help along the fly in the ointment Cyril! So to start with, as we all felt a little bit sorry for him in the end, some of the lads gave up some blankets, as it was summer and didn't need them all, so we made a bed up for him on the floor. Someone had a torch and took it out to him in the ablutions so that he could find his way back without crashing into anything and possibly waking up the Corp. Then lights out and we climbed into our pits, wow, 6 hrs sleep!!

As ever, 6 am, in comes Corp, shouting a little louder and banging his stick on the beds a bit harder, bad mood I think. But when he got to Cyril's bed, he noticed he wasn't there, and that all his kit had been put away all nice and tidy! And all the blankets the lads had lent him were neatly folded on the bed. Also Cyril was already in the ablutions washing and shaving! The Corp shouted, "Breakfast parade in 30 minutes" and I'm sure as he marched away, I saw a little grin on his face.

After breakfast it was out onto the parade ground to try and get some sort of correct order into our marching, mind you, I think it was getting better and better even after only a few days as things appear to be clicking into place, and strange as it may seem I was getting to enjoy it, in fact the Corppicked me out to be a 'right marker', which meant that I marched at the rear on the right hand side on my own, and if we came to a halt on the parade ground for a review or something, and the call came out, 'front face' then 'Company, right dress,' everyone took one step forward, turned their heads to the right, then put up their right arm straight and touched the shoulder of the person next to him, then everyone shuffled into as near as dam it a straight line. Then it was my job to look down the first line and call out to anyone who wasn't quite straight, E.G. 'number 4 forward or back' then I would turn and march a couple of steps to the middle row, turn and do the same thing there, and then the 3rd row, then march back to the front row again, halt, then the Corp would shout "Company, eyes front" then everyone would snap their arms down and face the frontand If we were being reviewed The Corp would then march up to whoever was doing the reviewing, usually an Officer of some rank or other. The Corp would say "Company ready for your inspection Sir" then the Officer would walk up and down the ranks inspecting everyone. We always made sure Cyril was in the middle somewhere so as to hide him, as unfortunately, he had two left feet, as sometimes when he marched his left arm would go up at the same time as his left leg went forward, and the same with the right, now we don't know how he managed to do that because it's difficult, but it looked as if it came naturally to him! Hence sticking him in the middle!.

Unfortunately on this particular morning the W.O. was wandering around the parade ground, observing all of the squads in action. He was particular interested in the four squads that were rehearsing for their passing out parade on Friday. He would go over now and again and march up and down with them barking out his orders, then stand back and observe. h e was looking around and suddenly started to march over to where we were, he told the Corp to halt the squad, and I heard him say, as I was standing at the end next to them, "There is an airman in the middle of your squad with two left feet, call him out and have him report to me "Oh! oh! We thought, Cyril, The Corp shouted out "Airman Coombes, fall out and report to the Warrant Officer". Now Cyril really surprised us all, we all thought the world was going to fall on his head, but he smartly came to attention, took one step forward out of his line, right turned and marched,correctly, around to the Corp and the W.O. came to a halt in front of them and said "Airman Coombes reporting as instructed, Sir", well everyone was looking gobsmacked until the Corp shouted "eyes front, you lot" I then heard the W.O. say "Airman, I am going to take you somewhere quiet on the parade ground and give you some one to one instructions on the art of marching, so quick march", so off the two of them went, the W.O. marching at the side of Cyril, they looked fine until suddenly Cyril started swinging the same arm and leg together again, they stopped and you could see the W.O. talking to him, not bawling at him, then off again, and Cyril was o.k. again.

Our lot carried right on until lunchtime, and then again after lunch, we were absolutely exhausted when we finally finished for the day, and our boots took a hammering as well, so more bulling tonight. The parade ground was all concrete but there was a covering of fine gravel which was there to accentuate the sound of marching boots, it does sound good when there are 60 blokes all marching in step. There is also one rule about the parade ground that was drilled into us, no one is allowed to walk over the parade ground, say as if to take a short cut or something., it's a hanging offence!!

Before the dinner parade the Corp came in, we were all lying on our pits exhausted, we all jumped up, he said "stand easy", then we all noticed that Cyril wasn't in the billet, then the Corp explained something to us all, and why the W.O. had taken Cyril to one side, he said "The W.O. is a military career man and very experienced in dealing with men, and turning them from civilians into military personnel, especially misfits, which unfortunately Coombes seems to be. the W.O. has a 100% record in that field, and aims to retain it. He had noticed that Coombes was struggling, as he pointed out" there's always one" so he sorts them out and keeps an eye on them, he will take them to one side sometimes for a little extra tuition, quietly, you can shout and scream and threaten some people, and they do it, but to some it will have the opposite effect, so as to obtain progress you have to use a different approach, and that's what the W.O. is good at. Now as to using two left feet, the W.O. explained it to me once. Cyril was trying too hard, he was frightened that he wouldn't be able to keep up, and let everyone down, so he tried too hard and that scrambled his brain and he loses all co-ordination, and the harder he tries the worse he gets, so you have to shut everything off in the brain and then start again from scratch, after all walking is a natural action, so forget about trying to do it, let it be natural, simple, and that's why the W.O. took him to one side to teach him that, and if he sees him left foot again, he will do the same thing until he gets it right, and he will. Just then Cyril came in, he looked knackered and red faced, but he was smiling, so perhaps the psychological approach works. We asked him if he was ok, he said "Yes", and he enjoyed his session with the W.O. With that off we went to dinner.

So it came to the end of our second week, and funnily enough we all began to feel much fitter after all that P.T. marching and early morning runs, but it was nice to have a Sunday off, although we still had to march to the canteen for our meals, and of course the never ending bulling of our kit and boots, apart from that just resting and writing home, you didn't phone as not many people had phones in those days believe it or not. We sometimes played cards, and that's where I leaned to play 'Brag' in all its shapes and forms, 3 card, 5 cards, 7and9 card, deuces floating. we didn't have much money as our first pay parade wasn't until Monday, so after that Monday nights was Brag night, if you liked to gamble, also as from Monday we can now use the NAAFI, also, big day, as we go and pick up our rifles, so square bashing is going to be a little bit different from now on! So 6am Monday, a one hours run around the camp perimeter, back, showered, dressed, on to breakfast parade, after breakfast, pay parade in which we marched up to the offices near the main gate,and guardroom, you could actually look out onto the main road and see cars going by, civilisation, wow. so we are not on another planet! Anyway we all lined up outside the pay office door. and when your name was called, you marched up to a desk where three officers were sitting, halted, saluted, said your name, rank, and number as follows, "Sir, Aircraftsman Warden, 4107300,(still remember it)Sir, then with your left hand hold out your 1250 (a sort of RAF passport with your photo in it and other details) you were then handed a brown envelope with your money in it, you saluted and said "thank you sir" about turned and marched out, now the Corp was watching all this and if you didn't do it smart enough you had a rollicking and he made you practise it back in the billet.

We then marched over to the armoury to collect our rifles with the Corp shouting all the time, "shoulders back, swing those arms, heads up, straighten those arms, every ones watching you so try and look like military men, and not as if you're on a Sunday stroll ! In the armoury, and at the counter, you showed your 1250 it was checked and then you were handed your rifle from the rack, plus a webbing strap, the rifle number checked and written against your name, also a small pouch, Outside we lined up and the Corp said, "as you have probably never handled a rifle before, let alone marched with one, you will march with your rifle ' At Arms' which means rifle in your right hand arm straight by your side, and rifle level, don't move your arm, just swing your left arm whilst marching, and when we get back to the billet I will tell you all about your new toy" Then in another two weeks you will get some instructions on the Bren gun, and the opportunity to fire both on the rifle range. I couldn't wait for that having shot guns before, in fact, myself and one of the other lads, who worked on a farm, had ever used a gun before. When we got back the Corp set up a table at the end of the room and put a blanket on it, and we all gathered round, "Right" he said," The weapon is a Royal Enfield 303, that means the bullet size is a 303, which is also the same in the Bren gun. The rifle weighs around 12 lbs, the thick wooden end is called the 'butt' which fits into your shoulder when firing, the 'grip is along and underneath the barrel which you grip with your left hand, the' Barrel' is the metal tube on top of the grip, it is gun metal grey, not polished, as you do not want any light reflecting off it which could possibly give your position away in an engagement situation. The bolt on the right hand side pushes a bullet into the barrel when pushed forward, you then squeeze the trigger to fire, and then releases the spent cartridge when pulled back. the trigger is the little

lever underneath, you never pull a trigger, you squeeze it, remember that."
he demonstrated the bolt action. that thing on top above the chamber that
flips up and down and also that little notch on the end of the barrel are
your sights, you look through the little hole on the flip up and line it up
with notch on the end and onto your target and then gently squeeze the
trigger, the metal box underneath the chamber is called a ' magazine' it
holds five rounds, but you will be instructed more thoroughly on the range.

In the little pouch you were given you will find a cartridge clip with
5 blank cartridges, some small pieces of cloth, a long piece of cord and on
the end of it a piece of brass rod about 3 inches long and the other end a
loop, and lastly a small tin of gun oil. All of these things you guard with
your life. In your locker you will notice a clip on the side, this is for your
rifle to stand, always make sure your locker is locked if you leave the billet,
now the brass thing and cord is called a 'pull through' it's for cleaning the
inside of the barrel, you put the brass end into the barrel, breech end, and
let it drop through until it appears out of the end of the barrel, then you
take one of those small pieces of cloth which are called, 4x2s, put a little oil
on it, thread it through the loop on the end halfway, get hold of the brass
bit and then pull on the cord so that it pulls the cloth though the barrel,
thus cleaning it, you have to do it several times to clean it properly, also the
bolt is removable, best to clean that with an old toothbrush. The wooden
bits, the butt and grip, you polish, and the strap you blanco, the same
as your webbing. Your rifles will be inspected when you're on parade by
myself and the W.O., and woe be tide anyone with a dirty rifle, remember
that in certain situations your rifle can be your best friend, so it's no use if
it's dirty and not working properly. Oh! and if you happen to lose one, it's
a hanging offence!, now I'll show you how to put cartridges (bullets) into
the clip, then place the clip on the rifle and push the cartridges into the
magazine, load and then fire, and extract.

Now I found that demo very interesting, having loaded shotguns and
air rifles, and also cleaned them, as for shotguns, as the barrel is much
wider, you use a metal rod with a slot in the end and a thicker piece of
cloth. The Corp said to go and sit on your pits and get used to handling
your rifle, the weight of it, learn how to clean it, strip it down, blanco
the strap, also on the end of the butt is a flap, lift it and there's a little
compartment with which to keep the cleaning kit if ever you were out in

the field on combat, so that you can still keep it clean. After dinner he was going to come in and show us some drill movements with the rifle. He said he didn't have too, but he wanted a bit of one up manship over the other squads, he's certainly after winning the two weeks leave at the end of the course. Jim and I were going to have a look at the NAAFI after dinner, but had to postpone that. The Corp came in as he said he would and bought his own rifle. He told us to get our rifles and stand at the end of our beds, and try and copy what I do, he would do it slowly, one movement at a time, first, slope arms, we copied, he walked around checking everyone, then order arms, and so on and so on, every movement we needed to know with a rifle, now practise and practise he said, also check each other as that's a good way to learn, especially Cyril he said with a wink. I think we were beginning to warm to the Corp a bit by bit. Mac was right, the more we co-operate and try our hardest to please him, the easier it would be, mind you, he was still capable of biting, and biting hard!

Well the next few days flew by, we were on the go from 6am until 9pm, there was always something to be done, even after lights out, We had gotten some torched from the NAAFI and were still at it until late at night. Jim and I went up to the NAAFI a couple of times, and we could walk to it on our own without marching. The NAAFI was divided into two half's, one half was the shop where you could get anything you needed, the other half was the canteen, where you could, if you wanted, get hot food and drinks. If you wanted to, you could miss a meal parade and have something later in the NAAFI canteen, some did now and again, but we mostly went over for a coffee and a 'Depth Charge.' Which was a piece of thick dark pudding like cake that weighed a ton, but it filled you up. Also to chat and listen to the tales from some of the other lads in the other squads, and from some of the tales we heard we were having it really cushy. One billet on a kit inspection, two lads had their kit thrownout of a window, and they couldn't fetch it back until the following morning, and it rained during the night!. Another billet had a billet and ablution inspection at 9pm at night, and evidently it wasn't up to standard, so they had to do it all over again, they were at it all night! So we are either really lucky, or are doing some things right. i know one thing that does strike me is that when you enter our billet, is the floor, it really shines and its like it all the time, that's because of the felt pads that everyone skates around on all the time, the Corps idea, and it seems that no one else does it as well. So we just keep our mouths shut and listen to the horror stories from the others. The NAAFI didn't sell alcohol by the way, only in the NCOs mess, (Non commissioned Officers) and Officers mess.

In between all the square bashing and P.T. sessions, that means physical training, by the way, there were lectures and films, lectures all about the RAF and all the various ranks, an Air Chief Marshall down to us lowly 'erks' as we new recruits are known as. films on germ warfare, camouflage, Nuclear war, One afternoon we were taken down to the bottom of the camp where the rifle range is situated, and there was along hut that looked like an air raid shelter, a small door one end and a chimney out of the roof. There was an Officer there to meet us and he quietly explained that the hut behind him was a gas chamber, and that each of us was going to experience what it is like to be gassed, don't worry too much it is only tear gas !! Only tear gas, shit! Now put on a pair of these overalls, and a woolly hat, and then the gas mask, and be sure it fits properly, as we don't want any fatalities, gas!!, fatalities, is the man mad! He said. "Now listen carefully and you will come to no harm. When the door opens you will all file in, wearing your gas mask, it will be pitch black in there so hold onto the person in front of you, when you hear a whistle you will stop, take of your gas mask, and stand still for two minutes, then when you hear another whistle the rear door will open, and you will file out. There will be some bottles of water on a table outside and I advise you all not to rub your eyes, just swill them out with the water the best you can". We lined up at the door holding onto the overall of the chap in front of you, the door opened and we quickly filed in, he was right it was pitch black, we stood there and then a whistle blew so we cautiously took of our gas mask, a dim light came on in the corner, and what looked like steam, was in the air, we were looking around at each other, when suddenly my eyes started to smart a bit, and I started to cough as everyone else did also, now my eyes were really smarting and running and everything seemed very claustrophobic, someone shouted" let me out" Just then another whistle sounded and the large door at the rear opened, and we all shot out coughing and spluttering and some were lying on the grass," Don't rub your eyes if you can help it" someone shouted. I made my way, half blinded, to the table, grabbed a bottle of water and poured it into my eyes, blinking and pouring more water into them. There were a couple of 'sqaddies' going around with water, treating those lying on the ground. Someone shouted "take off your overalls and hats and wash your hands, as you will probably have gas residue on them, so don't touch your face or eyes until you have, oh, and just swill your boots a bit when you get back to your billets, and have shower, and thank you all for coming." Cheeky b-----d! He must be a sadist, as he seemed to be enjoying himself. That was a bloody horrible experience, my eyes were still running a bit two hours later. the Corp said" he knew how it felt as he'd been though it as well, it was to show what a gas attack would be like., and that was only tear gas, think about those in the first world war when there were mustard gas attacks". It puts it all into perspective I suppose, which made me think about Dad.

On Saturday morning when we got back from breakfast, the Corp came in and put a box on the table and said open it and take out one each" inside the box were Bayonets in a sheath, he said "on your passing out parade in 3 weeks time you will all be wearing your dress uniforms with a white belt and a bayonet hanging on it, part of your drill will be 'fix bayonets' then marching past the C.O. who will be taking the salute. There is a special drill for fixing a bayonet onto a rifle, so I'm going to show you all how to do it now, but don't tell any of the other squads, as I've pre-empted them as they won't be getting their bayonets until Monday or Tues, so you lot will have all the weekend to practise and be one step in front of them, charming. I could think of better things to do at a weekend! But if we can get some Brownie points, all well and good, a bit more one up man ship. The Corp showed us how to do the fixed bayonet drill, and we practised and practised, poor old Cyril, he was really struggling, at one point his bayonet shot off the end of his rifle and stuck quivering in the floor, the Corp was watching, He picked it up, and patiently gave it back to him, and quietly said "when you place the bayonet onto the end of the rifle, push it down hard and turn it to the right and it will lock it in place. Then you can't kill any one !! Then he said that next Friday we are all going down to the parade ground to watch an intake do their passing out parade, so as to see what goes on and pick up some points. oh! yes, I nearly forgot, on Monday you are all going on a route march in full battle kit, and then on Thursday you will tackle the assault course, which should be fun for you all, it will be fun for me, as I will be watching you. So something for you all to look forward to, Oh! yes!!.

Sure enough on Monday after breakfast, we had to put on full kit, plus webbing, which we had finally found out how it goes, and where it fits. We assembled outside, the Corp checked us over, then we marched up to the guardroom, halted, and then the other 2 billets joined us. So the whole platoon was going on this jaunt. He had also pre warned us at the weekend to make sure your canteens are full of water (Tin water bottles) and put them in your chest pouches, also get some chocolate or something sweet to chew on. Sweets were still on ration believe or not! I think they were until 1957, the very last thing to come of ration. Anyway, there we were all 60 of us lined up, then out of the guardroom came the W.O. And the Corp barked out "Platoon, attention, Officer on parade", the W.O. said "stand easy" and he addressed the platoon, "you are all going on a little fitness walk, to Assess your fitness levels after your first 3 weeks on this course. It is not going to be easy, but not so bad as to kill you, we don't think!, a vehicle will be following you most of the way where it can, with a couple of Medics on board just in case anyone falls ill, if you do, just drop out and you will be attended to, it is not our intension to kill you, as its very inconvenient as it messes up the numbers, right, over to you Corporals and carry on. Well after that very re-assuring little chat, we were all brought to attention, right turn. Then our Corp said to us "this is not a march as on the parade ground, but you will keep in step, try to relax as you march, keep sipping your water and eating your sweets at intervals, you don't have to swing your arms as on the parade ground, you will find it relaxing if you stick your thumbs into your chest webbing now and again, this is a route march not a parade, but keep it smart and tidy, don't do what the other squads do, do as I say, and you'll find it much easier, as we are the front squad, we set the pace, if you start to fall out of step, I will call it out, the first 5 miles we march on the roads, then across country, and then 5 miles back to camp on the roads again, we should be out about 6 hrs, if you must talk, only whisper, but you shouldn't talk at all, so be careful, across country its o.k., I will be marching with you at times, just to check things, otherwise I will be in the vehicle following, lucky aren't I, so that's it, By the way, the W.O. could be watching you through binoculars from somewhere or other, so do your best, as I reckon he thinks we are the better squad, so try to live up to that. Good luck, you know, all these tips he keeps giving us, he doesn't have to, but it certainly makes life a bit easier.

With that little pep talk we came to attention, right turn, by the left quick march as we marched past the guardroom, the 'Snoops' (RAF Military Police) were watching and smiling, did they know something we didn't? so onto the road and back into the civilian world. As our camp was on the edge of the countryside it was a fairly quiet country road, and with 60 men marching in big studded boots it was quite a sound. The weather was a little cloudy with a nice breeze which was in our favour, it must be murder with the summer sun beating down on you, even after only a couple of miles we were sweating, actually the first 5 miles weren't too bad, much better than we thought, so our fitness levels must have improved over the last 3 weeks. as back home I wouldn't walk anywhere if I could go on my bike, or catch a bus, plus the fact I suppose that I hadn't had a beer for three weeks, god, I'd love a pint at the moment.

After the first 5 miles we had to turn left, through a gate and into some fields, there was a well worn path across these fields, so a lot of men had come this way before us, I say march, but of course you couldn't march across fields. We must have crossed 6 or 7 fields, climbing over gates and squelching through muddy patches and cow shit, we then came onto another road, a small country road, or lane, just wide enough for three ranks of men to walk side by side, also in the dips water was running the road nearly ankle deep, so we had to wade though that, oh my poor bulled up boots! After a couple of miles on this road we again went into some more fields, and in the distance you could see a huge hill, and we were heading straight for it. By now we must have been out about 3 hrs, there just in front of was a small wood with a path running through it, and as we got nearer we could see the truck that had been behind us on the first stretch amongst the trees. Now our Corp had left us when we entered the first field, he told us just to keep following the path, and one Corp had stayed with us to make sure we did. When we got to the truck(a 3 tonner), we were told that here was a packet of sandwiches for everyone, and also to fill up your water bottles from the urn, which was good as mine was empty. We were given a half hours break which was very welcome, we were told not to take our boots off, as we wouldn't be able to get them back on again. I wished we could have as my feet were burning despite all the water that had gotten into them.

After what seemed like only 10 minutes, we were told to form up again, and to set off towards the hill, which was about a mile away, no, not to go around it, but straight up it and down the other side, this time our Corp came with us to make sure we all did just that. he told us (his squad) that we were doing good and setting the right pace, as he had been watching us from a distance with binoculars from the truck, so keep up the good work. We arrived at the hill and started up it, now after 3 hrs marching and then climbing uphill made your legs feel as if they were going to split open, it was pretty agonising and it was just as bad going downhill on the other side as you are bracing yourself against the downward slope. When we got to the bottom of the hill everyone was blowing hard. The Corp then calmly said," two minutes rest, then back up and over the hill again, and then make your way back to the camp the way you came!!" I didn't believe what I was hearing, I said to Jim "did he just say to do everything again in reverse" and he said, "I was just going to ask you the same thing!"

So our squad gathered ourselves together, checking on each other, especially Cyril, who seemed remarkably well. So we started back up the hill, but more or less scrambling on our hands and knees this time, and going down the other side mostly on our behinds, there were 4 lads who just couldn't get up the hill, they were still stretched out on the ground. Also when we got to the bottom there were another 3 who hadn't even managed the first side! Not one from our squad though. Whilst we were waiting for them to catch up we at least managed a bit of a rest whilst they walked around the hill. When everyone was there our Corp got everyone into some sort of resemblance of 3 squads, and we started on our long journey back, as we approached the wood where the truck had been we saw that it was still there, which was good as our water bottles were empty again, and we still had about another couple of hours to go, we approached the truck and was able to get a few minutes break whilst filling them. our Corp said he was going back in the truck and another Corp would do the final leg, he also said quietly to us that our squad had done very well, much better than the other two squads. all of them had had someone retire for some reason or other, in fact there were 7 lads who had to go back in the truck. I think mostly Blisters. so if you can, as you approach the camp, and the guard room, try and summon up something, and show everyone that you are the best squad, I'll be waiting there and probably so will the W.O. o.k.?

We had now been out about 4 hrs, it seemed like 4 days, so only a couple of hours to go, I think it will be a little easier when we get out of these fields, as trudging through fields was murder on your leg and back muscles, plus the webbing straps were cutting into you, I don't know about my feet, as I couldn't feel them anymore! So it should be better when we get back onto the road again, but walking back along the little lane my feet started burning again, but this time when we came to where the water was running across the road it was a relief to let the cold water get into your boots again!. Once back on the road it was much easier, and only a few miles to go. No one seemed to be bothered about keeping in step. it was a case of just keeping your feet moving.

After about half an hour you could just see the two huge hangers of the airfield in the distance, so only another half an hour to go. The road to the camp was, thankfully, on a downward slope which made it easier, so when we were about 300 yards from the camp entrance, the word went through our squad from Mac to hold our heads up, backs straight, and get into step, and he quietly called the steps out, and swing your arms. I reckon the other two squads wondered what had gotten into us, the other Corp couldn't see us I don't think as he was right at the back, and as Mac was at the rear of our squad and I was at the front, I started to call out the march time as well, softly, left, right,left, right, we soon got into the swing of it, as tired as we were. And as we marched through the gates and past the guardroom, I could see out of the corner of my eye the W.O. looking through the guardroom window at us all. Our Corp was outside and he called the platoon to a halt, and the W.O. came out and stood in front of us and shouted," Platoon, right face, stand easy, right gentle men, I hope you all enjoyed your little walk," sarcastic b-----d, "If any of you require medical treatment, blisters, sores, and that, report to the sick bay,(medical centre) it is now 3pm so back to your billets and get yourselves cleaned up, Corporals, take charge of your Squads" Our Corp bought us to attention and we marched, smartly, back to our billets, we halted, the Corp said dismiss, and don't forget to use the floor pads with the state your boots are in" Give it a rest mate!! We went into the billet and all I wanted to do was to get out of these clothes, have a nice shower, a rest, then dinner, and perhaps sort out my kit later. So at 5pm we all went to dinner.

After dinner when we were all cleaning our kit and bulling our boots, the Corps came in, we all jumped up as usual, and he said relax. He walked up and down the billet looking to see what we were doing, offering a bit of advice here and there. After a while he said "listen up you lot, I just thought that I would come in tonight and tell you that today's performance on the route march was excellent, I thought your discipline and personnel endeavours were A1. You clearly were the best squad out there, and the best bit, which I don't think we have ever seen before, was when you came marching down the road to the camp entrance, just your squad, at the head, and marching as if you were on the parade ground, and after a 6 hrs route march, very impressive, and so did the 'Snoops' who stopped what they were doing to watch you march in. As you know the W.O. was there as well, he was watching, but made no comment. I actually felt proud of you today, but don't let that go to your head as I can still bite, and bite hard!! So goodnight and get some well deserved sleep. After he had gone we all clapped ourselves and it made us feel good.

We all sorted out our laundry, which was done once a week, wholesale, we had all marked our kit with marker pens, we threw everything into a large bag in the store room, then someone would take it down to the laundry on the camp. It was operated by civilians, but 2 or 3 from each billet had to go and work there one night a week for a couple of hours, it wasn't too bad, but it put you all behind on your bulling, it was the same with the cookhouse, but that was run by RAF cooks, you could be sent there as a punishment as well, but for a whole week. And that's where I learned why the tea and coffee tasted a bit peculiar, as once I was making some in a big urn, when a corporal cook came and dumped some yellow powder into it. I asked him what it was and he said it's Bromide, something I'd never heard of before, so I said is it some sort of vitamins, and he laughed and said, as this is an all male camp, with no women around, it's to stop you getting randy, No further comment on that.

We carried on cleaning our kit. The Webbing needed cleaning again, brasses polished, and the state of our boots was something else! After 3 weeks of bulling and meticulously polishing them, they looked as if we had only just gotten them! They should give you 2 pr, one for doing all the mucky stuff in, plus, 1 pr for parades and such, or wear the shoes sometimes as we only wear them to go to the NAAFI. It would make life much easier, but of course we are not here for an easy life.

On the Friday morning we did our usual thing, early morning jog, breakfast, and onto the parade ground, We have started rehearsing for our passing out parade, so we are drilling with our rifles and also have the bayonets on our belts. we all practised fixing bayonets in the billet with the help of the Corp quite a lot, so that we would look semi proficient right from the start, another bit of one up man ship from the Corp, as when the other squads started practising it, you could hear the clatter of bayonets and rifles hitting the concrete and the swearing of the other Corps. Another movement with the rifle is 'rifle inspection', you are at slope arms, that's the rifle on your left shoulder, then the order' rifles inspect' you grab the butt with your right hand and bring it down across your chest grabbing the barrel butt with your left hand, you grab the bolt with your right hand and pull the bolt back, (open the breech) then return your right hand to the butt, you do each movement in time counting to yourself, one two and one two, all together, then you stand there at attention waiting for whoever is doing the inspection to get to you. They inspect the 'breech' (where the bullets go in) to make sure it is clean and that there's not a bullet up the spout (in the barrel) then stands back and says 'inspect' you swing the rifle around and put the butt of the rifle into your belly button, point it forward and up, and stick your right hand thumb into the 'breech' with your nail pointing forward just behind the barrel, that's done so that the light reflects up the barrel off your nail, then whoever is inspecting looks down the barrel to see if it is clean, the more light the cleaner it looks, so there's an old trick told to us by the Corp, put some clear nail varnish on the thumb nail and it will reflect more light up the barrel, and for the passing out parade he keeps some in his room for us to use on the day! He knows it all!!

There are other moves to practise as well, (hope I'm not boring you with all this technical stuff, just thought it might be interesting to some) One is the slow march, that's quite difficult to maintain your balance, it's used on funerals, and also 'reversed rifles' that's if you are standing on guard at someone laying 'instate' in a coffin. you stand there usually one at each corner of the coffin with your rifle upside down, both hands on the butt and your head bowed. Then there's 'present arms', when you salute with a rifle, 'slope arms', 'trail arms', 'shoulder arms' I hope I've gotten all the commands and movements right, but it was a long time ago.

Today, Friday, is also the passing out parade day for the company that have finished their 6 weeks basic training course, lucky sods, so we are going along to watch it and perhaps pick up some pointers as it will be our turn in 2 weeks time, So we marched up to the parade ground, all 3 squads. Along one side, opposite to where we were, were rows of chairs for the guests and families of the lads passing out, plus in the middle of them was a platform with 4 chairs for the persons taking the salute, usually officers. Also there was a band setting up, which will make it easier to march to.

After a while when everyone had settled down, someone blew a whistle and the band started to play a good roaring marching tune, and from around the corner of the barracks came marching the 3 squads and around the parade ground and halted in front of the platform, then they 'open order marched'. (The front row 2, steps forward, and the rear row 2 steps back, then present arms(salute) and the band played God save the King, then back to attention, One of the Corps marched up to the platform and said "Company ready for your inspection, Sir." with that a couple of the Officers stepped of the platform and proceeded to walk up and down the ranks, stopping occasionally to chat to one of the airmen. then after that the band struck up again and off the company marched to start their marching routine. I must say they looked very smart in their dress uniforms with a white belt and white boot spats, white !!, ours are grey, but we get white ones for the parade evidently, plus a white rifle strap. Also, evidently, this is the very last time that forage caps will be worn ! As they are being withdrawn from the RAF and new peaked caps are being issued, we get these on Monday. It's a shame because I think forage caps look smart and typical RAF, also when you take them off, say to go indoors, you can tuck them into your shoulder epaulettes. Like you do with your berets. The parade went on for about an hour all told, the finale was the march past the platform rostrum so all of the Officers could take the salute, and then they marched off, and everyone was clapping, once they reached their billets, the tradition is everyone throws their hats into the air, stick your rifles in the billet, then you can go and meet up with your relatives and friends, show them around the billets if you want too, then over to the NAAFI, but they had to leave the camp by 1800 hrs as you had to take your rifles back to the armoury, and all other kit webbing,spats, then pack your kit bags as you were off in the morning for a week's leave. Everyone knew where they had been posted to after their leave, which would be a trade training camp somewhere, it depends on what trade you had chosen, to how long it would be before being to be posted to your permanent camp.

When we got back to our billet we had a surprise waiting for us. The Corp came in and said " you have now been here for one month, so tomorrow you can all have the day to yourselves, and from 10 am you can leave the camp if you wish to, either walk down into Cardington, or catch a bus to Bedford, but you must be back in camp by 21-00 hrs (9pm) If you do go out of camp, you will wear civvys,(civilian clothes,) but look smart and behave yourselves as there are 'Snoops' in the town, and they will know you are RAF believe me! I'm going to town myself to do some shopping and have a drink, I go in the pub near the cinema, so if you are near there pop in and I'll let you buy me a drink!"

Jim and I decided that we would go into Bedford for a change of scenery, and also have a couple of lovely pints at last! So we got our civvys out of the trunks under the beds, and ironed everything ready for the morning. So after breakfast the following day we got dressed into our civilian clothes, which seemed very strange wearing them after a whole month. We walked around to the guardroom, checked our dress in the big mirrors, and could see that the 'Snoops' were watching us. We went inside to sign out, we showed our 1250s and signed. The 'Snoops eyed us up and down, asked where were we going, told us to behave ourselves and if we came back slightly inebriated we would go straight into the 'slammer' (forces jail) and probably stay in there for a couple of months on b& w (bread and water) charming! I reckon all 'Snoops' must have been hated by their Mothers when they were children also they couldn't have had any Fathers!

There was a bus stop opposite the camp and there was a bus due, It's only a few minutes to Bedford, and we checked at the bus station and there was a bus back to the camp at 8 pm. which was just right, It was a nice day so we walked up around the shops, stopped for a coffee, real coffee, without that funny taste like back at camp! We then walked down to the river past the cinema, which we decided we go to after lunch, we found a pub that overlooked the river and did food, so we had a pint, lovely, and a pie and chips. Window shopped a bit, bought a few things I needed. Then we went to the cinema, can't remember what we actually saw because we both dropped off, it must be fatigue!! When we came out we went for a coffee, then bought some fish and chips and sat by the river eating them, by this time we were ready for a pint, so we went back to the pub by the cinema as it was near the bus station. I think the beer was M&B at that time, not bad. We were sitting at the bar when I felt a tap on my shoulder, I turned around and there was a chap looking at us and he said "What are you two doing in here" for a few seconds we didn't recognize who this chap was, then it suddenly dawned on us. It was our Corp, dressed in civilian clothing, no wonder we didn't recognize him. He said he had just dropped in for a pint and then he was going to meet some friends. I didn't think drill instructors had any friends, just joking, Thinking back, he did say if we did drop into the pub and he was there we could buy him a drink, which we did. Overall he was quite a nice bloke. He was a 7 year regular with 4 still to go and hoping to be made up to Sergeant at the end of the year, he asked us where we came from and what trade we had chosen to do after we had finished our square bashing, and he said that for that trade we would probably be going down to Wales, a place called St Athens near Cardiff, a big RAF station with lots of amenities on site, which sounded o.k. as we would be there for 13 weeks on our trade course. He also reiterated, with a stern look on his face, that his squad, us, would win the best squad award so that he would get the two weeks, as he wanted to go to Oxford where his girlfriend lives, and as it seemed to us that you will win it or, else situation !! We said that everyone was trying their best, including Cyril, and he laughed, and again "there's always one" was said. With that he said he had to go but would not try to wake us all up when he gets back, probably in the early hours, cheeky b-----d.

It was getting on to nearly 8 pm, so we caught the bus back to camp. We checked back in at the guardroom, we were eyed up and down but nothing was said. as It was still early we went over to the NAAFI for some beans on toast and coffee and then back to the billet. Some of the lads were playing cards and we sat chatting. Told them that we had seen the Corp and his surreptitious remark about winning his two weeks leave, or else! and Mac said we can but do our best, we all came here on a bit of a low, not knowing what we were in for, so it would be nice to go out on a high knowing that we had all done our best. Wise man, he should go far in his service career.

The next day, Sunday, we spent quietly bulling our kit, and contemplating the following week, as we knew it was going to be hard, there was the rifle range and then the assault course to contend with apart from everything else. The week after would be all bulling, and then having to rehearse for the passing out parade on the Friday afternoon. A couple of the lads said their parents would be coming, but I don't think mine will be coming as it takes too long and a lot of waiting around on stations.

After breakfast on Monday we were told to change into our gym kit as we would be going onto the parade ground for a couple of hours workout with the gym instructor, a couple of hours!!! First of all though we went for a couple of miles jog just to warm up, all of the 3 squads were present and the instructor stood on the platform showing us all the exercises, whilst the Corporals wandered around shouting and bawling if we weren't doing it correctly. Poor old Cyril was suffering a bit but he was trying his hardest. He was a bit over weight when he first arrived, but I am sure he has lost quite a bit in the past month, but also he seems to recover quickly which is a good sign of getting fitter. His Mum and Dad won't recognise him when they see him! Evidently his parents own a manufacturing business, electronics and instruments of some sort, but he worked in the office. He said his parents thought he was a bit too delicate to work in the workshops, but when they weren't around he used to go and help out in the workshop as much as he could. Maybe a couple of years National Service will make him a little bit more assertive as to what he wants to do. He has in fact signed on to be an instrument fitter, although he told his parents he was going into Administration! The little devil, there is hope for him yet!

After a quick shower we were off to the Admin building for another lecture, this time on the Commonwealth, and the different tours of duty that were on going at that time. We didn't mind the lectures so much as we didn't have to wear boots and gaters, just shoes, plus the fact it was nice just to sit still for a while. On some of the lectures though, it was hard to keep awake.

After the lunch break it was off to the stores to pick up our new peaked caps. As I've said before, I like the forage cap, it symbolises the RAF I think, all the other mobs have peaked caps, but why should we, anyway I was determined to try and keep mine if I possibly could, one by one our cap sizes were measured, then given a ticket and then walked along to the counter, you handed in your forage cap, as they handed you your peaked cap, it was busy at the counter so as I went to hand over my forage cap I pretended to drop it, then foraged around on the floor to pick it up, the queue was pushing forward, so tucked my cap under my jacket and just moved along and out of the door and lined up outside! When we got back to the billet Jim said, "What were you smiling about when we came out of the stores." So I took my forage cap out from under my jacket. He smiled, and then, bugger me, he did the same! Great minds think alike. The peaked cap, of course air force blue, with a black shiny peak fitted ok. Didn't like it much though, looked like a bloody bus conductor, ding, dong, hold very tight please I called out! The Corp wasn't amused "Shut it Warden, all outside with your ticket machines, ding, dong, too." I don't think he likes them either. We went up to dinner and then afterwards we were all sitting doing our bulling as usual, and of course parading around with our new caps on. We had everything from train guards, bus conductors, airline pilots, ticket collectors, train drivers, ship captains, gestapo, postmen, someone said street cleaners, he must come from a posh area! The Corp came in and told us all to put on our dress jackets as he wanted to make sure we were going to wear them properly on the parade. He checked everyone, some needed a bit more pressing, but all of them needed the buttons cleaning again, "so get on with it, o.k. and don't forget the cap badge, Also I've just been told that the assault course has been bought forward one day, so tomorrow after breakfast it's on.! so here are a few tips, firstly don't eat too much breakfast, you'll only bring it up, then pray that it's a cool, dry day, as there will be enough mud around without any more rain churning it up. The course itself is kept permanently dowsed with water just to make it more interesting, also after breakfast in the store room you'll find a bag with overalls and woolly hats in it, put them on, now what you wear underneath is up to you, my advice, vests and gym shorts, socks and plimsoles, and tie some string around the trouser bottoms, and button right up the neck collar, you don't want the collars catching in the barbed wire, (barbed wire!) Jesus! You will start off as a squad and timed as to the last man finishes. The winning squad will get a little bonus at the end by the way, and it had better be you lot, or else!! Now if you have anyone in your squad who you might think may need a little help now and again." I wonder why everyone looked at Cyril, poor lad, he looked sheepishly at the floor, "Try and stick together and help each other out as it's the last one over the line that counts, oh, and don't tell anyone I've given you these tips, and try not to worry too much about it, take it in your stride, and don't panic. O.K. now get some sleep and see you in the morning.

After he had gone, Mac called a huddle, and we decided we would keep in pairs as much as possible, but Mac, Jim, myself and Cyril, would keep together, for which Cyril said "thank you guys, I promise I'll do my best" "I know you will" said Mac. So we all turned in to try and get a goodnights, or rather apprehensive, sleep, which was rather difficult after some of the horror stories we had heard about the assault course.

So after breakfast, 2 glasses of fruit juice and a slice of toast, back to the billet and change into gym kit, put on the overalls and tie the bottoms of the trouser legs and await the call to fall in outside. Outside on the road were 3 three tonners, so evidently we were being transported to the Assault course. I had wondered as there was no sign of an assault course on or around the camp as far as I could see. It was probably miles out in the middle of the countryside so that civilians couldn't hear the screams!! Also, very ominously, was a Land Rover with big white circles on the side with a red cross in the middle. It couldn't have been more obvious than if a hearse had been there too!

We all boarded our trucks and off we went, it was only about a 20 minutes ride, when we pulled into a field down a country lane, jumped out and lined up in squads. Evidently our squad had been drawn to go first, which, according to the Corp was the best place, as all of the other squads would be following in all of the mud that we had churned up, mind you at the moment we couldn't see anything that looked like an assault course, in front of us all we could see was a wood, a thick wood. The Corp then gave us our final instructions "In front of you is a wood about 50 yards away, you will run over to it, as you get nearer to it you will see a well worn path, and entry into the wood, the path is only wide enough for single file, so as you approach it sort yourselves out into single file before you get to it, then you won't bunch up, and it'll save time. So run straight in and follow the path and watch out for the brambles on each side, the path will twist and turn for about 100 yards and then you come onto open ground, the start of the assault course, you can't go wrong as the course is roped off on each side, and there will be Marshalls on each side, just keep up a good pace and keep together just in case anyone falls by the wayside, you are the first off and the other squads at 10 minute intervals, o.k. lads, and good luck.

Right this is it we thought, we lined up at the start, the whistle went, a big gulp and grit your teeth and off towards the wood, as we got nearer, the lead chap aimed for the entrance and the rest of us gradually filtered into single file and straight in, no stopping, the brambles did catch your trousers and the branches were low so you had to duck all the time. I did catch my foot in a tree root or something, stumbled, but managed to keep going without stopping, the path twisted and turned, but the pace was good, the other lads were in front then it was me, Jim, Cyril, and Mac. Then all of a sudden we were out of the wood, then in front of us was what looked like a battlefield, I thought the wood path was muddy, but this was just one big mass of mud! The course was roped off, so you could only go one way, it was about 20 yards wide with all sorts of obstacles, each one about 20 yards apart, it was like racecourse, and we were the horses!. The first obstacle was four lines of tyres in two rows, so you ran, one foot in the left tyre and the other foot in the right tyre, I know it seems easy enough but there was thick mud inside each tyre, a couple of the lads went base over apex into the mud, but luckily didn't hold anyone up, Jim had Cyril by his side and Mac and I behind, there were 10 tyres each side so we were puffing a bit, also, something we were not warned about, on each side of the course the other side of the ropes, on the nice grass of course, were some instructors running along with us shouting and bawling all the time, that we didn't mind until they started throwing some sticks around us, which without any warning started exploding with an ear shattering explosion, I nearly s—t myself when one landed really close to me!.

So on to the next. Which was a water filled trench with 4 logs across it about 4 feet apart. The logs were thick but muddy, the trench was about 15 feet wide. It was best taken at a run as it was slippery and your momentum could take you over, but one lad went in, luckily feet first and only up to his waist so he got out quickly with the help of his partner as we were running in pairs as agreed. The trouble was it wasn't just water, it was thick water! One instructor threw one of those sticks into the trench just as Jim and Cyril got to it and it threw up a wall of muddy water which caught Jim and Cyril, also Mac and me, charming! A good start. The next obstacle was another mud filled trench, about 30 feet wide, but it had an overhead frame with bars about 2 to 3 feet apart going across the trench, so you had to jump up and grab the first bar and then swing hand over hand grabbing each bar in turn across the trench, obviously trying not to let go. As Cyril and Jim got to it Mac and I lifted Cyril onto the first bar as he was a bit short, gave him a swing and surprisingly away he went, and Jim was waiting for him on the other side and grabbed him and pulled him in, but those b------d kept throwing those sticks at us, I was going deaf by now. We had another casualty there but he managed to pull himself out o.k. Another 30 yd dash to the next one, now we could see what the Corp said about barbed wire catching in the collar of your overalls. There was a large area of crisscrossed barbed wire lifted up and held off the ground by poles only about 18 inches high, so you had to belly dive onto the mud and then crawl along on your belly using your elbows and toes to propel yourself along, Jim showed Cyril who was next to him how to do it, he did get his collar caught once, but Jim managed to free him, when we came out of the other end we were absolutely covered in mud, also back along where we had just crawled there were a couple of woolly hat hang on the barbed wire !!

Next was another mud filled trench, about 25 ft wide with tripods on each side and a pole going from one side to the other and along it four ropes hanging down, now the ropes were hanging down but they were in the middle of the trench just out of reach, so how to get at them and to be able to swing across? One of the lads up at the front immediately came up with a solution, brilliant!, he took off his overalls, swung them around and caught each rope one at a time and pulled them in so we could grab hold of them and swing across one at a time, then swing the rope back for the next one. By the time it got to our turn the lad who had taken off his overalls had them back on now so we all got across safely. The thing was that when you landed on the other side you had to make sure you didn't swing back that's why someone was there ready to catch you so that you didn't, as if you did you would just hang there in the middle until you couldn't hold on any longer, then you just dropped into the trench, and this one was shoulder deep!! We did hear that a lot from the other squads had dropped into the trench! That's why when Cyril took his run up Mac and I gave him an extra little shove to make sure he landed on the other side where Jim waswaiting to catch him. Another 50yd dash and by this time we were all getting a bit slower and blowing hard, next was the net, a huge climbing net, up one side about 50 ft and down the other side, this was high!, The Corp had told us to take a run at it jump up it as high as you can, find a place to put your feet, then climb one square at a time, then flop over the top, grab the net again and lower yourself a bit at a time, everyone got over that quite quickly, Cyril surprised us, because, as he was small he went over it like a ferret! Of cause don't forget whilst we were flogging our guts out, those sadistic b------d were still throwing those things at us. Next the water tunnel! now this obstacle was manned by a couple of instructors, it consisted of a long trench, of cause water filled, up to your shoulders, halfway along the trench was a bridge at water level, about 15 ft wide, an instructor stood in the water on one side of the bridge and one on the other side, they of cause had on wet suits. What we had to do was get into the water at one end of the trench then walk along it up to the first instructor, (That water was cold, God knows what it's like in the winter!) The instructor put one hand on your head and one on your back, told you to take a deep breath, and keep your body straight, then ducked your head under the water, pushed you in the back, and if you had kept your legs straight he would give another push on your feet, and you should theoretically travel along underwater as far as the other instructor is able to grab you and pull you out of the tunnel. now I'm a good swimmer but that scared me a bit, even non swimmers had to do it, if you refused, you were disobeying a direct order and would be put on report and get a long stretch on 'Jankers' (doing horrible jobs in your own time) I suppose it was to teach you to obey orders from someone of senior rank to you. When I surfaced I couldn't see for the mud in my eyes, but was given a bottle of water to swill my whole head with. O.K. Cyril, he only got halfway under the tunnel and one the instructors had to duck in and pull him out, but he came out laughing his head off, and said "I wouldn't mind doing that again" everybody laughed including the instructors, and he was ready for the next thing!! We had to wait until everyone was through, and the clock was stopped to allow everyone to swill off, then it was started again and off we went.

We ran to the next obstacle to try and make up a bit of time, this was the final one, thank God, we were all of course soaked to the skin but a lot of the mud had washed of us in the tunnel which made it easier to run. In front of us was 'The Wall'. It must have been 30 ft high and 20 ft wide, it was a brick wall, smooth both sides, so no hand holds or grips of any sort, but you had to get over it using your own ingenuity and team work, now this is where we had cheated a bit as the Corp, although not supposed to, and he wasn't sure whether or not the other Corps had told their squads what to do at the wall, but just in case they had, he decided to tell us how to tackle 'The Wall', which is supposed to separate the men from the boys. Firstly, the leading pair will run up to the wall, face each other then cup their hands together, then the next pair run up one at a time, and put one foot into the cupped hands of the pair at the wall, who will then heave him upwards so that he can grab the top of the wall and then sit astride it, the same with the next man, so that they are both sitting facing each other on top of the wall. Then the next man will do the same, the two at the top grab him as he is heaved up and then lower him down on the other side. Then the next does the same, it's best to send your biggest blokes to do this. Now you have your wall crew in position, two heaving up, two catching on the top and lowering them down and two at the bottom on the other side also catching them. Now the last man is your best athlete, he has to run at the wall, leap up as high as he can so that the two on the top who are now leaning right over can catch his hands, then haul him up, and lower him down, then themselves just drop to the ground the other side. Job done.

We did notice that whilst we were tackling the wall no fireworks were being thrown at us, and the Corp told us afterwards that it was because the instructors were just standing watching us at the way we tackled the wall, he admitted he felt quite proud at the way we did it, not a bad lad really. Better than some of the other Corps from what we had heard. At last we thought the worst was over. Just make a mad dash to the finish line a hundred yards away. What we hadn't bargained for was the mud, the first 20 yards were o.k. then the mud got deeper and deeper, it was just a quagmire, a bog, it was up to our knees. Do they import the bloody stuff just for us! We were exhausted as it was but dragging one leg after the other was absolute agony, plus you can't keep your balance as most of us fell over, then trying to pick yourself up as your arms went in up to your shoulders, we were in pain so we tried to get as close to each other as possible so that if you did keel over perhaps someone was near enough to give you a hand up, which worked quite well, so everyone shouted to get close together in pairs and help each other, Mac and Cyril were in front of Jim and I so we could assist Mac with Cyril as he was really struggling, being short the mud was up to the top of his legs nearly. The next 20 yards were a little easier as the mud was getting thinner and not so clinging and not so deep, more sloppy than thick. Cyril, bless him, started singing "mud, mud glorious mud" I don't know how he had the breath to sing, I know I was gasping, but he made us laugh. then the mud started to get shallower so thankfully we were walking out of it at last, and then finally onto dry grass and the finish line 20 yards ahead. We all fell over the finish line and collapsed in heaps, gasping for breath. that last hundred yards just about put the top hat on it all. We won't forget that experience for a long time. Plus the fact it will be our turn and pleasure to relay all the facts to the next squad when next in the NAAFI !

Our Corp and some of the instructors came over with bottles of water which we gulped down, and poured some over our heads to wash away some of the mud out of our eyes and mouths. The Corp said "if I were you I'd peel of those overalls, you have your gym kit on underneath and it's hot, there's a water 'Bowser' (a truck mounted water tank) over there, there's a couple of hoses on the back, swill yourselves off and then lay on the grass to dry off, as it's hot now, and you've got at least half an hours wait for the others to finish as they aren't even in sight yet! So that's what we did, we swilled each other off, the water was quite warm, then lay on some clean grass to dry off a bit as the sun was now hot, I felt sorry for those still on the course in this heat, it was gratifying laying there listening to the explosions of the little sticks an knowing what the others were going through, and of course a wry smile when you thought of what lay in store for them, THE BOG ! Mind you it was nice just laying there doing nothing for a change. Our Corp came over and said "Instead of us just hanging around he had permission to take us back to camp whilst they tried to sort out the other squads. We had been out for 5 hours and a late lunch was laid on for the assault course groups, so we dumped our overalls in a bag, and still in our gym kit we climbed aboard our truck and back to camp, the Corp said have a quick shower, change and outside in 20 minutes, and he would march us up to the canteen and he would join us for lunch as well, and afterwards you can have the rest of the day to yourselves. He would await the results of the assault course and the assessments as far as we were concerned when the others get back, and perhaps let us know later, perhaps!!

When we got back to the billet we threw all our dirty things into bags and a couple of the lads took then down to the laundry, another 4 lads volunteered to clean up the showers a bit because of all the mud that we washed off ourselves. Then we all just flopped out on our pits exhausted, and had a couple of hours kip, well earned we thought, As we had had a late lunch we didn't bother with dinner parade until 1800 hrs. On our way back the Corp did say he would come in and see us all in a while. We wondered what we had done wrong as he didn't look too happy, or what were we letting ourselves in for next! Anyway we all sat around doing some bulling or writing letters. We all did at some time just to let people know that we were still alive, there was a phone up in the NAAFI but people didn't have phones in their homes in those days! So if you had any reason to make a phone call in those days, it was up to the red box with your pennies. Of course the only ones that did make phone calls were Cyril and Mac, because of their parents businesses. Mac said it was no use him ringing home as his parents were abroad at the moment, very middle class. You just knew there was something about him and that he came from good lineage, that was obvious, just like me, uhm !As the Corp promised he came into the barracks and we all jumped up as usual. He told us to gather around and sit down where ever. "Right you lot, do you want the good or the bad news first" let's have the bad news first we all said and get it over with. "Sorry to have to tell you but on Wednesday evening after dinner there is going to be a full kit inspection, plus barracks, and ablutions, by not only the W.O. but one of the Officers also, so just to pre-warn you, both of them will be wearing white cotton gloves, which of course they will be running their fingers over various surfaces checking for dust and such like, it will probably be your last kit inspection, unless someone does something wrong, remember what happened before, looking at poor old Cyril, so far you have all done well on these inspections, far better than some of the other barracks. my philosophy is if you want to get the best out of someone or people, treat them with respect, bawling, shouting, bullying, gets you nowhere in the long run, of course you make everyone toe the line and not take advantage, that's why I seem to turn out good squads, much to the annoyance of the other squad corporals, also I'll let you into a little secret now that I've got to know you all, now I am a military man and so was my father, and also several relations, and military life suits me, also I enjoy training people, erks, like yourselves. It puts a bit of discipline into your lives, and that, you will appreciate later in life" Mac cut in "We all appreciate what you're saying Corp, and you are absolutely right" there's something about Mac that I haven't quite fathomed out as yet. The Corp continued "But I have no intention doing what I do here for the rest of my career, as I am looking for a promotion and a transfer. The W.O. and one of the Officers are backing me, I would like to go to somewhere like the Officers Training college at Cranwell which would suit me better, and the W.O. thinks so as well, as I said before, this could be your last kit inspection, as next week, your last week, you will be rehearsing all week, and bulling for your passing out parade, talking about bulling, here is a little tip, if you want to do it, your dress jacket, the material is as you know Blue serge, and its rough and hairy, now to make it look like a smooth cloth, like an Officers jacket, you shave it!! Yes, shave it. with an ordinary dry razor, you can just do the front and sleeves if you like and you'll probably use two or three blades, but it's surprising how much smarter it looks, it's up to you, oh, and by the way, nothing I've said or told you leaves this room O.K"

Now for the good news. Your showing this morning on the Assault Course, now don't let this go to your heads, was excellent, as you know they let us come back early, that's because the squads behind you were making a real pigs ear of things, and the C.O. in charge didn't want any of you getting cold and cramps, all of the assault Corps and instructors thought that you had done the course before as you were very well organised and determined. The way you approached 'The Wall' and the tactics you used, it was if you had had some sort of Commando training beforehand. of course they didn't know that I had already warned you what to expect, but the way they were talking, also when they stopped doing what they were doing just to watch you going over the 'Wall' made me feel good and proud of you all, and I can tell you now, that you all broke the course record time"!! With that we all cheered and clapped and it made us feel good ourselves. I know it may sound all a bit cheesy, but remember we were just young men, now fit, and raring to go and achieve something. Must try that shaving thing!!

The next morning 6 am, a rude awakening by the Corp banging on your beds as he marched up and down the billet, I wish he'd use the bloody floor pads like we have to! "Right you lot Outside in your gym kit in 5 minutes". I think he was trying to shake us out of our comfort zone after last night and as there is still a lot of work to do so we've got to keep sharp, it was a good thing we had spare gym kit and that our plimsoles had dried out a bit. Outside it was still a bit misty and we all felt a bit stiff after yesterday, so the Corp said we will just do a gentle jog for about 5 miles, as today we are on the parade ground with our rifles, just to run through a few movements before we start real rehearsals next week, as tomorrow we go on the rifle range in the afternoon, but before that, instructions on the Bren machine gun, can't wait for that. We probably spent a couple of hours rehearsing with our rifles and things were starting to come together better now. I was having to do my right marker thing, I did slip a couple of times, so must try not to take such big strides as you do tend to skid a bit on the gravel. Marching back to go to lunch a couple of the lads had to fall out to go and collect our laundry, also another set of overalls to wear on the rifle range tomorrow. After after lunch the Corp came in and said to quickly give you rifles a clean and pull them through a couple of times and lock them away as we are now going over to the armoury to have your instructions on the Bren today, as tomorrow we will probably spend all day on the rifle range. Behind the armoury was a large room where all of the squads could get in, and also 3 large tables, one for each squad and an instructor, ours was a Sergeant. He said to gather round the table, on which stood a Bren gun, He first told us to observe everything he did as he started to dismantle the gun and hand the pieces around for everyone to handle, and then lay the pieces on the table, then he said "I hope you all took note of that". When it was completely stripped there seemed to be loads and loads of pieces on the table, he then said "The very small pieces i.e. the gas jets, trigger assembly, injection and rejection assembly, you needn't worry about them too much. The thing that will concern you is what to do if your weapon fails you, especially if you are in a combat situation, so I am going to show you how to deal with that problem that might occur in that scenario", He then explained what do about the various faults that may occur. It's too long to explain in detail, but basically, blocked barrel, lock ups, gas jets, faulty rounds, and so on, and how to deal with them. Then from under the table he produced two more Bren guns, and said to us all," Now look the weapon over, get the feel of it, the weight of it, as not only do you fire it from on the ground, but you could be in the situation where you are walking firing from the hip!. Take them to pieces and reassemble them if you can, if you need any help, I will work with you, as each one of you will strip down the parts that might concern you if the gun fails, and then re-assemble it. Take your time and do it slowly to start with. At the end of the session everyone will be timed to see who can do it the quickest. Then you can try it blindfolded, actually it's not as hard as you think. Then to make it more interesting each squad will go against each other on stripping and re-assembling the gun.

Well the next couple of hours we spent getting to know the Bren, and all the ins and outs of it really, what to do if it packed up whilst you were firing it, faulty rounds, changing the barrel, adjusting the gas jets, ejecting and reloading, (it was a long time ago so I'm trying to remember the details the best I can.) then we started timing ourselves, I must admit some of us made a real mess of it, time wise I mean. But we managed to complete the task. Then the Sergeant told us to try it blindfolded, as it could happen that the gun failed you when it was pitch black. Then he would take the best of the 3 times from our squad to go against the other 2 squads. So they left just one weapon on each table, the other squads do the same, now previously to this, the best time on our table was, believe it or not, was Cyril!, so he was to represent our squad in this little competition. I daren't look, and the Corp had his hands over his eyes. He had stand by the table, behind the gun, put on a blindfold, and when a whistle blew, strip and re-assemble the Bren gun. The whistle blew, Cyril calmly stepped forward, felt for the gun and then went to work, we all watched with our mouths open because it could only have been about 60 seconds when Cyril stepped back, finished !! you could still hear the clattering from the other two tables going on. Cyril cockily took of his blindfold, turned to us and smiled and said" it was just like stripping instruments in our workshop back home" even the Sergeant was impressed. Our Corp stood there with his mouth open! The Sergeant walked over to Cyril and said. "Well done lad, that was one of the quickest times I've ever seen, if ever I was out in the dark and in action, I'd like you to be at my side, again, well done." Cyril just stood there with a grin on his face. All of the squad were slapping him on the back on the way to the billet, he was certainly the toast of the billet that evening. Even the Corp said that wonders never cease.

The next morning arrived and I felt quite excited about going onto the rifle range, and so did some of the others, some with a little trepidation, but we all hoped Cyril wasn't going to kill anyone. After breakfast all of the3 squads jumped into the back of the trucks with our rifles and off we went to rifle range. The range was near where we had done the assault course. It was about the width of a field, flat and about 100yards long, at the far end was a huge hump of earth, obviously to stop the bullets, just in front of that was a deep trench, on the top and just in front of the trench were 6 pairs of targets which could be winched up and down by the people in the trench. The same trench was also about 50 yards down the range, but no framework, so the targets were just placed in front of the trench manually. At the front, the firing position, was divided into 3 sections, with a board separating them, in each section were 4 firing positions on the ground with 2 or 3 sandbags in front, obviously for resting your rifle on when firing. At the back were some open fronted huts with tables in, and lots and lots of instructors walking about with red armbands on, plus a field ambulance, ominous! Each squad was split into 5 x 4s, 4 at a time on the floor firing. Then we were given a lecture on what to do and how to do it. How to ly in the firing position, resting your rifle on the sand bags, how to load a five cartridge clip into the rifle magazine, live bullets now!! Tuck the butt into your shoulder. Now I have a protruding collar bone so I was pre-warned about this and had a couple of dusters tucked under my jacket to protect the right one from the recoil of the rifle. Then how to set the sights, and to remember to squeeze the trigger, not pull. Everyone had an instructor kneeling beside them, and two in the hut behind shouting the instructions.

The first 4 were told to assume the prone firing position, I was one of them, my instructor adjusted my legs and elbows which felt more comfortable. I tucked the rifle into my shoulder tightly, flicked up the sights, set them for 50 yards. The people in the first 50 yard trench had placed the targets outside, they were about 3 foot square, one target each.

Red flags were flying down each side of the range and a huge one at the end about 40 ft high. Then someone with a megaphone shouted, "Danger, range live" My instructor passed me my clip, he said "load" I put the clip into the breach and pushed the rounds down into the magazine with my thumb, 5 rounds, flicked out the empty clip, a shout from behind "load one round, aim and fire on command from your instructor" my instructor said" fire in your own time when I tap you on the shoulder, remember what you have been taught" so I blinked twice, took aim, deep breath out, a tap on the shoulder and squeezed slowly. The recoil wasn't as bad as I thought it would be, "unload" bolt back, empty shell flies out, relax, from out of the trench by my target came a pole with a big red arrow on the end, and it pointed to where my bullet had hit, at least I hit the target!! "Well done" said my instructor," inside the inner ring, slightly to the left, so compensate o.k. now reload" bolt forward, relax, breathe out, tap on the shoulder, squeeze. the red arrow came up again, "bang on" said the instructor "now let's see how you do with the remaining three" last one gone, "unload, make safe weapon" bolt back and forward three times, close, pull trigger. Got up and moved back.

Now it was probably just luck, but I had two inner circles and three in the bull, Our Corp said "Well done Warden," After all the others had had their turn, poor old Cyril was holding his shoulder, so I gave him one of my dusters to pad it. It was time for the Bren gun. There were four of them lined up in the firing position. the same procedure, I was in the first lot again, the same instructor, only this time the magazine, which is separate and is clipped under the Bren, had 20 rounds in it and on the side of the Bren is a lever so that you could fire either single shot, or automatic rapid fire, The Bren has a tripod on the front so you don't have to hold it up with your left hand, that, you put on top the butt by your right cheek to hold it steady. My instructor said. "At your target in front, single shot set, five rounds only, take aim," tap on the shoulder, I wriggled myself more comfortably, set the sights, breathe out, squeeze, five rounds, one after the other, up came the red arrow, all five in the inner circle, a 3inch grouping, wow!!. I love the feel of the Bren, Then, switch to rapid fire, now when you fire the Bren you don't pull the trigger and blast away non- stop, as it would overheat the barrel and not give the gasses chance to escape and probably seize up. So as you squeeze the trigger you say to yourself, "Johnnie get your gun" and release the trigger, then squeeze and say it again, you can do that until your magazine runs out, which I did. Then unload and stand up for the next chap to get ready to use the Bren. My instructor was looking at my target with binoculars, and he said "very good grouping lad" I suppose it was through firing guns before had helped. When everyone had finished firing on the 50 yard range it was time for lunch, which was sandwiches and tea, we sat on the grass talking about our efforts and the majority of our lot seemed to have enjoyed it so far, even Cyril said he enjoyed firing the Bren as it made his toes tingle? Our Corp came over and said" two or three of you are doing very well, so keep it up this afternoon"

Right, now it was time to get back into position for this afternoons stint. So it was a repeat of what we had done this morning only his time it is the 100 yard range, the actual target looked a little bigger and this time it was pulled up and down on a frame by the people down in the trench, the only exception from this morning was that you only fired when the target appeared, both for single shot and rapid, and after each single shot the target disappeared and you waited until it appeared again, the time in it appearing and disappearing was only 2 seconds, then you waited for it to appear again with no set time, it could be a couple of minutes, so you had to aim and fire pretty quickly, or just lay there waiting for it to appear. I think the lads in the trench liked playing games with you! Luckily there was no wind that day, just a slight breeze, so really you only had to calculate the speed and arch with the distance, and not the yawing or air density, as it was a fine day. I really enjoyed it all, and could have stayed there for ages, and was sorry when it was all over.

So when everyone was finished we all gathered around for the results, and it appeared that our squad had recorded the most points, but apart from that, so the Officer in charge said, there were 5 of us out of the 60 who's individual points tally gave them the right to wear on the left arms of their uniforms the badge of a ' Marksman' which was crossed rifles, and Mac and myself were two of them! I was chuffed and everybody cheered us. Then the Officer presented us with our badges there and then, so we were happy bunnies on our way back. But there's always a sting in the tail, Our Corp said "after dinner you will all clean your rifles, and I mean clean them after you have fired them, they need a special clean and I will come in later and inspect them, and don't forget that tomorrow is full kit inspection after dinner and apart from inspecting everything, they might ask to inspect your rifles as well, oh! by the way, well done you lot on the range today, especially the two Marksmen, another feather in our cap! so after dinner it was rifle bulling time, it was surprising just how dirty it was after firing. I must have pulled through the barrel about twenty times, and you used an old tooth brush to clean some parts, but the woodwork looked good as when we were in Bedford I bought some high gloss wood polish, it really put a glossy shine on the butt and grip, and we all used it, even the Corp said they looked good when he inspected them later. a couple of the lads needed just a little bit more attention. Thankfully we haven't got to use them again before tomorrow night's inspection.

After our pre breakfast jog next morning and then 3 hrs on the parade ground which was pretty exhausting to say the least at last we were getting things right without being bawled at like the other squads were experiencing. Plus Cyril is now marching without swinging the same leg and arm, also standing more upright than ambling along like a great ape!. Straight after lunch we were marched over to the two huge angers, which were empty at that time, just to have a look at them. They are amazing, and you cannot appreciate the size of them until you stand inside them. they say that they are so high that they have their own weather systems inside like clouds in the roof. My Dad said that he had worked here for a while when he was in the RAF, or rather RFC, in the 1914-18 war.(Royal Flying Corps). the instructor was interested in that and said he must have worked on the Airships of those days.

Back in the billet the Corp said that this evening's inspection would be at 1900 hrs (7pm) so until dinner time and afterwards get the place cleaned up, and then lay out your kit ready for the inspection, so we split up into two groups, the stoves were given an extra polish, the floor still looked great, just dust around the edges, some cleaned the windows inside and out, then a couple went up and the billet dusting everything in sight, 6 went into the ablutions and blitzed the place, you could have cleaned your teeth in the toilets, so until after the inspection use only one toilet, even if you have to queue!! if you have to use a thunder box go over to the NAAFI !! The store room was cleaned up, you could even hear the Corp doing his room! Mac asked him if he had a minute, could he come and look at what we had done. He came in and walked up and down running his hand over everything and then went into the ablutions, he came back and stood at the end, looked up and said "has anyone cleaned the lamp shades ?" knowing that we probably hadn't, Mac s said

"Er no" said Mac" so 4 of the lads, two on each other's shoulders did just that. "Oh! And by the way" we all stopped and waited. "The ablutions look good, and smell nice as well" we had bought a couple of bottles of Pine disinfection from the NAAFI and thrown it around all over the place! There is an old saying in the forces, ' Bullshit baffles brains' and it's true.

Time now to start laying our kit out and giving a final iron to anything that looks creased, and also a good polish to your boots as they have to be on the floor at the front of the bed with shining toecaps to the front, I must say that the toecaps and heels after 5 weeks of continuous bulling, that they do look like patent leather, good old 'spit and polish' I only hope all the marching and final rehearsals next week doesn't knacker them up!! Time for dinner now, so I'll finish things off when I get back.

A good dinner tonight, fish and chips, and peas, Jelly and blancmange sort of thing, quite nice though, Back in the billet we all finished off laying out our kit, and decided that everyone check each other's kit before we ask the Corp to do a final check. I checked Jims and he checked mine. I told him his knife, fork, spoon, were the wrong way around, and he told me, that he could still see some hairs on my hair brush. Mac went and asked the Corp, could he come and check our kit layouts. He walked slowly from bed to bed, touching this, moving that, picking a rifle out of a locker and checking it. When he had finished he said that everything looked o.k. but it depends on what standard the W.O. and the Officer would be looking for, Now all get changed and smarten yourselves up a bit, so we put on our shoes, slacks and shirts, and awaited the dreaded inspection. We posted someone on the door to pre warn us when they were coming. Then at precisely at 5min to 7, he shouted and ran back in, we were all sitting on our beds, we heard them come in and go into the Corps room, and they were talking for a while, then the Corp came in and shouted" Officers in the room, stand by your beds" and in came the Officer, a lieutenant, and the W.O. the Lieutenant stopped at the first bed which was Macs, he looked up and down his bed and just glanced in his locker and then spoke to Mac, they were chatting and smiling, and it seemed ages before they moved on to the next bed. Meanwhile the W.O. was doing his bit, running his finger over everything and sometimes grunting and talking to the Corp, he picked one lads rifle out of his locker, and both he and the Corp examined it thoroughly. The W.O. got to me. I thought I just know he's going to find something wrong. He stood in front of me looking me up and down, and then walked to my locker, he took out my dress jacket, took off one of his gloves and ran his hand up and down the sleeves and the front, put the jacket on the bed then walked back and stood in front of me and stared at me. I thought I'm going to s---t myself any minute now!, He asked me my name, rank, serial number, I snapped to attention, and told him, then where do I come from, I said "Coventry Sir", he said" ah, Coventry, I have some relatives who live in Coventry, they had it a bit rough in the war, I suppose you were only a young lad then, how did your family fare, I told him we were bombed out twice he tut, tuttered, and said "rough on your family as well eh! And by the way congratulations on getting your Marks mans' badge on the range yesterday, and I also noticed that you have shaved your dress jacket like most of them in here have. I wonder who told you that old trick", looking at the Corp, "actually, going by the book, you could face a court martial for defacing a military uniform, but no one worries about that now, beside it looks smarter" and then moved on. The lieutenant got to Cyril's bed, but looked at it touched a couple of things, picked up a boot, looked at it and put it back down. Then both of them walked out and into the ablutions, the Corp followed them, after telling us to stand easy. We all sat down with a sigh of relief, as on the whole things seem to have gone o.k. We will soon know when the Corp comes back

Jim and I went over to see Mac and to see what was going on between him and the Lieutenant, when he and the Officer were chatting for so long. Mac said the Officer asked him his name and where he came from, I told him John Macdonald and I come from Slough and I worked in such and such a bank. The Officer had laughed and said that his parents were retired and had just moved to Slough and were now using the bank where Mac had worked, so they both had something in common, which seemed to break the ice. Also he told the Officer to tell his parents that they had made a wise choice in choosing that bank. The officer also congratulated him for obtaining his 'Marks man' badge yesterday. The word gets around doesn't it! After about 20 minutes, I think they were out there having a smoke, the Corp came back in. I tried to read the look on his face, but it was just blank. He walked up to the stove and stood looking at his clip board, but still with a blank expression he said" "the Officers thought the place was a complete mess". There was complete silence," he paused and looked around, then smiled and said" They were both very impressed with the overall standard of everything, and could see that you had all worked hard to achieve that standard, the lieutenant had already received some good reports about this squad and could see why, and they both congratulated me for bringing and instructing a squad up to such a high standard, so all in all lads, a good result don't you think! Now put your kit away, and well done. Now I am going for a beer, so sorry you can't join me," sarcastic sod. I can't wait until next Saturday and 7 days leave at home and to be able to go out for a few beers with the lads. So in the meantime it was over to the NAAFI for a cuppa and a fag. Before we went Mac called a huddle and said that we all should congratulate ourselves and it just shows what can be achieved when you all pull together.

I know I have talked about these kit inspections briefly, but let me try and explain in more detail what is exactly expected on these nerve racking and frightening times, and believe me they are frightening. Firstly there is the photograph showing you how the kit is laid out, but it does not explain how to get it looking like that. So from the start your blankets are folded in the way you leave them every morning, except one which is stretched tightly over your bed and tucked under the biscuits, no creases, then you place your peaked cap on top of the blankets with the peak sticking over the edge precisely 2 inches and exactly in the middle, you use a rule to do that as there are plenty going around the billet! now,on the bed your shirts are folded in a special way with the sleeves folded over the front, buttons on top, and just touching the third button down of the shirt, no creases, then your stiff collars in a row on top,(I think they now have shirts with collars) and inside the collars your collar studs, nice and shiny, now place your shirt on the left hand side of the bed 1 inch from the blankets and 3 inches from the edge, in the middle your jumper, folded exactly the same as the shirt, on the right hand side your vests, all with an inch gap in between, your socks laid flat (ironed flat) one pair each side, long ways with the heels facing outwards, in between the socks goes the towels folded twice and laid flat, on top of the towels goes your washing kit, soap, toothbrush(new), shaving soap and brush, razor, open with blade showing, hair brush and comb, make sure the soap is dry and wiped clean, and the shaving bowl spotless, no hairs in your brushes, (not that you have much hair after your initial haircut) I forgot to mention that episode! But it's starting to grow a little after five weeks! But we still have to have another one for the parade! Next comes pyjamas, folded neatly with the cord in a nice little bow on the top, your ties are rolled up and put on each side of your cap with the V at the front laying just 3 inches out, your gloves one each side next to the socks, your jackets and overcoat are hanging in your locker. Haven't had to wear the overcoat as yet, good job it weighs a ton. your gym kit folded and ironed laid in between the socks and gloves, the plimsoles clean and the bottoms polished, as with the boots, laid on the floor under the foot of the bed, 5 inches in from the legs and 2 inches in between, on the bed and below the gym kit is your housewife, which is a cloth bag containing black and white cotton a small ball of black wool, pair of scissors, a folded pad with an assortment of needles, which believe it or not have to be polished!, a button cleaning plate, it's a piece of brass plate about 6 inches long and 2 inches wide with a slot up the middle halfway about ¼ inch wide, you slide it under a button to polish it then the polish doesn't go on the clothes, and as it's brass it has to be shining, all these things are laid out individually so that they can be picked up and examined, then your boot and shoe cleaning kit and brushes, the black polish tin would be polished, the brushes are white wooden ones, and the wood has to be clean and white, imagine using black polish with white wooden brushes, the trick was to tape up the handles as you used them, or buy a spare set just for polishing,! Next all your webbing, and the belt, which has been blankowed white, and it's all laid out in a pattern strictly to precise measurements. I know it's a bit long winded but it gives you some idea what goes into a kit inspection, I wonder what it's like now a day's? I wouldn't mind actually doing one.

The next couple of days were spent either on the parade ground or going to lectures, some were boring but some were interesting, On the Friday we were told we could go out of camp tomorrow if we wanted to, so Jim and I decided we would go into Bedford again, also Mac and Cyril said they would like to join us. So on the Saturday we changed into our civilian clothes, signed out at the guard room, again very carefully scrutinised by the 'Snoops' and caught the bus into Bedford. I must say Mac and Cyril were very smartly dressed in their civilian clothes, smart and conservative. Cyril even had a tie on. The first place we looked for was a cafe so as to get a decent cup of coffee, then we did a bit of shopping, and wandered around, and by this time it was near lunch, so instead of getting fish and chips and eating them by the river, we would find a pub and have some pub grub, there was a nice looking pub overlooking the river that we had noticed last time, so in we went and sat outside overlooking the river. We all had steak and kidney pie and chips, and a pint, but poor old Cyril had to show his RAF 1250 to prove that he was over 18! They thought he looked too young to drink!

We all got talking and finding out a bit more about each other and we all agreed that all of the lads in the billet were a great bunch, never any arguments or fall outs and we all pulled together, a mixed bunch but we all gelled, which fortunately had made life much easier, especially after all the horror stories you have heard about square bashing. It was going to be a shame that after next Saturday we will all be going our separate ways, and we won't know just where until next week, probably next Wednesday or Thursday. Mac said he knows he's only in doing his National Service but he was seriously considering taking the W.O. advice and signing on for a few more years if he could be accepted for Officer training, as he was having second thoughts about going back and working in his Fathers bank. (his Fathers bank ? I don't remember him saying that!!) Even though the prospects were good, as he really wanted to travel and perhaps going for a commission would enable him to do that. I remembered then that one of the lectures we attended was all about making the RAF your career, and that afterwards Mac was talking to the Officer who gave the lecture for some time. At the moment he has signed on in Administration of some sort. Cyril on the other hand had obviously been a bit of a Mothers boy, not entirely his fault I don't think. Especially when he told us the times he used to sneak into the workshop for a change from the office so that he could work on the instrument when his Father wasn't around. That's why he had been looking forward to National Service so that he could sign on to be an instrument fitter and perhaps go abroad, but I didn't like to tell him that being only National Service, and only in for 2 years, that by the time you had done your square bashing, and your trade training, as that is also a long course, it wouldn't be worth sending you abroad. In fact I think he was lucky to get a job as an instrument fitter in only 2 years service, perhaps he told them his father owned an instrument factory! But I could really see him signing on for extra years as well. Plus you could see that it would make a man of him, because after only 5 weeks here at the moment, how much he had blossomed.

Jim and I asked the other two what did they fancy doing after lunch, it was too a nice day to go to the pictures, so Mac said why don't we have a boat out on the river, as I had seen him looking at the boats as they went by. There was a hire place just a little way up so off we went and hired a dingy or rowing boat or whatever you call them, so Jim and Cyril sat at the back, and Mac and I did the rowing. We sat side by side with an oar each., Mac asked me if I had rowed before, I said does paddling with a piece of wood, sitting in a tin bath across a water filled bomb crater count, he said probably not! So he started to show me. and he made it look easy, firstly dip the oar, blade upright, gently pull back, lift the oar, feather it back, and repeat, He made it look easy as you could see that he had done it before. He said that where he lives in Slough, it's near the Thames, and he often goes out on a 'skiff' I think he said, as he was a member of a boating club. Now sitting on a 'skiff,' if I'm thinking correctly, is like sitting on a kitchen chair on a long plank of wood, about 3ft in the air with two oars, the kitchen chair moves backwards and forwards as you row. I think that's about right! Tricky! Anyway at my first attempt I missed the water altogether and went flying backwards into the front of the boat, much to the amusement of them all, I clambered back and tried again. I did manage to dip into the water with the oar and then pulled back as hard as I could, unfortunately the blade did hit the water, but only when I was halfway through my stroke, consequently when it did hit the water at some speed, it shot a big column of water up, which engulfed Jim and Cyril, that'll teach them to laugh at me! Anyway after that episode Mac took charge of the rowing and I sat up front, in the bow as I was told, anyway the pointed end. So we all enjoyed a pleasant afternoon on the river Ouse. At one point we passed three girls sitting on the bank having a picnic, and they waved to us, If only we didn't have to catch the 8 o'clock bus back!! So after that watery excursion we decided to go for a pint. By this time Jim and Cyril's clothes had just about dried off, not quite, so we had another pint. Then we caught the bus back, Back at camp we felt a bit peckish after all that exercise. so we went for some beans on toast and a chat to some of the lads who were on their second week, so we put them in the picture as to all the tragedies and horrors that await them, rotten sods aren't we ! Sunday was another day to ourselves so we sat on the grass, writing or reading, some played cards, some were bulling, but just resting, and building up some extra strength for next week's Rehearsals.

6 am Monday morning, another noisy and rude awakening by the Corp. "Hope you all enjoyed your peaceful weekend as it's time to put the finishing touches to your wonderful stay here, and then to send you all out into the wide, wide, world, much wiser and fitter, and better men! Well that was the idea, but looking at the state of some of you at the moment, it didn't work." does he have to be so comical so early in the morning! "So outside in 10 minutes, in marching order, as we are going for a little stroll before breakfast, just to loosen you up a bit" So we marched for about an hour around the roads in the camp, then we would stop and he would tell someone just to correct something they weren't doing quite right, also it looked as if we were the only squad that was out at this time of the morning. then two things struck me, either the Corp was trying to show everyone what a good squad he had, or just to polish up on a few things as the rehearsals we were going to do this week were with the other squads as well, together as a Company. And he was hoping that his squad would stand out from the rest. He really was bucking for that two weeks leave!

After breakfast it was back onto the parade ground with the other squads. No rifles, we were just going to practise the marching and the sequences and the order in which they came in, the inspection parade, and the march past, and so on. We were to be the lead squad, on the W.O.s orders! Which was another feather in the Corps cap. We rehearsed until lunchtime with a couple of breaks, and then the same in the afternoon, but we did at least finish up at 1600 hrs (4pm), so we were able to get a shower and a little rest before dinner. Then, of course, 'bulling' again. That routine went on until Thursday,with the exception of Wednesday afternoon, when the whole platoon were marched over to the assembly room in the admin block where we were going to be told where we were going to be posted to after square bashing and our weeks leave. There were some career Officers there as well. Briefly, what happened was that your name was called out and you marched up to the table that had called out your name, there were 4 of them, saluted, said your name rank and number, then told to sit down. They checked the list, and one of them said" Ah, Warden, I see that you are a three year regular, good, and that you have chosen Aircraft Airframe fitter as your career, well done, there's always a need for you technical chaps don't you know, you wouldn't be doing that course if you were only National Service don't you know, also if you do well in that trade there is a good chance that if you signed on for a few more years, the promotion prospects are very good don't you know". (Why does he keep saying that, of course I bloody well know!!). "Anyway, your trade training course is 13 weeks in duration, and you will be stationed at 'RAF St Athens', which is near Cardiff in Wales. (O.k. boyo) Here is your 7 day leave pass, also your train travel vouchers from Bedford to Coventry on this Saturday, then one week later the same for you travelling to Cardiff, you will have to check the route and times at your station, but make sure you arrive sometime on that Saturday. Cardiff is a very big station, and there is always a lot of movement going on there on Saturdays, so make yourself known and there will be transport laid on for you and all the other personnel who are going up to the camp. St Athens is a large camp as it caters for a lot of the technical trade training courses. Here is also your weeks pay and a little extra for travelling expenses, and we wish you luck and all the best in your new career, they both shook my hand, I stood, saluted and went and sat down.

Back at the hut we all were finding out where everyone was going. Jim and I were going together of course, plus Cyril for his instrument course. Now Mac had been assigned to a large recruitment centre in the centre of London! the jammy devil. also it meant that he would be able to get home every evening as there were no barracks nearby! The other lads were spread out all over the country, 4 of them were going on an M.T. course. (Motor transport), and 3 were also going to St Athens on Aircraft Engineer Mechanics courses, so perhaps at least some of us will be able to keep in touch when we are there. The Corp came in to see where we were all going, we said St Athens, and he said "he once spent a couple of weeks there in transit, he also said that it was a big camp and the amenities there were very good, there was a large indoor swimming and diving pool, football and rugby pitches, an athletics track, a huge dining hall for O.R s (other ranks) a cinema come theatre, a large gymnasium, catering for all indoor sports, one of the best NAAFI s in the forces, where you can actually get a beer! The billets are good, and centrally heated. They were in blocks of 6 dormitories all over the camp, with 3 floors, and 3 on each side of a central entrance, each one sleeps 15, 7 one side, 8 the other, at one end, toilets and showers and store room. It sounded pretty good, he said it would make a good permanent posting as Cardiff was only a bus ride away, but the only problem was its location, depending on where you live, as there could be a lot of changing stations and awkward times, for instance if you had a 72 hr pass, to get to some places it wouldn't be worth it as you would probably only get 24 hrs at home, but apart from that there's plenty to do on camp, and as it's a trade training centre it's pretty relaxed as far as discipline is concerned, just keep your head down and your nose clean and concentrate on your work, and I think you'll enjoy your stay there, as long as you pass all your exams, because they'll keep you there until you do! 'Exams'!! I knew something would spoil it.

Thursday morning came, and we think it's going to be hot today, our last full day of rehearsals, only two days to go and then home for a whole week. There was a surprise in store for us though as the W.O. had told our Corp to only let us rehearse for this morning, as it's going to be really hot this afternoon and he didn't want anybody finishing up with blisters, which was a distinct possibility as my feet were getting sore from what we had already done this week. Also he said our squad were up to scratch as it was, and he didn't want us to be over trained. That was nice of him. So this afternoon after lunch we of course spent more time on our kit, and the Corp came in and sat chatting to us again and picking up little points on our kit and watching us doing our final preparations and giving tips where needed and telling everyone to get a goodnights sleep, and not to worry too much as it will all be fine tomorrow, and just look forward to Saturday and your 7 days leave, also, my 2 weeks as well, or else!. No worries then!!

Friday morning was bright with a slight breeze, ideal for a parade, so after breakfast the Corp told us to put our gym kit on and assemble outside, we were just hoping that we weren't going to go on a run, not before a big parade surely. I think that would be a bit stupid, but the Corp just said that we are going for a walk just to loosen and warm up your muscles and joints. It seemed strange just walking along quite casually instead of marching or running. Our route took us along past the parade ground and it looked as if they were getting it ready for this afternoon's parade. There was a small tractor going back and forth with a large rake on the back and it was levelling and striping the gravel, the stones around the ground were being white washed. Also along the top end the raised platform was being erected and chairs put on one side of it, and a row on the other side, presumably for the band. The Corp pointed out where the markers were being put, small white discs, which we knew what they were and for what they were for, as we had practised with them. I think that with seeing all this going on, the old butterflies were beginning to flutter a little, but after about an hours walk we began to feel a bit better, and when we arrived back the Corp said that we would be having an early lunch and then come back and get ready. but in the meantime lay out all your parade kit on your beds and do any last minute things that need doing, and I will come in and have a look. so we all set about doing last minute spit and polishing, and the Corp was walking around checking everything again, He told one lad to go and have another shave and put a blade in this time, another had a little scratch on the toe of his boot and he showed him how to disguise it. we had all been issued with white belts and gaiters a couple of days ago and they had been whitened and kept in the store room ready to put on, so by the time lunch arrived, I think everyone was as ready as they were ever going to be, plus the Corp seemed happy enough, so off to lunch.

The parade was due to start at 2-30 pm, and it looked as if some of the parents had arrived and were being entertained in the Officers mess. Mac and Cyril's parents had evidently arrived. I bet Cyril's parents will be surprised to see how much he has changed in the past 6 weeks, even we are! He is much more self assured and confident in himself now, and on the whole I think that all of us have changed in one way or another, and I think a lot of that is down to our Corp as he didn't shout and scream at us as some of the other Corps did with their squads, he let us learn and sort out our problems by ourselves, or amongst us all, and I believe, as we all did, that working as a unit we achieved more that way. I forgot to say, that a couple of weeks ago Mac had said that to show our appreciation to the Corp we should get him something, we all agreed and each one of put £1 in a kitty, and when Mac myself, Jim and Cyril were in Bedford we looked around for something for him and decided on a wrist watch. It was quite a nice one actually, I know £15 doesn't seem much nowadays but that was a lot of money in those days, a week's wages for some, anyway we wouldn't present it to him until after the parade. When we came back from lunch the Corp said "Line up and stick out your right hand, thumb nail upwards" and he went along and painted each thumb nail with clear nail varnish, and we all knew what that was for, rifle inspection, reflecting the light up inside the barrel to make it look cleaner, just another of many tips he had given us.

We all started to get dressed in our best, we kept checking each other to make sure everything was correct and in place. One lad had panicked when a brass button came of his tunic, but Jim sorted him out. The spats were a bit tricky to put on, and you had to make sure your hands were clean because of the whitening, the same with the belt. The Corp came in as he was ready, he looked really smart as it was the first time we had seen him in dress uniform, someone whistled, "cut it" he said "right stand at the end of your pits and I'll have a look at you all" so he went from one to another, adjusting, straightening, making sure your cap was firmly in your head because if it fell of whilst on parade, you were hanged afterwards! He also said if you want to have a pee whilst on the square, just do it where you stand! also if you faint, make sure you lie at attention on the floor! Just at that moment the W.O. walked into the room," Officer in the room, stand by your beds" Now I didn't think you saluted a W.O. as it's not a commissioned rank, oh well, The W.O. said to stand easy, and that he had just come in to wish us all good luck, and try not to let your Corporal down, and off he went. "Right you lot, it's 2 pm, so line up outside after you've been to the loo, so we lined up on the road outside which led to the parade ground, and so did the other two squads, some of their Corps were still shouting at them. We were all standing at ease with our rifles and I thought everyone looked so smart. What a difference six weeks makes to people when at the start we looked like a ragbag of civilians.

Our squad was the lead squad, three rows of 7 as I was at the rear in the right hand lane as the marker and the Corp on the left. The W.O. was to lead the parade onto the square as the parade commander. When the band struck up, the W.O. bought us all up to attention, then slope arms, left face, and by the left, quick march. Marching with a band is quite easy as the beat helps you to keep in step. We marched onto the parade ground and you could see that quite a few people were seated there and watching.

On the platform were three Officers, the middle one the C.O. of the camp. The band looked very smart also, they must have bussed them in from somewhere. We marched around the perimeter of the square then in the front of the saluting platform the W.O. halted us, right face,

Then, General salute, Present arms. He marched up to the platform, saluted, the Officers saluted back, the W.O. said something like Company so and so ready for your inspection Sir, The C.O. mumbled something, the W.O. came back and shouted 'slope arms', Open order march,' the front line took one step forward and the rear line one step back. Then he said' Right Dress' everybody swung up their right arm, turned their heads to the right and shuffled into a straight line. Then came my little play, I slopped arms, marched to the rear line, checked the line was straight, the same with the centre and the front line, I was so pleased that I didn't have to shout to anyone to get into line!. I then marched back to my spot, and the W.O. shouted 'eyes front', hands down. it was a bit nerve racking but it went off without a hitch. The officers split up and walked around the squads stopping now and again to chat to someone and asking some inane questions. The C.O. was inspecting our squad with the W.O. The C.O. did stop to talk to Mac and also Cyril. I bet his parents were proud of him at that moment. When they had finished, the W.O. turned and saluted the C.O. and he said" Thank you very much Warrant Officer, a very smart turnout, please carry on".

I know it's probably a bit boring, but it's just to let you know the procedures that go on. Anyway, the band struck up again, the W.O. shouted slope arms, left turn, by the centre quick march. He then went and stood at the side of the platform to watch us do our little marching routine, which was now commanded by our Corp. So we marched up and down, around and around doing all the stuff we had rehearsed. The music the band was playing was very stirring and easy to march to. We did stop once and back again to the platform for our rifle inspection, why couldn't they have done that the first time? The inspection was done by all 3 Officers, one to each squad, but the big surprise to me, and also Mac, was that the Officer who inspected my rifle said. "I am very pleased to present you with your dress uniform 'Marks mans' badge and certificate, well done" and he shook my hand, even the W.O. was smiling! Our final stint was to march up to the platform again, open order, slope arms, 'General Salute, Present arms", and the band played 'God save the King', and all the Officers and spectators stood to attention, We then shouldered arms, turned and awaited for the order to march off, but before that the W.O, marched over to our Corp, spoke to him, and escorted him up to the platform, some words were spoken and the C.O. shook his hand, he saluted and marched back. Don't know what all that was about.

So now it was our final march, and that was off the parade ground, hoping to never march on it again. As we marched off to the sounds of the RAF march. The spectators all stood and started clapping, it felt great. We marched around to our billet and the Corp halted us and told us to go and change into our battle dress as we were going over to the NAAFI so that some of the lads can meet up with their parents. We were all inside changing and talking and laughing with relief that it was all over at last, you could feel that all the tension had faded and everyone was now relaxed. Just then the Corp walked in, "NCO in the room" shouted Mac, we all jumped up as usual, "Ok relax you lot said the Corp", grinning. "Right you horrible lot, I just thought that you would like to know that you were voted the best squad in the Company, which means that as I am your Corporal who has had to put up with you shower for 6 bloody weeks, my reward for doing so is 2 weeks leave"!! We all cheered and clapped and shook hands, then he said" seriously though, I have been instructing for a few years, and I would just like to say that you lot are the best I've had to work with, and also the easiest, so I'd like to thank you all for enabling me to receive my 2 weeks leave, so get outside and let's go and get a well earned cuppa. Then Mac stepped forward and added "Excuse me Corp, but before we go, the lads here have really appreciated all the help and indeed the patience you have shown us, which has made our 6 weeks stay here much more tolerable, which in some way makes it a shame that it's come to an end and we will all be going our separate ways, so just to show our appreciation, we would be honoured if you would accept this small gift, and we all hope that you do get the promotion and station you wish for." With that Cyril stepped forward and presented him with our gift, and everybody clapped. The Corp opened the box and looked at the watch we had bought for him, and he just kept looking at it, and looking at it, then he lifted his head, looked around at everyone of us, I could have sworn I saw his eyes watering, and he cleared his throat and just said "Wow, I really don't know what to say, except that you really are a great bunch of lads and I will treasure this watch always, thank you all so very much, then he walked around and shook hands with everyone. "it's a shame I can't invite you all around to my mess for a drink, but not allowed I'm afraid, but let's go for that cuppa, now outside".

Over in the NAAFI there were tea and sandwiches and everyone mingling. Jim and I were introduced to Mac and Cyril's parents, they were very nice, and I don't think Cyril will be her Mummy's boy anymore as I reckon he is his own man now. Some of the lads took their parents back to show them the billets, but Jim and I started packing some things in our kit bags and suitcases ready for the great off tomorrow.. We just have one thing to do early in the morning and that is to return our rifles to the armoury and some of the kit back to the stores. That night in the NAAFI there was quite a lot of jollity and laughing, it is a pity they didn't serve any beer, but as it's a training camp it wouldn't be wise, never mind, I will make up for it when I'm home. The Corp came in to tell us the arrangements for the morning. At 6-30 outside with all the stuff to be returned, then breakfast, make our own way over to the mess, wow, no more marching! Then back to the billet and clear out our lockers of everything, ready for the next batch of poor sods to arrive, it's a shame they won't be getting our Corp to instruct them. In one way I feel sorry for the whole of the next Company, as all of the other Corporals must be a bit p------d off at not getting the 2 weeks leave that our Corp had won again. so they won't be in very good moods me thinks!

So after we had done everything, we were told to gather up at the guard room to check out, as there was transport laid on for anyone who needs it to the station at 10-30 as I imagine that most of us will be going from Bedford to Rugby to catch other connections. We all have the train times and connections. Jim and I will catch a train from Rugby to Coventry at 14-00 hrs (2pm) so we'll be able to have a drink in the buffet, if it's open! Mac and Cyril's parents spent the night in Bedford and came up to camp to pick them up in their cars, must be well off! We all made our way up to the guard room, and who should be there but the Corp, all packed and ready to go, he was off to Oxford to spend his leave with his girl friend. We all of course asked him what the time was and he kept having looking at his new watch to tell us, until he caught on! We all laughed and we got the V sign back. We said farewell to Mac and Cyril. Sorry to see Mac go, but we will no doubt catch up with Cyril down at St Athens. So onto the wagons and down to Bedford station. When we got there the station buffet was open and as the train to rugby wasn't for another half an hour, we went in and had a drink. Our Corp was already in there and he generously bought us a pint each which went down very well, he was, as most of us, going to rugby for connections. The train arrived and this time there were more than 2 carriages, but still no toilet, but at least it went a dam sight quicker than it did 6 weeks ago when we arrived.! They must have found some more coal from somewhere!

At Rugby we had an hour's wait, but a lot of lads had good connecting trains, quite a few to London which came in more or less straight away. The Corp caught the London train but gets off before then and another train on to somewhere else. The buffet bar was open so we went in and had a pint and a pork pie, which I'm sure it walked onto my plate and squealed when I cut in two! I think it was with the second pint that we began to relax and enjoy a smoke and look forward to our few days leave. Our train finally arrived and it was one of the fast trains from London to Birmingham which only sometimes called at rugby, so it wasn't too long to Coventry. at Coventry station we went outside with our large kit bags and suitcases and looked at the bus stop. Jim's was just across the road, but mine was up the hill and around the corner. Jim said "sod it, I'm having a taxi ", now Jim lives at the opposite end of the town to me, so it was no use me going with him, so I also said sod it, I'm having one too! I didn't fancy lugging all this kit around anymore. We both said see you at 9am next Saturday here at the station, and enjoy your leave, and off we went. it seemed as if we had been away from home for months instead of just 6 weeks. When I got home the front door was open as usual. Mum gave me a big hug, and Dad was in the front room tinkering on the piano, and when he saw me the first thing he said was" when are you going back" it became a family joke with me and 'our kid' after that. Mum said that I looked thin and that she had a good meal waiting for me. It was also a shame as 'our kid' was home on leave last week with his mate Alan from across the road. They had just come back from abroad for a couple of months and were stationed in Weymouth, where, according to Mum and Dad he had met a girl, he could only have about 18 months left of his 7 years in the navy left to do.

After I had a good meal, there's nothing like home cooking, I had a quick swill and a shave as Mum had said that she had seen one of my mates, John Mac, and told him that I would be home on Saturday for a week's leave and he had said tell him to meet us all in the "Old Ball' pub on' Ball hill' around 7pm as the gang were all having a drink and then onto the GEC dance hall, which sounded about right to start of my leave. Before I went I told Mum and Dad all about my experiences at square bashing, and Dad about the airship hangers at Cardington where he had worked for a while when he was in the RFC. I decided to keep my battle dress uniform on as I suppose everyone will want to see me in uniform, and of course take the Mickey. I'm going to wear my forage cap which I had illegally kept, and not my peaked cap as I don't think there will be any 'Snoops' about. I asked Dad if he wanted to come and have a pint with us, but he said no, go and have a good time with your mates.

When I walked into the 'Old Ball' a big cheer went up and everyone looked around, I felt a bit embarrassed. There was a pint waiting for me and it was good to see the gang again, plus John Mac had bought his two sisters with him. Now I had always fancied both of them, but one had her boyfriend with her who had been in the Army, his name was Jack and I was introduced to him and we hit it off straight away, and he remained a good friend, with his girlfriend Dorothy(Dot) and later his wife, for about 60 years, but sadly he passed away just recently, bless him, now john Macs other sister, Eileen was also very attractive, I think she was seeing someone, but I made out that what I had heard was that he was much older than her, and probably as she was the same age as me, and more or less all the others, he might feel uncomfortable in our company! I'm a swine aren't I Apart from that we were having a great time, the beer and gin flowed quite nicely, and we all played darts, which was a good laugh, especially with the women playing. About 9pm we decided to make our way as we usually did down to the GEC ballroom, which was about just over half an hour's walk away and as it was summer and still light it would be a nice walk, so there we were laughing and joking and fooling around, when all of a sudden a land Rover pulled up at the side of us and in it were a couple of 'Snoops' I couldn't believe it, 'Snoops' around this area, mind you they were Army 'Snoops, or MPs as they are called, Military Police. They called me over and John Mac and Jack came with me, they asked me for my Identity, so

I showed them my 1250 and leave pass, Jack was chatting to the other one as he had just been demobbed from the Army. The MP looked at my forage cap and said he thought they were now obsolete, so I said I had just come back from Germany and was probably a bit behind the times as we only wore forage caps out there, but should get it changed when I get to my next station. They were only a couple of young blokes, probably only been in a short while, so they wouldn't know what I was talking about, it was a good job I had my 1250 and leave pass in my pocket when I came out, or they could have hauled me off. The two girls were starting to chat to them by this time, which helped, one of them said to me to check out about my forage cap when you go back, and enjoy your leave, and smiling at the girls, drove off. I couldn't believe there were 'Snoops' around in Coventry, it's a good job they weren't RAF 'Snoops' or my feet wouldn't have touched the ground, better watch my step. Anyway, time for some more beers, so off to the dance.

Luckily we only just made into the dance as they close the doors at 10pm, but the bar doesn't close for another hour, so the usual £5 in the kitty for the blokes and get the first round in, when it gets to nearly closing time we get a couple of rounds in for later. The local resident band was playing the usual waltzes, quick steps, foxtrots and perhaps a tango now and again. the music in those days was a mixture of Victor Silvester, perhaps a little bit of Ted Heath jazz, and if you were lucky perhaps a bit of American big band music, Jimmy Dorsey, Stan Kenton, well the local band tried to sound like them. Mind you if they did manage to play jazz, you weren't allowed to do that improper thing called 'Jive' oh no! They didn't allow that for at least a few years. If you did try they would turf you off the floor. In the intervals they would play some records, but not disco stuff, Disco's weren't around then, but on the whole we really enjoyed ourselves. As I've said the bar closes at 11pm, and you were only allowed 10 minutes drinking up time, Very strict licence laws in those days and if you hadn't drunk your drinks after the ten minutes they would come around and take your drinks off the table. By closing time of the bar we would still have a few pints on the table, so we would put the drinks on the floor and pull the table cloths so that they hung right to the floor sometimes it worked sometimes it didn't, it depended on how keen they were on collecting. if it didn't work and they found the drinks under the table, you were given 20 seconds to drink it all or away it would go, obviously they never took any away, it was a case of 'down your necks lads'. The dance finished at twelve, so we all staggered our way back, a couple of the lads took off with some girls they had landed up with, but myself, John Mac, jack and the two girls went back to John Macs for coffee. His parents were long in bed, and I had pre warned Mum and Dad that I might not be home that night, just like I used to before I went into the Forces! So Jack and I crashed out on the settee and armchair. Next morning we awoke to the wonderful smell of bacon and eggs, which Mrs Mac had started already, she was a wonderful lady, a real cockney, and I had a nice cuddle when she saw that I was there, so all in all a great first night home.

The next few days just flew by, from what I can remember of course, I know a lot of the time was spent in an alcoholic haze and hangovers, well it would be some time before I was home again, so had to make the best of it. One evening we all went over to Hinkley dog track, that was good, I remember when we were kids sometimes we would catch a bus to there and spend the day walking the dogs around the track on race days, it was good money too, worth the bus fare! All too soon Friday was here, so got all my kit ready thanks to Mum, went for a pint with Dad at lunchtime, then at night just a quiet drink with the lads, to get to the station by 9am. Dad had arranged a taxi for me as well., I think one of his friends worked for a taxi firm, so that would save a lot of lugging kit about, so I said cheerio to my mates, I didn't know when I would see them again, but I would let them know. So onto another phase in the struggle of life!

I was up and about at 7am, having just started getting used to a bit of a lay in, had a good breakfast as no idea when I would be able to eat again today. said cheerio to Mum and Dad, into the taxi and off to the station. Jim was already there, as his uncle had dropped him off in his van on his way to work. We only had 10 minutes to wait and as it was a fast train it only took about three quarters of an hour. Once there we went to sort out the next move, and it appears that Cardiff is a bit of a bind to get to from Birmingham where we were. From what I can remember we next went to Worcester. Changed and then on to Gloucester, Changed, then onto Newport, changed, then Cardiff. No wonder the Corp said you wouldn't be able to get home even on a 72hr pass as you would only have about 24 hrs at home. The connections weren't too bad but it still took over 11hrs of very weary travelling. We couldn't carry our kit bags any more so we had a trolley, actually we pinched it when a porter left it outside the toilet, it was a long platform and a lot of people still about even though it was nearly 21-00hrs, so I don't think he could see us when he came out.

In the entrance hall there were a lot of RAF lads about, and there was an RAF kiosk there too, so we went and reported in and showed them our documents and so and so. they told us to get on bus No 2, and when we arrive at camp, the Corporal will show us which billet we were in. the bus ride took about ¾ of an hour and as we went by the camp we could see just how big it was with lights on everywhere, once through the gates we arrived at some billets, and the Corp was right about them, anyway we stopped at one block and the corporal called out our names and told us our room number. Jim and I were on the middle floor, also our mess was luckily just across the road, and the Corporal said, get your kit upstairs and grab which ever bunk you want, put your kit on it. Then if you want to, go across to the mess and get some food and drink as its open most of the night on Saturdays and Sundays with all the new inmates arriving, so it's a big coming and going weekend as lots of courses are starting and finishing. So Jim and I lugged our kit up the first flight of stairs and into our room, it was a long room with, as our Corp had said. 7 beds on one side and 8 on the other with plenty of room in between each bed, a double wardrobe and a bedside table to each one with a light above and a window above each bed, down the middle of the room were 5 tables and chairs, also the room was heated with hot water pipes. At the end of the room before the stairway entrance were 2 rooms, one each side with showers and toilets, it looked really comfortable. On the landing outside were store cupboards, better than the old wooden huts at the last camp. Jim and I were the first in so we chose the two far end beds opposite each other where there was plenty of light. We dumped our kit and took a walk over to the mess. We were starving, dirty, and thirsty. It was now dark so we couldn't see much, so we'll have a look around tomorrow. The mess was quite a big place, and busy at this time of night as there must have been be a lot that had arrived tonight. You just grabbed a tray and a plate and walked along choosing whatever you wanted and the cooks dished it out to you, some good choices as well as good helpings, they must do catering courses here as well. at the end were cups for tea or coffee (I wonder if they put that yellow powder in !) and weapons. All very civilised I must say. We felt much better after we had eaten, I think the order of the day is a quick shower and then put all our kit away. On each bed were already blankets and sheets. Before I went for a shower I had a quick look at the notice board for any rules and regulations, and as far as the locker lay out was concerned as long as it was neat and tidy it was ok as they could be inspected at any time, also it is requested that as the floor is light pine that everyone walks around on floor pads that are in the store room, I thought the floor looked nice and shiny, used to using floor pads anyway! So I took it upon myself to get them all out and pile them by the door to remind everyone when they came. One thing I had said to Jim was that when I get home after square bashing, I Was going to bring back with me a dressing gown, and so did he, as I was fed up with walking around with a wet towel around me. Another thing I noticed on the notice board was that every Wednesday morning there is a room inspection, and one person in the room is allowed to stay behind when everyone else has gone to classes to make sure the room looks tidy, classes start at 8-30 am and the room inspection is at 9am, after the inspection, usually by an Officer, he then joins his class.

More lads began to arrive in the room, and sorting themselves out until there were only two beds left. We all made ourselves known to each other as we were all here on the same course for 13 weeks. We told them to go over to the mess and get something to eat. I had my quick shower after reading all the notices, and Jim did the same. When they were all back we were a mixed bunch again from all over the place, 3 from Birmingham, 4 from Leicester, 5 from around the London area, one from Wales, one from Manchester, and one from Norfolk, so a really mixed bunch, 2 of the lads from Leicester said they had eaten at the station while they were waiting. One of them had the bed next to me, quite well spoken as well, he was also a 3year regular, as it seemed most of us were. He said that he has always wanted to work on aircraft, and what he wanted to achieve was to pass the course with good grades. (I don't know how they grade you, it must be on your exam results) then do sometime on a permanent station, then volunteer for an overseas posting, get demobbed out there and then try for a position on a civilian airline, as evidently they try to snatch British trained aircraft fitters and engineers before they are sent home, with offers of very good salaries and 5 star accommodation. he certainly had it all worked out. and I wish him luck.

Now that all the lads were back and had sorted themselves out, we sat at the tables chatting and getting to know each other, they seemed a good bunch of blokes. there was no stipulated lights out time and on the wall by the entrance was a bank of switches which turned the lights off two at a time in the room, I suppose that was to help with any late night swatting by anyone. Also there would be no bed banging at 6-30 in the mornings! A bell rang at 7 am and then another at 8am for breakfast, then at 9am another bell to assemble outside on parade to go off to your classes or workshops, it was like working hours. We sorted out the person who would be the room orderly on the Wednesday morning room inspection, we sorted it in alphabetical order, obviously it would be next week, it first fell to Tony (Anthony) job done. We were also told that someone would be in after breakfast in the morning (Sunday) to fill us all in as to what was going to happen, and the procedures for the next 13 weeks, so we had to make sure everyone would be present at 10 am. By this time I think the majority of us were just about knackered after such a long and tiresome day, so a last smoke and lights out, and see what tomorrow brings.

Sunday morning at 10am we were all sitting around in the room when in walked a J.T. (Junior Technician) one stripe upside down on his sleeve, some of the lads jumped up, but he waved and said that there was no need for that here, only if an officer enters. He introduced himself and started to explain what would be happening in the next 13 weeks. Firstly he explained that this was a trade training camp, and the top 2 floors of this block is solely occupied by, hopefully, future airframe fitters like yourselves, you will split into 3 classes of 20, the bottom 2 floors are Engine fitters. Your classrooms and workshops are just a short distance away, and each morning you will form up outside at precisely 8-45 am into your own individual classes, you will all be in the same class in this room, and then march, quite informally, to your allotted classrooms and tutors. This is not a square bashing camp, but you are still military personnel so you will obviously abide by the rules and Regulations, and if you disobey you will be punished in the same way, you are here not to march but to learn a trade, 13 weeks is not a long time to teach you, and turn you all into tradesmen. Some of you may fall by the wayside as the course is quite intense and there is a lot of swatting to do in your own time, if anyone should fail, you will be offered an alternative trade, so don't worry too much, after all you must all be, or feel mechanically minded, or you wouldn't have chosen this trade! As I have said a fitters course is not an easy one, so you will all have to put your heads down and study hard, both in class, and in here. There are hundreds of personnel on this camp, with lots of different courses. But on a lighter note, it is not all work and no play, Cardiff is only a bus ride away, if you fancy that, and there are some excellent facilities on the camp, there are 3 large NAAFIs, which do sell alcohol, but don't go O.T.T. ok, A large gymnasium, that will teach you many things if you wish to, such as weight training and lifting, gymnastics, fencing, indoor tennis, squash, badminton, and all the kit is there to use. The swimming pool is one of the best in the country, a lot of international events are held in there. There is also football, rugby, cricket, hockey, also a cinema, which doubles as a theatre, and occasionally there are variety shows on, also if you fancy a bike ride, you can get a bike from near the guardroom. So you can see everyone is well catered for with plenty to do. In fact a lot of the camp staff have their names down to be posted here permanently, especially those who live in Wales! I know it's a bit of a bind to travel anywhere to some parts. One important thing is, payday, which is on Thursday's, Dress around the camp is battle dress and berets, except if you go into Cardiff, it's best dress and peak caps, but you can wear gym kit if you are doing something around camp.

Now in the morning I will be taking this room and the room opposite as you will be in my class whilst you are here plus other instructors, so I will be shepherding you about. On the way to your first lesson we will call into the stores and you will all get a satchel containing books, pads, both for writing, and drawing in, pens and pencils, rulers, and all the stuff you will need for your course. Now any questions before I go next door and fill them in too. So if I were you I'd take a wander around the camp today, and try to get to know your way around, and I welcome you all to St Athens, and hope you enjoy your stay here and all the best on your course. So Eddie stood up and thanked the J.T. for explaining everything so clearly which we thought was very civil of him. Eddie is the chap in the next bed to me, from Leicester, he has a posh voice, but a nice lad. So Jim and I and Eddie decided to go for a wander, The camp was huge, like a small town, there were chaps riding around on bikes, permanent staff I suppose, they only needed a bus service and it would look like a town. We found the gymnasium, and there was a lot going on in there, I suppose because it was Sunday. In one corner they were fencing, I wouldn't mind having a go at that, as I did a bit of it when I was in the sports shop. The swimming pool was enormous, you could train for swimming the channel in there, and an enormous set of diving boards with its own pool, near the perimeter were a lot of hangers and workshops. As it was getting near to lunch we decided to go to one of the NAAFIs, the one nearest to our billet, well, inside it was like a supermarket, with a bar and a restaurant, you could buy practically anything, they say that in the bigger NAAFI there is even a shop where you can buy civilian clothes. We went into the bar which was very comfortable, very much like a pub really, had a half each as they only sold the draught in half's, why? and you could also get bottled beer, the half of beer was 6 pence, 6 old pennies, you try to equate that to today's prices, ok. 5p! We had 3 half's then went to lunch. This afternoon we'll take another walk in the opposite direction and see what's what

So after what was quite a decent lunch we went for another stroll. There were a lot of chaps walking around wearing tracksuits, instead of uniforms I suppose, must have a look in that civvy shop and see about getting one. When we had gotten past all the housing blocks we came upon rows and rows of classrooms, then beyond that were all the playing fields, football, cricket, rugby, and so on, then an airstrip and chopper pads, which led up to the hangers. On the way back we veered right and came upon the huge Administration block and Medical centre. This camp has everything, no wonder people try to get here on a permanent basis. Afterwards in the evening we just sat around chatting in the billet, some lads were playing cards. I could see some sessions of 'Brag' being played in this room in the future!

Next morning we went for breakfast and then back to the billet to tidy up the room. Everyone folded their blankets in the usual manner, and made sure the showers and toilets were clean, everyone one was now getting used to using the floor pads, and you only had to use them if you had footwear on, but once you were in the billet, most of us walked about in stocking feet. As Tony was this week's room orderly, he had been told that on Wednesday after the room had been inspected he was to make his way to classroom A, so we told him where it was as we had found them on our tour around yesterday. It seemed that as long as the place was clean and tidy and everything in its place, it was pretty relaxed as far as bulling was concerned. That is all except the floor, which it seemed was high priority. as it had to be extra clean and highly polished, I can see why really, as it was a lovely light grained polished pine and needed looking after obviously, so we were all told that every two weeks it had to be polished, everyone was responsible for their own patch and up to the centre of the floor, hands and knees job. The polish and dusters were in the cupboards at the top of the stairs on the landing.

At 8-45 the bell went and we all went outside and lined up, our room and the next were one class, which was 'Intake A, class I'. There were three J.T.s outside and it seemed that it was their job to Sheppard their classes to where ever they had to be. I think I should now try to explain the different ranks for airmen and NCOs. When you first join up, you are just an airman, no badges, then you promoted to LAC, leading aircraftsman, a single bladed propeller badge, then SAC, senior aircraftsman, three bladed prop, Corporal, two stripes, Sergeant three stripes, warrant Officer, a Crown badge worn on the bottom of the sleeve. Now in the Technical trades, if we pass the courses, the same, first LAC, then SAC, but then its Junior Technician, one stripe upside down, then Corporal Technician, two stripes upside down, and Sergeant Technician, three stripes upside down. Your first badge you get when you pass your course, after that consecutive badges are awarded by your superiors on merit only. In my three years I was made an SAC within 15 months, if I had stayed and signed on for a further 2 years I would have been made up to a J.T. straight away, but declined their generous offer! Especially where I was stationed the last 2 years of my service! But more about that later.

Further more, I see no point in attempting to relay events on a day to day basis for the next 13 weeks, too boring probably, so I will attempt a synopsis of events in a concentrated form.

Initially we spent the next weeks in classrooms, a lot of theoretical stuff on the workings of flight, Aerodynamics, flight controls. Aircraft structure and materials, stress factors on materials, metal fatigue, hydraulics, everything that makes aircraft fly. You would think that we were training to be pilots, not making them fly! We wrote pages and pages of notes and drawings, and spent hours swatting as every two weeks we would have an exam, after the third exam we noticed that one or two were missing from the ranks, none as yet in our room. Then there were lectures on tools and equipment, aircraft procedure's, ground handling, marshalling, refuelling, towing, fire drills, type's of fuel, safety, crash procedures, then into the workshops, hands on servicing of components, fault finding and correction procedures, actually working on aircraft, They had a Dakota and a Chipmonk in the hangers, and various parts to practise on, i suppose some things were familiar to me having worked in an aircraft factory, but even so after a full and intense day, swatting in the evenings, and even classes sometimes on a Saturday, it was hard going.

After the third exam and one or two had been reassigned, we were given a 72 hr pass, a long weekend, as it was no good us trying to get home and back in 72hrs, we were going to just relax and try and clear our brains. I decided I was going to get a bit of exercise for a change. The swimming pool was great as I used it sometimes in the evenings after swatting to ease the tension a bit, also I had signed up for a course on fencing, which was really energetic, I actually bumped into Cyril one day in the gym. He said he was really enjoying himself on the Instruments course and had passed all his exams so far with flying colours, I thought he would, remembering how he stripped and assembled that Bren gun blindfolded! Good on him, (His course must be slightly different to ours, as we don't get any results of our exams until the end.) He had really come out of his shell, he was also thinking of signing on for another couple of years if he gets his LAC badge, as I'm sure he will. Jim and Eddie had taken up football and were trying to get a team together from our block. I did say that if they were short I'd join in, but I hope not! As rugby is my game, but I didn't feel like joining any team whilst I was here in case I got crocked. That weekend was great, we all did our own thing during the day but met up for meals and went to the NAAFI at nights. We went to the cinema on the Saturday evening, plus you could have a bit of a lay- in, in the mornings if you wished to, and you didn't have to go to the mess for all your meals, you could use the NAAFI again, if you wanted to. Some of the lads caught a bus into Cardiff, but too many RAF blokes around and loads of 'Snoops' as well. There were a lot of Welsh people there as well one chap said! But it was a good weekend and I felt rested and ready for the next two weeks slog.

By now we had filled in about 3 note books with writings and the same with drawings, you were also marked on your standard of drawings. In one workshop there was lots of machinery of various types, lathes, drilling, planers, bending, and so on, I had used most of them at school in the metal work classes, also when I worked in the factory, so I got some pretty good marks for that so I was told. After the forth exam two more lads disappeared, one in our room, one of the London lads, he had to pack his things and move to another block which was a transit block, then go and see a careers Officer for reassessment, it was a shame after 8 weeks already, but he didn't seem to mind as he was only National Service so they will fit him in somewhere, I was surprised that being N.S. that he even got on the course.

I had done my stint as room orderly by this time and it wasn't too bad either, you didn't have to get up when the others did if you didn't want to, and you could wander over to breakfast on your own, and usually the showers were empty by that time, just as long as you were back by 9am so that you could go around the room and the toilets checking everything so that it all looked clean and tidy, the floor pads put away in the cupboard and everything ready for the inspection which was usually around 9-30 to 10-00. It was usually an Officer, a young Pilot Officer, who came, with an NCO who would make notes if needed. You could hear them around so when they came in you stood to attention, saluted and said" Room ready for your inspection, Sir," He would take a walk up and down the room looking at something here and there, perhaps say something to the Corporal who made a note of it. He would come and say "thank you airman" you saluted, and out they went. It all seemed a waste of time as we never did get any feedback from theses inspections. Then I would make my way to where my class should be and join them.

On our 10th week the exams were getting harder and very technical, so that meant more time spent swatting, but only three weeks to go and one final exam, so you either pass or you don't, then you are assigned to your permanent station. We were all getting quite used to this camp and I wouldn't mind staying actually if it wasn't for the distance from home, but as our trades are airframe fitters, and aircraft technicians we would be transferred to a flying station somewhere. Two more weeks went by of classes and practical and in the second week we had three days of exams, written and practical, also, oral, you were given a piece of equipment or a situation, and you had to explain to the rest of your class what that piece of equipment was, and what it did, and what to do if it malfunctioned. The situation was that if something wasn't working correctly on an aircraft, as reported by the pilot, what would be your course of action, depending on what it was, would you ground the plane, repair it straight away, or leave it until its next service, ? The exams finished on the Friday, but we wouldn't be getting the results until next week. so it was going to be a worrying weekend as to how we got on, I must admit I was fairly optimistic, as was Jim, Eddie was not so sure, well at least we had finished the course and not been thrown off, so that was something to celebrate, so over to the NAAFI for a drink, but we were so mentally exhausted that we only had a couple of half's, we'll make up for it over the weekend.

Saturday, Jim and Eddie went off to football and I went and had another lesson at fencing for the morning, I have really enjoyed that, as I've said it's really exhausting and your reactions have to be so sharp. Perhaps take it up again at some time. It was the same with squash, a relatively new sport at that time, I had a couple of lessons, they say it's one of the most strenuous sports going, and I could see why. After lunch and a couple of beers I went up to watch them playing football, and lay on the grass soaking up the sun. After dinner we went to the cinema then into the NAAFI for a few half's, can you get drunk quicker by drinking half's,? I felt quite merry when we got back to the room. Some of the lads were playing 'Brag', there were four of them around a table with a blanket over it, and by the look of it, it was a serious session. I have played it many times but only for 1p or 2p at a time, evidently the word had gotten around about some serious sessions going on in our block, with lads getting paid on Thursday mornings and then broke by Thursday evening, not for me at the moment thank you! Sunday I went for a swim quite early, didn't bother about going back for breakfast, had something in the NAAFI next door to the pool. Wrote a letter to Mum and Dad, told them I would be home for a few days, maybe next Thursday or Friday, as we had been told that might be the case for all those that had actually passed all their exams. If you had failed on any of them, you had the opportunity to retake them as there were still 3 days left before the course closes. After lunch had a quick drink and then a little kip, when I awoke went for a little jog to liven myself up a bit, then dinner, then over to the NAAFI to play snooker for a couple of hours, so that was the last weekend we spent in wonderful Wales, it was said that in some places in Wales the pubs don't open on Sundays, now that's a shame Boyo!

On the Monday we went up to classrooms as usual, the first two sessions were taken up by talks from Career Officers, and then by the C.O. (Commanding Officer) of the camp. It was quite informative on various aspects of military life, O.K. I suppose if you didn't mind your life being a bit regimented. Making it a career would have its advantages, most of all a secure job and future, the pays not too bad, plus everything found, and also a chance to travel the world, also to be able to retire when you are about 40 if you wanted to, with a good pension, and as Eddie said if you were abroad, you could possibly get a job with a civilian airline. After lunch we knew we were going to get the results of our first two exams, so we apprehensively waited for the instructor to come in with them. He said the results of the exams are never read out or posted on any bulletin boards. You will each receive personally an envelope containing the results of your exams to open in your own time. In the first month you had two exams on 6 subjects, then another month and 6 more subjects, then your last month also 6 subjects, so 36 subjects in all, the pass rate is 30 subjects or more, any failed subjects are graded at 30%, 60%, 90%, which is attributed to the effort made. 60% and 90% will be regarded as a provisional pass, although lower graded. 30% and you will have the opportunity to retake that subject in the 3days remaining, or be reassigned. All those with pass rates will be leaving on Friday, but before you leave you will be issued with orders as, and when to join your permanent stations. Personnel who didn't take any of the 48hr and 72hr passes whilst stationed here will get 6 days leave as from next Monday. You will all report back here in the morning as usual so that we can sort you all out for the rest of the week.

We couldn't wait to get back to the billet to open up our envelopes for the results, I think my hands were shaking as I opened mine, and it was very quiet in the room for a start, well, low and behold, 33 subjects passed, and 60% on the other 3, wow! I had to read it all again just to make sure. Jim also passed with 31 and also Eddie with 32, a good result. We congratulated each other. One lad sadly only had 10 passes and 8 at 60% so he is for reassignment, there were 4 with 26 passes, but they want to take the failed ones again, I don't blame them because taking 36 subjects in 13 weeks is a bit nerve racking, I think it all depended on how good you were at swatting, also being able to remember things. So tomorrow we will know just where our next stations will be, I hope Jim or Eddie are on the same as me. and of course we are now LACS, LEADING AIRCRAFTSMEN, sounds good to me. a bit more pay as well, but of course from now on we will be working on aircraft, not sitting in classrooms all day. as we had finished early I went for a quick swim, then dinner and over to the NAAFI for a couple of celebration half's, A very satisfactory day all round.

The next morning back up to the classrooms, we found out that 11 had failed out of the 60, and so would be re assigned on our course, and a further 16 were going to retake some of the exams, so 33 would be leaving at the end of the week. Also the 33 of us were given our LAC badges to sew on to our tunic's, I think my uniforms looked good with the LAC badge and also the Marks Mans badge on as well! Also we were given a folder telling us which station we had been assigned to, our travel warrants, both for back home and then warrants to the new station. The following Thursday. As luck would have it Jim and I got the same station with 3 others, Eddie is off to somewhere up North to a bomber station with some of the other lads, so we were distributed all over the country so it seems, Jim said he will see what our next place is like then he will put in for an overseas posting, I think I prefer to stay in the U.K. Our next posting is to a Flying Training School, at a place called Feltwell somewhere in Norfolk, about 8 miles from Downham Market, where ever that is, I bet it is in some God forsaken place miles from anywhere, and after looking it up on the map, I was right. I know that Norfolk is as flat as a pancake. That's why there were a lot of airfields there during the war, and evidently RAF Feltwell is near a huge American air base called Lakenheath. Now getting there is going to be a nightmare from Coventry, as its right across country, and as far as we can see numerous stations to change at and mostly just side lines which entails a full day's journey to get there again. So, once more, no more 48hr or 72hr passes, save them up for a week's leave now and again, anyway, something to sort out next week.

So we had two days now to pack up everything and get ready for that terrible journey home. We did see Cyril and he had also passed all his exams and had been posted not too far from where he lived, just an hour and a half's journey. Plus the fact when he goes home from here he can get a train straight through to London, and only 3 hrs, Jammy sod! On the Thursday we said farewell to our instructors and had a bit of a do in the NAAFI that night, not too much to drink though as we had to be up early for breakfast and get up to the guardroom to check out, and get the wagons to the station at Cardiff. It looked as if it was the same way old way home, Gloucester, Worcester, Birmingham, Coventry, or something like that, I'm sure it would have been quicker going to London and that way home, but probably cheaper our way! The train left at 8-30 am and I finally arrived home at 8-30 pm totally knackered. Still Mum had a nice supper waiting for me and a bottle of beer. I had arranged to meet Jim next Thursday at 9 am at the station. Mum said she had seen John Mac and told him that I would be home today and he told her to tell me to meet up in the 'Old Ball' on Saturday night as they would all be going down to the GEC ballroom afterwards, as usual. So 6 days to get used to civilian life once again, good beer, good home cooked food. Mum said she was going to re-wash all my clothes that were in my kit bag. I don't mind as I will be wearing only civilian clobber this leave.

As usual it was good seeing all the lads and girls again, still fancy Eileen though, I guess it's being without female company for so long, it's like being rescued from a desert island, you want to go mad for all the things you have missed for so long,. Not that it would be any good, not with all that yellow stuff they keep putting in the tea! Had a great night though, and a few good days, went greyhound racing, ice skating in Birmingham, that was hilarious, but all too soon it was time to repack my kit bag, taking a suitcase with me this time with all my good civilian clothes in as it's going to be my permanent station. Mind you I suppose to go out anywhere where we are going it would be more appropriate to wear a straw hat, brown smock, and wellies so that you blended in with the locals and wander around chanting ooh,ar,ooh ar, ooh ar. Not that I don't suppose there will be anywhere to go to, more about that later. Anyway met Jim at the station as arranged, and tried to find out the route but just told to catch a train to so and so, get off and then get the next train that comes in and so on, I think they were all one stop stations. To this day I cannot remember the way we went, or how many stations we got off and got on again, all I remember is, we finished up at a place called Brandon. I remember that name because there's a place called Brandon near Coventry, Brandon Woods, used to play in there when we were kids, also there's a motor cycle speedway there, who were called 'The Brandon Bees'.

Anyway the chap in the ticket office, when he saw us standing on the platform with our kit said" if you are RAF? (we were in uniform, very observant of him!!) "You'll be a wanting a lift up to that there airplane place won't e" He's got sharp eyes that chap. he picked up the phone and evidently rang the RAF station, it must be an arrangement they have. He said that they will be picking us up in 20 minutes, sure enough a land rover arrived driven by an LAC the same as us." Watcha mates2 he said "welcome to the land that time forgot" he laughed "no, it's not that bad, a bit isolated, but a good camp though, jump in". As we got nearer and drove around the perimeter you could see that it was a large camp with several hangers and the billets were just like the ones at St Athens only they were only two storied. He drove slowly so that we could take it all in, there were several aircraft outside the hangers and from my aircraft recognition classes I could make out some 2nd world war American Harvards, and some Chipmonks, along the wings and tails were broad yellow stripes which denotes it's a Flying Training School. We checked in at the guard room, allocated our billet, the lad drove us around to our billet, we were on the ground floor this time. We went in, there were 3 or 4 lads in there already, so we grabbed a couple of empty beds. The rooms were furnished the same as at St Athens but only 10 beds instead of 15, which of course made it all more spacious so you had now 2 lockers, plus the bedside table locker, very comfortable, better than home actually. 4 of the beds were still empty so we wouldn't be the only strangers. The 4 lads who were already in there had only been there themselves a couple of days, so we were all new. They were just going across to dinner so we went along with them, unpack later.

The housing blocks, 6 of them, were arranged around a huge parade ground, but it was tarmac, not gravel, at one end a huge building. Administration Block, and beyond that another housing block, which was the WRAFs quarters (Women's Royal Air force). I thought I had noticed a few walking around, it might make life a bit more pleasant! Beyond that about 200 yd's was the training Officers quarters, Pilot Officers, just out of Officers College, here on initial flying training. Also in the village of Feltwell were some married quarters where most of the permanent NCOs and Officers lived. Then beyond all of the buildings were the hangers and airstrip, the NAAFI and the mess and gym were behind another housing block, large buildings all joined together. Everyone ate in the mess, but the NCOs were separated from us Ors (other ranks) and of course the Officers had their own mess, but the WRAFs ate with us, so it was quite cosy. I did notice as we went and queued up for food some of the WRAFs were looking at Jim. Oh! perhaps I forgot to mention about Jim, probably because I was envious, but he was a really good looking bloke, black wavy hair, lean looking, good body, and he knew it (bastard) I had already decided to stick close to him whilst we were here when I saw that there were WRAFs about, you never know I might catch a bit of fall out !!

After dinner we decided to have a quick look in the gym and the NAAFI, both very good, and well equipped, also you could get anything in the NAAFI and it had a good snack menu, also some local real ales, and in pints too!, so overall first impressions were good, just wait until tomorrow to find out what the working conditions are like. We went back to the billet to unpack and whilst we did we chatted to the other 3 lads, two of them were Engine mechanics and the other instruments. They had been in about 6 months and this was there 2nd posting, the instrument chap had been in for a year and he was in transit at the moment waiting for an overseas posting which he had put in for. Just then a Corporal tech walked in and asked for Warden and Taylor, Jim and I, and he told us that in the morning to make our way to hanger no 3 and to make yourselves known to the Sergeant there. The instrument chap said that that was where he was working so he would show us the way. By now it was 7pm and we had unpacked and put everything away. Another thing that was the same as at St Athens was the bloody floor pads! Can't get away from them can we. One good thing about this camp was that if you were off duty you could walk around in civilian clothes or track suits in the evenings, so we changed and went over to the NAAFI in our track suits so that we didn't look too conspicuous as new boys in camp. There were quite a few WRAFs in there and some of them looked quite good in their civilian clothes, also, again I noticed that Jim was getting a few glances from some of them (I hate him!!) not really as we are good mates now. I must say it was nice to relax with a drink and a smoke after a long day and now knowing that we were here to stay for a while, we hope.

Next morning after breakfast we made our way up to hanger No 3, This was another nice thing, no more lining up outside and marching everywhere, you were trusted to make your own way to work, but you had to make sure you were not late for any reason, which was fair. Our workplace, or hanger was quite large, there were 4 aircraft in there at the moment, 2 of each, all along one side of the hanger were the offices and small workshops, hydraulics, electrical, welding shop, tyre bay engine bay, and then rows of cupboards and drawers with the tools for all trades. We went in and made ourselves known to the Sergeant in charge, he was a very nice chap, kept calling everyone lads, he fixed us up with overalls and a pair of plimsoles, for climbing on the aircraft if needed, you hung the overalls up each evening and they were changed every week. This particular hanger was a servicing hanger, where aircraft came in for various services according to the how many hours they had flown, so that was to be our job. Also as this was a flight training school, the aircraft took a bit of a bashing form these raw pilots. Each aircraft has a Log book which tells you the hours flown, and when it is due for a particular service, and any remarks written by the last pilot, so if it had done say 50 hrs, it would come in and you would look out a particular service schedule manual for those hours flown, and then follow the schedule step by step, if everything is ok on that one item, you sign it as checked and serviceable, then on to the next item, If any item is faulty in anyway, you change it or repair it up to standard. It might be a hydraulic pump that operates the ailerons, (flaps on each wing) So you remove it, take it to the hydraulics workshop, if there's no spare available they will repair the one you took in. servicing an aircraft is similar to a car, but much more specialized, as you don't have to look for hairline cracks or metal fatigue on a car. To do a major inspection can take a week or two, or even longer depending what you find, and these are only small aircraft.

At the end of the servicing schedule you have probably inspected every square inch of the aircraft except the engine, which of course is the engine mechanics job, then you can sign off the aircraft as serviceable, and just hope that you haven't missed anything, because if anything goes wrong, or it crashes, all servicing records are immediately impounded and scrutinised, and if it was something that was missed or repaired incorrectly and it has your signature on it, you are for the high jump. so you can see that servicing and repairs are taken very seriously apart from that it could be someone's life that you're dealing with. I hope that this is not too boring to read.

It didn't take Jim and I too long to fall into the swing of things on the camp, it was more or less the same as going into work in civilian life, you get up in the morning, have breakfast, go to work, lunch, back to work, back to your room, dinner, and the evening is yours. You might be called upon to do a bit of evening work, marshalling, or refuelling on the airfield if they were doing any night training flights. The Pilot instructors were o.k. but one or two young trainee pilots were a bit snobby. Some of them thought they were the cat's whiskers because they had finished Officers College and were training to be pilots, but usually the old sweat instructors would soon put them in their place, and they were only kids anyway. I remember once an instructor came into the hanger and asked me about a certain aircraft, and I told him that it was standing outside hanger no 2 and the service on it was complete and ready to go,. He thanked me very politely and as they started to walk away, the trainee pilot turned to me and said "Airman, pick up my bag and carry it over to the aircraft will you" The instructor stopped dead in his tracks, turned to the youngster and said "come with me for a minute please" they walked about 20 yd's and stopped, I could see the instructor talking to the trainee and waving his finger, then they both walked back, the trainee picked up his bag and walked away and the instructor said to me "I do apologise about that" smiled and walked away.

There was a parade once a month on the square, usually on a Sunday morning if you weren't working, as occasionally they might be doing some weekend flying, We reckon it was some of the more senior Officers taking the aircraft and flying home for the weekend or down to London! We always tried to be on duty on those Sundays! The turnout for the parade would be about a hundred personnel, WRAFs as well, it was more like a church parade as there was a Padre there, who read a piece from the scriptures, and then we had a march past, the salute taken by the C.O. or any other Senior Officer. It only lasted about an hour and it gave your best dress an airing, and when it was over it was straight into the NAAFI for a quick pint before lunch. Leisure time was spent in various ways, there was of course football, where each block would have a team and play each other in some sort of a league, I believe Rugby also, then there was the gymnasium, then there were the tennis courts down near the Officers quarters, snooker and table tennis in the NAAFI, also bingo one night a week, it was called housey, housey in those days. There was also a cinema in a large room attached to the NAAFI, 3 times a week, Sat, Sun, Wed. A lot of the time was spent though reading, writing letters, some playing cards, or in the NAAFI, chatting up the WRAFs. There was a little pub in Feltwell if I remember, but the only largest place was Brandon, which I never did bother going to, only to catch a train. As for trying to get home on a 24 or 48 or even a 72 hr pass, you had no chance, you could if you had a car or motorbike I suppose, but just not worth it by train, so most saved their weekend passes up and took a week's leave now and again. There were quite a few lads from Birmingham and one weekend on a 72 hr pass they all hired a bus to get home, but they said it took too long, and really only had one day at home. As I've said a lot of the time was spent in the NAAFI just sitting around and chatting in mixed company, and as far as Jim was concerned, flies round a jam pot, springs to mind, I didn't mind, as I said, there could be fallout, or crumbs, I am now demeaning myself! So Jim was a good looking guy, and he knew it, at least it did attract the WRAFs. And in particular one girl, who came over with her mates to join us one night. I myself quite liked the look of her and I'm sure she kept glancing at me, I knew this as I was looking at her all the time!! I shouldn't stare, can't help it though, but we were all in a crowd so there was no pairing off or anything like that. Now one Saturday evening I went to the cinema on my own as I wanted to see a particular film, and Jim had a date already. So I was sitting in the cinema before the film started when in came the girl that I had fancied before. So she looked around and saw me, so I waved, and blow me she came over and sat next to me. Now believe me or believe me not, but basically I am quite a shy person when it comes to women until I get to know them well, so at that particular moment I was rather tongue tied and I said" have you come to see a film" I could have bitten my tongue off, what a stupid thing to say, (no, she had come to practise swimming the channel), butshe put me at ease by saying by saying she wanted to see this film so she came on her own.

After the film had finished I plucked up courage and asked her if she would like to go for a coffee or a drink in the NAAFI, and blimey, she said she would love to, so I was quite pleased, pleased!! I was over the moon, anyway we settled on coffee and we sat chatting. We were both dressed in civilian clothes and she had on a lovely floral printed dress and a cardigan and high heels, and to me she looked gorgeous. Her name was Margaret, the same age as me, she was small and petite, lovely curly blonde hair. great figure and so easy to talk to, in fact at the end of the evening it was as if we had known each other for years. She had only been on the camp for 4 months and worked in the Admin block. She was also an LAC, and she came from Hemel Hempstead near London and had worked in a dress shop after she left school and had become Manager, but she couldn't see herself doing that for ever and wanted to see a bit more of life before she eventually settled down, she was an only child so decided to join the WRAFs, and she was enjoying it and mixing well with all the other girls, she would, as she had a lovely bubbly personality, so she could mix with anybody. We had several coffees and sat talking until the NAAFI closed, so then I walked Margaret back to her block and as it was Sunday tomorrow we arranged to meet up at breakfast. No, no kiss goodnight, play it easy and see how it goes. Jim was asleep when I got back so didn't bother to ask him how he got on, although I was dying to tell him how I got on! I couldn't get to sleep myself, I don't know whether it was all the coffee, or thinking about Margaret.

Up and shaved early this morning for some reason or other, put my track suit on and told Jim I would see him down at breakfast, got a quizzed look, went and got my breakfast and got a seat away from anyone. Then Margaret came in, she also had on a track suit, she saw me, got her breakfast and came over and sat with me. I tell you she was like a breath of fresh air, so easy to talk to, she had put her track suit on as she was going to have a game of netball with some of the girls in the gymnasium and if I wasn't doing anything in particular would I like to come and watch, I would, I would, I would, steady on lad! After the netball, interesting, I could see that Margaret was pretty fit. After that we decided to go for a walk around the perimeter of the camp as it was a nice morning, it was November by now but it was still nice and warm and sunny, and also it had been a good summer this year. Walking around the perimeter and at the end of the runways it was like taking a walk in the countryside, and we just walked and talked as if we had just met up again after years apart and catching up on everything, but if you asked me what we talked about, I have no idea, as it was nice just being with her. We got about halfway around the camp and it was time for lunch so we made our way back. got a couple of wolf whistles from one of the blocks, saw Jim and sat with him, he said he was going to meet one of the WRAFS in the NAAFI tonight and would we like to join them and make it a foursome for the evening so Margaret and I said yes. After lunch we both weren't doing anything in particular, so we decided to go for another walk around the other half of the camp as it was still nice and warm and sunny and a shame to be indoors, we walked and talked and when we came to some long grass we thought we would sit for a while, we stretched out and relaxed and we both dropped off to sleep believe it or not, I awoke first and leant over to see if she was awake, but she wasn't, and I just couldn't resist the urge to kiss her, so I bent over and kissed her gently, she opened her eyes and I was dreading what her reaction would be, and she said "that was nice Ray" so I kissed her again, or rather we both kissed each other. So I guess you can say that was the start of a sort of romance as we both agreed it probably was, we started walking back holding hands but we were careful not to as we got nearer and in sight of anyone, as we both knew that fraternising with the opposite sex in a camp is frowned upon by the establishment, so we would have to be careful from now on and not be too obvious about it.

After dinner we met up with Jim and his girl, her name was Barbara, ' Babs', Margaret didn't actually know her but had seen her about, as there were about 60 WRAFS on the camp altogether, but they hit it off o.k. also Jim thought Margaret was a little smasher by the way. So we had a very enjoyable evening together. we played darts and skittles and snooker and had a good laugh. From then on we knocked about together as a foursome, at the same time though trying to be discreet about it. We would sometimes arrange to meet the girls in the pub in Feltwell, and the girls would leave camp on their own and we would join them later. So life went on in camp and things just became routine, but much more pleasure able now with the two girls. I actually managed to go flying a few times as that's when a kite has had a major overhaul and inspection that an instructor usually took it up for a shakedown, as we called it, to see that everything was in order, also all the aircraft had dual seats so we would ask if we could go up with them as we had done all the work on it, and they would usually say yes, also as we had done the work on it, we wouldn't want to fly in a kite unless we had done a good job! There was one instructor, a nice guy, and if you ever went up with him he used to let you have a go at flying it, he would say "right you have control of the stick" it was great fun once you had got used to it, and that's where I learned the basics rudiments of flight, not theory, but hands on!

Christmas was fast approaching and Margaret was going home to be with her parents and family for a week, I couldn't get any time off as I was on 'duty roster' over Xmas, as was Jim, his Babs lived in Cambridge, which wasn't very far away, so she was going home for 3 days, still there would be plenty of things going on in camp over the Xmas period. Xmas week we saw the girls off, but the weather started to turn nasty, but before it did, a surprising number of aircraft disappeared from the camp and there weren't many senior Officers around either, so it was obviously a case of, ' those who can, do' they were lucky to get away though before the storms hit, so there wasn't going to be much flying done, also there was no inspections due, so we hung around in the crew room playing cards. for something to do I decided to make a ring for Margaret. I had thought about it before, but to get the right size I'm afraid I was a bit deceptive, as once in the NAAFI, I had said that I'd thought about getting a Signet ring, so I asked Margaret if I could have a look at the ring on her 2nd small finger on her right hand as it looked nice, so she took it off and I just slipped it on to my little finger to see how far it went up, made a note of it mentally, as I reckoned the same finger on her left hand would be the same size as the right! I just casually said that it was a nice ring and gave it her back, so I had the size?. In the workshop there were lots of pieces of piping, and one piece of nickel alloy was just the right size, so I cut a piece off and started to shape it into a ring, well it passed the time, in the instrument shop they had an engraving tool which they used to engrave part numbers on pieces of metal, so I used that. It was quite intricate work and I engraved a heart on the top. I thought it looked good when I had finally finished it, as it took a whole day. On the plus side, also in the instrument shop was a silver plating vat and one of the lads said he had to do some plating tomorrow so he would put it through all the processes and pop my ring in as well. Great.

Christmas Eve there was carol singing in the NAAFI by a church choir from one of the villages, and hot toddy and mince pies. There were still quite a few people on camp and also a lot of WRAFs still here, so the old mistletoe was going the rounds of course and everyone was getting merry, I reckon someone had spiked the hot toddy as it had a hell of a kick! When we finally staggered out of the NAAFI, some lads were flat out on the grass, but someone would pick them up I suppose. Jim and I couldn't as we were escorting a couple of girls back to their dormitories, either that or the girls were escorting us back to ours, can't quite remember which way it was, and also how the hell did we get lipstick on our shirts ? Hope the girls don't find out!

Christmas morning we both had hangovers, but we both managed to get to breakfast as it was going to be a huge fry up, full English, also it was served an hour later which helped, whilst we were standing in the queue two girls walked by and said" Good morning Ray and Jim, o.k. this morning" giggled and walked on. Jim and I just looked at each other "Don't bloody well ask me" I said and carried on! Today was going to be a late lunch which was a good job as when we got back from breakfast we both crashed out for a couple of hours. After a shower and a shave I didn't feel too bad so got dressed and we went over to the NAAFI for a pint before lunch, and in there were the same two girls who were looking at us and giggling again. I don't know what it was but I don't want know

I don't think! In the mess the tables all had cloths on and knives and forks and napkins, plus a Christmas cracker, then we were all told to be seated and a load of Officers came in from the kitchen carrying jugs and glasses, put a glass in front of you and then filled it with rum punch, another one following put a glass dish of prawn cocktail down in front of you also. The Officers were mainly the young trainees, but the C.O. was doing his bit as well. It's a bit of a tradition in the forces that the Officers wait on the O.Rs at Xmas lunch. Before we started the Padre gave the blessing and we pulled the crackers and put on the paper hats, then a toast was given to the C.O. and the camp. That rum punch is lethal, you could fly a plane on it! Never mind fill it up again, what the hell. I must say the dinner was superb, turkey and beef and all the trimmings, Xmas pudding and thick cream, there were nuts and things on the tables. One of the lads, with a bit of encouragement, went up to the C.O. and spoke to him, so the C.O. stood up, a little unsteady, I reckon he had had a few samples of the rum punch beforehand! Then banged on the table and told one of the young Officers to go tell all of the cooks to come out from the kitchen and line up. when they were all out, he took up his glass, and we all stood, and he said "I have been requested that on behalf of all the personnel here, I been told to say what a wonderful lunch you have prepared and given to us on this Xmas day and we would like to thank you sincerely, so everyone raise your glasses and a toast to the catering staff" we all raised our glasses and said "The catering staff" and then we gave them a big round of applause. They all looked embarrassed, in fact one of the girl cooks was crying, bless her. Well after that lunch I was stuffed. So a quick pint to wash it all down and then a little kip is called for before this evening's festivities begin.

When we walked into the NAAFI later there was a Father Xmas standing at the door and he gave everyone a present as you went in, a present from the NAFFI organisation. Carols were being played and as you went up to the bar for a drink you had a hot minced pie given you. So we all sat around singing carols and drinking and everyone was enjoying themselves, also an area of the room had been cleared and dance music was put on later. Even some of the Officers came up to the NAAFI and politely asked for permission to come in and join us. The NAAFI Supervisor came in and asked us if we minded them joining us, so we all shouted "The more the merrier" so in they came, there was about a dozen of them, couldn't be much going on in their mess tonight, anyway they joined in and we all started playing silly games and it got really hilarious, and nobody cared as everyone was getting rather merry. I was sprawled out in an armchair with a girl on my lap, I have no idea who she is, but we kept getting up and dancing away and having a bit of a snog, well it was Xmas! I just hope that no one is taking photographs. The NAAFI also laid on a free buffet which went down very nicely later on, soaked up a bit of the beer anyway. I reckon that by midnight 90% of us were smashed out of our brains, a couple of the Officers were spark out on a settee and were evidently still there in the morning, these youngsters can't take their beer! Some were outside on the grass, it might be a bit chilly tonight as they will find out later. Now tonight, two of the girls took Jim and I back to the block, that I do remember, but they wouldn't come up, which reminded me to stop drinking that tea with the yellow powder in it!

Boxing Day hangovers were quite rife throughout the camp evidently, and that was quite evident at breakfast as there was hardly anyone there, and those that were there, plus anyone who was about, looked pretty awful and very subdued, but the cooks, bless them, had come up with the answer, strong coffee and a full English again. Jim and I were very glad that we had made the enormous effort to get here, despite having to drag a couple of blokes out of the showers where they had slept all night, and laying them on their beds, like corpses, and they never even opened their eyes. After breakfast and on the way out we saw one of the cooks and we said "Thanks for that breakfast mate" and he said "I don't even remember cooking it". Outside it was getting a bit nippy now so as to get some fresh air, and as we were in our track suits we decided to take a quick walk over to our hanger and see that everything was O.K, as we were still on call on the duty roster. It was quite bracing and I think there had been a bit of a frost, well it was that time of year, as we had already had a fluttering of snow in the storms at the beginning of the week, evidently the rivers were pretty high in some places for the time of the year, plus as we were nearly into January 1953, the spring tides which were very high tides would be due soon which sometimes caused some local flooding, clever aren't I, not really, the reason we know this is because one of the lads in the room works in the so called meteorological centre on the camp, they do the weather forecasting for the whole of East Anglia, they even have their own plane, so he used to tell us what the weather was going to be like, and sometimes he even got it right!

Everything seemed to be alright in the hanger, but it was bloody cold in there as all the blast heaters had been turned off for the stand down. We did find one of the Junior Techs asleep in the crew room with an empty bottle of Scotch near him, but we decided to let the poor lad sleep it off! but being very sympathetic, we did switch on the coffee machine and left him a note to that effect stuck in the empty bottle. When we got back we went into the NAAFI, which had now been cleaned up a bit we sat and had a coffee and relaxed a bit and laughed at some of the stories from the previous night. Evidently around 4 am some Snoops came around and chucked the two Officers that were asleep on the settee in the NAAFI, plus the two who were outside on the grass, into the back of the land rover and took them down to the Officers mess, dumped them outside, rang the

175

bell, and left. i bet the two who were outside got a touch of hypothermia. also a corporal and a WRAF were discovered wrapped around each other, dead to the world, under the snooker table, the Snoops must have missed them, so a night to remember. Tonight is going to be a bit quieter because I believe a choir from a local school is coming in to sing some more Xmas carols to us, besides the girls will be back tomorrow, and then it will only be five days to the New Years Eve, so that will be a bit of a ding dong as well, still I will be able to see the new Year in with Margaret. I forgot to mention about Xmas presents for us both, well I got Margaret a nice bottle of perfume from the NAAFI, which I was told was very chic, and Margaret bought me a bottle of aftershave, something I had never used before, but was told I should do, it was called 'Brut' I think, new on the market, smelt ok, but when I used it for the first time after a shave, it said to plash it on, which I did, but then I thought my face had set fire to itself, I had to dowse my face in cold water until it calmed down, after that it was just a dab here and there, but I told Margaret it was lovely!

Today we went up to the hanger to see if anything was going on. The sergeant was there, also the lad in the instrument shop, he said he had done the ring and gave it to me and I'm telling you it looked brilliant I never in a million years expected it to look that good, Jim said it looked as if it was from a shop. The Sergeant said that there was nothing going on today, so we might as well go, so we did. Both girls arrived back at about the same time, late afternoon so we met up in the NAAFI after dinner as they were late. They both said that they had enjoyed their Xmas with their families, but missed being with us, Ah! We said that we had had a nice a time as possible, considering that they were not with us !!! I gave Margaret the ring I had made and she said it was lovely, especially as I had made it just for her, also it fitted perfectly on the ring finger. I did say perhaps the next one will be real, and she said. I suppose that I can take it that we are engaged in some sort of way or other, to which I replied "no comment" but got a big kiss anyway.

The next two or three days we went to work but there wasn't much going on and no flying because of the lousy weather, and no servicing either, but there were a couple due next week so the sergeant arranged for them to come in now. One of them was a Harvard which had a problem with its landing gear so that was a priority and it would perhaps take some time to sort it out, Probably the hydraulics as the undercarriage was retracting too slow, it dropped and locked ok but something was amiss, so that meant jacking up the whole plane onto stands clear of the ground so that we could plug in the electric bowser and retract and drop the landing gear (up and down) until you found the fault, so we raised and lowered the undercarriage several times with your head stuck up inside and it turned out to be a faulty non return valve, but a tricky job replacing it, and then of course having to bleed the whole system again, then double check everything and getting the Sergeant to check also so that I could sign it off on a F 700. Actually before I had started the work a couple of young pilot trainees had been sent down to see and experience what goes on during the servicing and repairing of aircraft, and they were put with me, so I had to show and explain what I was doing and why every step of the way. I must say that they did seem genuinely interested in what was going on and that they would like to ask to come back the next time if there was no flying if that was alright, I said that you would have to ask the powers that be. The component that I removed I took into the hydraulics workshop and stripped it down and found a little mark on one of the baffle plates in the hydraulic exchanger. I showed it to the Sergeant and we wondered what had caused it, it was nothing serious at the moment but worth checking other units, so he had it written into the service manual, but only on a major service was that particular component to be checked, unless it was reported as this one was, also a circular would be sent to include it in all further Harvard service manuals everywhere, a feather in my cap!

On New Year's Eve we finished work at lunchtime and went to the NAAFI after lunch for a drink, and to relax for a while to build up our strength for this evenings New Year's Eve extravaganza, but also the NAAFI had asked for volunteers to help clear the big room as a dance was going to be held in there tonight as well. There was going to be a group playing, plus someone playing records on a new type of sound system (one of the first disc Jockeys) plus an invite had been sent out to any of the local girls who would be welcome to join us. I bet the local lads didn't think much of that! But what the hell, there wasn't enough WRAFS to go around so why not, both Margaret and Babs had said that. They had bought new outfits whilst they were home to wear for this evening, so did I, clean underpants! We all helped to get the big room (cinema) ready for the dance. The decorations were still up from Xmas so it really did look like a Dance Hall, especially as it had a nicely polished wooden floor, as it was getting near lunchtime we stayed for a drink then went into the mess for lunch with Margaret and Babs, when we came out the girls went off to do their thing. Both Jim and I had noticed that opposite the mess entrance was a land rover with two Snoops in it who seemed to be interested in who came out of the mess for some reason or other, strange. Back in the room I dropped a few lines to Mum and Dad hoping they had a nice Xmas and wishing them all the best for the New Year, and would try to get home soon. Decided to have a little nap after I had ironed a shirt for this evening, and of course Jim asked me to do his as well, lazy git.

(Just to put a few things into perspective, as I know it may seem that we were having a good time all the while, drinking, and making merry, and a lot of time off, but that was only at this time of the year as everything was wound down with a lot of change around in the staff, coming and going, plus, some of the Trainee Officers had finished their courses and new ones were drafted in. During normal times we worked pretty hard every day, especially if you were on flying duties outside in all weathers, marshalling and refuelling and towing, especially on night duty. Most evenings after dinner you just wanted to have an early night, or Jim and I would just go and have a coffee with the girls in the NAAFI, or spend an hour in the gym. We couldn't afford to drink a lot as we always seemed to be broke, so in the period we were in at the moment it was nice to let our hairs down a bit. I hope that explains a few things)

We went for dinner and met the girls for a chat and a coffee in the NAAFI afterwards, then back to the billet to get ready for this evening. Time for a shower and a shave and some 'splash it all over' stuff, actually I think it was Methylated spirits mixed with lavender water, just joking, we dressed and went over to the NAAFI to get a good table and save the seats for the girls and it wasn't long before they both came in, and they looked stunning. They certainly turned some heads as they made their way to our table. I knew Margaret would look good, as she did work in a dress shop and was quite up on the fashions. There were eight of us on our table with some of the lads from our room and we chatted and laughed and another couple of WRAFs joined us so things got off to a good start, and in between we had a game of snooker and darts. The NAAFI bar/lounge was separated from the cinema/dance hall by large folding wooden doors which were now open, it reminded me of the GEC ballroom back home. I bet the lads are all in there at the moment living it up. In our dance hall there were some nice background records playing as the dance wasn't due to start until 10pm, We weren't going mad on the drinking, just steady, it's going to be a long night I reckon so plenty of time, I must say that say that all in all, with all the other lads and the girls, plus the music and dimmed lights the whole atmosphere felt great, so I think it's going to turn out to be a great evening, and my first New Years Eve, out of three, to be spent in "H.M.S. ' His Majesty's Service'.

At 10pm the group struck up, well it was more like a band and I reckon that most of them were RAF chaps and they were very good, a good mixture of music, jazz, swing, slow and quick, and smooching ones, so we all got up to shake a leg, there were a lot of girls there, and you couldn't tell who were WRAFs or village girls so the mixture was pretty good, about 2 to 1. I enjoyed dancing with Margaret as she was so light on her feet, and she could jive as well, she said the girls used to practise in their rooms. The time was now getting near to the countdown to midnight, so we made sure our glasses were charged, there were balloons and popping things on the tables also streamers. the speakers had been linked up to the radio and one of the band was out front looking at his watch and we all stood up and started to count down on his mark as Big Ben rang out, 10-9-8-7-6-5-4-3-2-1. Then the first stroke of the New Year and everyone cheered with "Happy New Year" Margaret and I were holding hands, and we looked at each other and said quietly' Happy New Year' darling, and slowly kissed, a long kiss, and an equally long hug, and then Margaret whispered in my ear" Ray, I love you so much" I swallowed hard as my knees went wobbly and I croaked "I love you too darling" we were absolutely oblivious of anybody else as we hugged. Didn't know that I was so romantic! So the rounds of kissing and hugging and shaking hands began, I have never since, kissed, hugged, and shook so many hands. I lost Margaret in the melee but we soon found each other and as we looked at each other we both knew that our relationship had gone to another level. Then everyone started doing the 'Auld Lang syne' and then the 'Hokey Cokey' They could have made a film of that night, I wished they had as I would like to see a replay even to this day. Everything wound up about

1am so we escorted the girls back to their billets, there were a lot of people still coming and going saying Happy New Year to everyone, even to the Snoops who were patrolling around in their land rover, poor sods having to work on N.Y.E. ah! It was their own fault, they should not have chosen to be a Snoop! When we got back to our digs it was a lovely crisp night so we sat on the wall outside and had a smoke, I hadn't seen much of Jim and Babs in the last hour after midnight, so I asked him how he and Babs were getting on together, he sort of shrugged his shoulders and said "no comment no commitments" and I understood what he meant. He then said that it looked as if Margaret and I were very cosy and close, but all I said was "maybe" We both half smiled and went in.

I can't quite remember what month it was in the New Year that things were beginning to look bad along the East coast with regard to high spring tides and the heavy raid that we were getting, adding to the flood risks that were being broadcast. Some places had already been hit and the emergency services were already rescuing people from their homes, and personnel from the American airbase at Lakenheath were out helping, and our base was put on standby also, as the Great river Ouse was dangerously high. Then all of a sudden the call came, evidently a section of the bank along the river was starting to leak and as one side of the river was low ground, if it went, then huge areas would be underwater including farms and villages, so we were all mustered around 10 pm one night, all forms of transport were bought into action, and we had to gather on the square and were issued with overalls and wellingtons and capes as it was raining hard, there must have been a couple of hundred personnel climbing onto the transports, trucks, vans, buses, you name it. We drove out into the night for only about three quarters of an hour then turned into some fields and down a slope to the river which you could see with all the arc lights that had been set up, was in full flood, Also a couple of bulldozers were in the fields, one in this field and one in the next. They were scrapping off the surface grass up and down the fields, there were loud speakers going and told us that half of us were to go into the next field, sort your selves out into pairs and collect a spade from a truck up at the top, also as many empty sand bags as you can carry, find a spot as near to the river as possible and one of you start digging and the other hold open the sandbag and fill as many as you can, don't go mad to start with as we could be in for a long stint, so Jim took the first stint at digging whilst I held the bag open, the soil was very sandy so digging wasn't too bad. When you had filled one you put it on one side and blokes came along and collected them and carried them down to the river bank and piled them up, for what reason I wasn't sure at that time. Jim kept going for about an hour and then I took over, and. so on. At about 2am we began to realise what the plan was, as a short while ago a motor launch had come up the river towing a couple of empty barges which were tied up to the our bank and gangs were throwing the sand bags into the barges. It was like a production line. To pass the time I thought I would try and work out mentally how long and how many sand bags could be filled in say an hour. so there were say 200 personnel, 100 filling the bags and100 holding the bags it takes approx; 30 seconds to fill a bag so that's 2 bags a minute, 60 minutes, just say average, 100 an hour with breaks, so 100 + 100 people = 1000 bags an hour, well that passed a bit of time. Every now and again someone would come along with a flask of coffee and mugs, usually a WRAF, and we would have a 5 minute break and a smoke. It stopped raining about dawn then we heard a cheer, we stopped and looked up and into the field came 2 caravans, one was a mobile canteen and out got 4 old dears, the Salvation Army girls, then over the tannoy(speakers) some officer said "the gracious ladies of the 'Sally Anne' have instructed me to tell you all that the tea bar is now open for tea, coffee and sandwiches, and will be until the job is done" a big cheer went up again, during the night a large marquee had been set up by the RAF and hot meals were being ferried from the camp, so you could take it in turns, 20 or 30 at a time to get some hot food inside you, and then back to sand bag filling which was dam hard work. It was cold and wet but keeping working kept you fairly warm, but you had to have breaks so it was up to the Sally Anne for a cup of tea and a sandwich to keep you going as we had worked through the night. An officer did come around asking if anyone wanted to go back to camp to sleep, they could, but nobody did. The object was to shore up that river bank to stop it bursting and possibly save property and maybe lives

The first barge was now looking as if it was ready to go, as it was, it was low in the water, so ropes were attached to the front and rear and gangs took up the ropes and the barge was cast off and it was held back by the ropes, but gradually the ropes were eased off little by little so that the flow of the river slowly let the barge drift outward and by controlling it with all the ropes it slowly drifted across the river to the other side of the bank where the leak was weakening it, two chaps stood on the bank opposite about 20 yards apart to indicate where the barge should go, also 4 chaps were on the barge holding ropes which were attached to the portholes on the barge and as soon as the barge was in place they would pull on the ropes and open the portholes which were now under water and the barge would flood and sink, and with all the tons of sandbags on board should stabilize the embankment. But then a bit of a disaster struck. The lads on the other bank shouted "It's going" and ran like hell away along the bank just as a section of the bank collapsed, probably about 4yds wide and there was a terrific swoosh as the river cascaded like a waterfall into the fields below. Everyone just stopped what they were doing and stood open mouthed and silent as the water started spreading like a fan across the fields. It all happened so quickly and everyone thought of all the effort that had been put into it had been in vain.

But just then as we watched, the barge which was about a yard from the bank when it sank, suddenly lifted out of the water a little and then slammed with all of the force of the water behind into the gap sideways, it was as if you had put a plug into a plughole in a sink. An enormous cheer went up as the water in the gap was reduced to a trickle, but the lads on the other bank shouted that there was another leak a few yards further along, And that the other barge needed to be put along there as soon as possible. It was already partially filled so everyone available set to, this time with a bit more urgency, so there we stayed for the rest of the day and all through the night again, and remarkably no one went back to camp either to rest, wash or work, and the best thing was the Sally Anne ladies, the 4 of them, took it in turns to rest, two at a time in the other caravan. I don't suppose they did actually rest as that's where they were making all the sandwiches, so for two days and two nights there were nonstop sandwiches and hot drinks always available, they deserved a medal, bless them.

By dawn on the second day the other barge was ready and thankfully the leaking bank had held, so the same procedure was adopted to get it across the river and sunk into place without any hitches. you could also see on the opposite side some lorries were now coming across the fields and dumping large stones and boulders and bulldozers were coming across as well, so it looked as if they were going to fill in the gap and re-enforce it as well, so job done. So we all started clearing things away slowly as we were all absolutely knackered, the Sally Anne caravans were being towed away to a lot of cheering. I suppose they will be off to somewhere else along the coast as we later learned about the disastrous floods along the East Anglia coast and inland, but we all hoped our little effort had averted some of it in this area. When we had finished clearing up, the fields looked like a battle field, as I suppose it was really! But they will soon re-cover, we climbed into the trucks and whatnots but by the time we got back to camp most were already asleep. We were all tipped out on the square, we must have looked a right bunch, about 200 blokes covered in mud, we stripped off the overalls and put them in some dustbins, and took of the wellingtons which weighed a ton with all the mud clinging to them, put on some pumps and staggered into the billet. it was now late afternoon and I just walked into the showers, stripped off and just soaked myself for ages until I felt myself starting to drop off, so into bed, put a towel over my head to keep out the lights, dropped straight off and I think that most of us slept for about 20 hrs, well I know we were woken when it was dinner time the following day. I was so stiff and had a couple of blisters on my hands even though we wore gloves. So after shaving and showering again, Jim and I thought that we deserved a pint before dinner, then we caught up with the girls who were a bit concerned as they hadn't seen us for 2 days, they knew that we were out helping with the floods, but they couldn't do anything as they were needed in administration to keep communications going. We weren't called upon again as most of the rescuing and dangerous floods were happening further down the coast. The C.O. did receive a letter from the Mayor of Downham Market thanking us for our efforts on the Great Ouse, and also telling us that thanks to our efforts, if the bank had collapsed, thousands of acres of land would have been flooded and many, many properties also. All the lads who worked on the floods were given the next day off, which was nice. So I took the opportunity to go to the gym and try to loosen up my stiff bones.

For the next three months things just sailed along as normal I suppose I did take a week's leave in May, and endured the horrendous journey there and back, I should have put in for a driving course to get a licence and then perhaps bought a motor bike or even a car, I reckon I could have gotten home in just a few hours instead of all day by train. There was one quite unexpected surprise that happened in May, I was made up to SAC, (Senior aircraftsman). I was evidently put in for it by our Sergeant and the Officer in our wor shops, I was quite chuffed really as I'd only been in the forces for about a year, also doubly chuffed because it meant more pay!!

But after the Lord Mayors show, there came a disaster. I knew things were going along too smoothly, so there had to be a fly in the ointment at some time or other and this was a biggy.

I was just going to go into the mess one day and meet up with Margaret and I could see her running down the road waving to me, and I could see that she had been crying, so instead of going in for lunch I said lets go into the NAAFI as it will be quieter in there and you can tell me what's wrong as she was so upset. She couldn't get her words out properly so we went and sat in a corner and I said to her take a deep breath and then talk to me slowly, this she did, and slowly and deliberately said "I have just been told that I have been posted to Germany" I just stared at her trying to let the words sink in, she caught her breath and continued "The station is called 'Munchin Gladback'. I have to go on a week's leave on the 29th of this month, which was in 8 days time, and report to the RAF office on Euston station at 9am on the 7th of June for my flight arrangements" My first reaction was that the bastards had finally caught up with us as they say they do, fraternising issues, my insides wereturning over and I had a heavy weight in my chest. Tears were beginning to run down Margaret's cheeks and we held hands tightly. I was still trying to absorb what she had told me, in 15 days time she will be in Germany, there's no weekend passes from there! And there's no retribution from a posting order, you are ordered, you go, full stop. We just sat there holding hands, and I was still trying to get it through my head.

I had to get back to the hanger, I didn't fancy any lunch any way, I couldn't have eaten as well. So we arranged to meet up for dinner, Margaret went to the ladies to swill her face and put a bit of makeup on to disguise the fact that she had been crying. I walked back to the hanger in a bit of a daze 'Don't let the bastards get you down' I kept saying to myself. I walked through the hanger and up to the Officers office, knocked and walked straight in, the Sergeant was in there as well. I just said "Sir, I wish to put in a request for a transfer to RAF Munchin Gladback in Germany" They both looked at each other and then at me and the Officer said "firstly when you knock, you wait to be called in, secondly, it's a sort of tradition in the forces to salute an Officer, and thirdly, what the hell's wrong with you Warden" there was a bit of a smile on both their faces. I apologised for my disregard of protocol, and just said that I was thinking of a change and to try life abroad somewhere as a different experience. They both looked at me steadily and quizzically, and the Officer said" there's more to it than that Warden, but I won't press it, and as you have made a formal request I will pass it on to the appropriate people as I have to, but don't build your hopes up, also I am surprised as we both thought you were settled here" with that I did saluted this time and left.

That night in the NAAFI the whole gang of us were a bit subdued, and Margaret had some of her friends with her and at one point they did get a bit weepy, also others came up and said they were sorry to hear the news, we didn't realize that so many people knew about Margaret and I, perhaps we weren't discreet enough about our relationship, well it's too late to do anything about it now, the damage has been done so to speak. So for the next 7 days before Margaret left we walked around holding hands or our arms around each other, so two fingers up to the establishment!! We did take long walks and talked a lot, and we both said that we would keep in touch as much as possible, and we could arrange to take leaves at the same time, plus there was the off chance that I may be able to get a transfer, we knew we would be out of touch for a while as she would have to write to me first with her new address and what she was doing and where, as I had heard that the camp was huge.

The last day arrived and Margaret was being picked up at 9am from the guardroom, which you could see from the end window in our room, I had arranged to do the room orderly bit that morning, so I should be able to see her leave so just before 9am I got a chair and stood on it and looked out of the window and as I was looking Margaret came out of the guardroom as a land rover drew up, and as arranged she looked up and saw me, she sort of half waved and stood looking for a good 30 seconds, half waved again, her hand went up to her face, she turned and climbed into the land rover, and was gone!! That was the last time I saw Margaret or heard from her for 3 years because of a set of circumstances that were totally beyond our control. We did have a brief reunion after 3 years but

I had lost the first real love of my life and at the time I didn't think that I would get over it. That night I went to the NAAFI and got absolutely smashed and the lads carried me back, but I evidently kept asking where Margaret was, sad aren't I.

Then to top it all, the second bombshell arrived. I think I did mention that when we first arrived on this camp, Jim had put in for an overseas posting, well two weeks after Margaret had left, orders came through that Jim had got his overseas posting, and bugger me, so had I! no it wasn't to Germany, we were both going to the Far East, no specific destination as yet, but we knew there were a couple of conflicts going on out that way. The big one was of course Korea, which we were heavily engaged in. the other was Malaya, which was the communist terrorists waging a terror war against the British and trying to force them out, because it was a colony of ours. Jim was pleased tobe going as that was what he wanted, I hadn't even put in for one when he did, but I was going anyway, I think that someone was trying to tuck me away as far as possible, perhaps hoping I wouldn't be coming back. So our orders were that in ten days time we were to have 2 weeks embarkation leave, then travel up to Kirby or was it Lytham St Anne, where we would be kited out for clothing for the Far East, then down to Liverpool to embark on a troop ship for. I'm not sure how many weeks trip it was or to where, we know not, so that was that. There seemed to be a lot of postings going around on the camp, with 3 lads going somewhere in our room alone, but so far it looked as if Jim and I were the only ones sailing over the big wide pond. I wrote to Mum and Dad and told them and that I would be home in 10 days time. The trouble was that I hadn't heard from Margaret as yet, so I hope I do before we go from here, as I don't know where she is, and she won't know that I've gone also. Plus the fact that I don't know where I'm going to also, a real cock up. It wasn't until only three days before we went that I managed to get Margaret's home address with a bit of wangling by Babs, so I wrote a letter to her mother hoping that when she hears from Margaret that she can explain to her what was happening, and that if she didn't mind I would write to her when I find out myself where I'm posted exactly and give my address to give to Margaret. It's not very satisfactory as it could take months before anything is finalised, but that's the best I can do.

The 2 weeks embarkation leave were o.k. although by now a couple of my mates were now courting, but I suppose it's to be expected as we are all around that sort of age when it happens, even the girl that I fancied once was now courting. So after the 2 weeks were up I said cheerio to my mates and Mum and Dad, no idea when I will see them again, I suppose it will be at least two years, wow!, two years and half way across the world, some adventure for a back street kid ! Jim and I met at the station as we usually did, it was amazing that we were still being posted everywhere together again. We arrived at Lytham St Anne later in the day where we were to be bunked up for two days whilst we picked up our Far East kit, first it was all the khaki stuff, dress jackets, shorts, slacks. socks, ect, then we had the same thing more or less all in olive green, o.gs, plus jungle boots,---- jungle boots!! and hats. The boots were rubber and canvas, calf length, They laced all up the front, plus two sun hats, one khaki and one o.g. We of course didn't know at that time what the significance was of all that kit, two kit bags full, we were also given a sea chest to put some of our RAF stuff in plus civilian clothes which we would get back when we reached our permanent station. Then we travelled by road to Kirby where we were to stay for 3 days before going on to Liverpool and embarking. At Kirby we were told we would have medicals and all the injection needed for the Far East. We would have these in the first morning, so we were laughingly told that you have 3 injections, and you will need 3 days to get over them! Really, really looking forward to those!

Sure enough, early next morning straight after breakfast, up to the 'sick bay' aptly named! then a medical exam, hold, squeeze, and cough sort of thing, then a jab in the right arm, then drop your trousers, and one in the butt, that bugger hurt, but not too bad if that's it, oh no, wrong! we walked single file into the next room, there were two medics and a doctor on the left and two medics and a doctor on the right, then we were told that one person goes to the left and one to the right, stand in between the two medics who will hold your wrist and upper arm and the doctor will administer the injection, the medics are only holding you just in case you faint, as some do, after you have had your injection, it is advisable that you go through that door and run around the parade ground outside waving your arms around as it will help to disperse the injection around your body so as to ease the after effects. I did not believe I was hearing all this ! They were going to torture us. The two lads in front of Jim and I went first, one to the left, one to the right, they stood there with the medics holding their arms, the doctor said look to the front, then from behind his back he produced the syringe, a syringe!! It looked more like a grease gun we use on aircraft, only in glass, and it was full of some yellow stuff. We watched as they stuck the grease guns into the lads arms, you could see them flinch, and one of them went a bit wobbly at the knees, and it seemed like ages as this yellow stuff was being pumped into them, I'm sure the syringe was emptied, they then led them to the door and pushed them outside. 'Next', was the cry, if there had been a window open I would have jumped through it, but no escape. Jim and I walked forward, I was s------g myself, they grabbed my arms tightly, I closed my eyes, then felt this terrible burning in my left arm, as if someone was stubbing a cigarette out on it, and it seemed to go on for ages, I nearly broke my teeth clenching them so hard, then Jim and I were pushed out onto the square, and we ran around like maniacs flapping our arms and swearing like troopers, I don't know how many actually made it to the door, but when we finally went back to get our jackets there were a half a dozen chaps slumped on chairs, and away with the fairies! I think we all spent the next 24hrs mostly on our beds, a couple of lads in the billet had bad reactions and were carted away, my arm was stiff and sore for nearly a week and we had to lug 2 kitbags around as well. I reckon whatever was in those grease guns would protect you from any disease in the world!

The next two days we spent at lectures and collecting documents, we were told that the troopship we were going on was called the 'Empire Fowey', and I'm sure he said there would be approximately 3,000 troops on board of all sorts, Army, and Navy. There were two or more troopships ploughing the seas, another one was called 'The Windrush', I bet a lot of ex-servicemen will recall those names. The planned route was arranged so as to call at several place to drop personnel and collect stores, when they told us the exact route it seemed such a long way to go, it's the other side of the world which I suppose it was really! Travelling abroad in those days was practically unheard of for ordinary people so I suppose in one way it an exciting thing to do.

The planned route, if I remember correctly was. Set off from Liverpool down the Irish Sea to the Atlantic, around the West coast of France, across the Bay of Biscay, down the coast of Portugal, first stop Gibralter, across the Med to Cyprus, stop, then to Port Said and the Suez Canal, stop, Down the Red Sea to Aden, stop, across the Arabian Sea to Columbo, now called Sri Lanka, stop, down the Straits of Mallaca, to Singapore, stop, and then on to Korea. I don't know if I was excited or apprehensive.

On the morning of our departure we grabbed our kit bags and jumped onto trucks to Kirby station, I suppose in our contingent there were about 100 to 150 RAF chaps, at the station a special troop train was waiting, there were already hundreds of forces personnel about, mostly Army, and everyone was being shunted about and onto the train, then more troops would arrive. We got on the carriages assigned to us and thank full to get rid of carrying those kit bags. We were given a packed lunch which was a good thing as we waited hours before we got away. The trains were able to go straight on to the docks at Liverpool, where we unloaded and went into huge warehouses, there were plenty of mobile canteens about so we were able to get a cup of tea whilst they sorted everyone out, There had been a train load in before us and they were still sorting them out, it must have been a logistic nightmare sorting out 3,000 troops. Evidently trains had been coming in all day and there were still more to come, but I suppose it was best to sort everyone out as they came in. We couldn't actually see the ship as the warehouses blocked the view, but finally our contingent had been sorted, so we filed out of the warehouse onto the loading Quay and we got our first glimpse of the ship, and blimey, was it huge! It was the first time I had been close to a ship, and as it was now getting dark, the lights were all on all over the ship, and all over the loading Quay, and everything looked gigantic and overwhelming. We filed up the gangplank and were given two number's, one was the deck number, and the other a bunk number. I'm not sure how many decks there were but luckily we were on the top deck, or rather upper deck. We went down some steps into what looked like a hanger to us and there were rows and rows of hammocks, one above the other and in rows and rows! Now a sun lounger or a camp bed or even a deck chair, but a hammock! We dumped our kit and were told to go to the end of our deck for a meal.

Afterwards we went back to our swinging canvas things. I was half expecting to be shackled and chained to the floor, Time was getting on by now and we had had a hell of a day, so we decide to call it a day as we could leave going exploring until the morning. Jim and I stood looking at the hammock and then at each other so I said "go on then, you are in the top one and I've been told its safer for the top one to get in and settle down first" I hadn't but it just seemed logical, besides why the hell would I have wanted to ask anyone about hammocks before! Above the hammocks was a bar which ran from back to front so I suppose the idea was to grab the bar hoist, yourself up and lay back down into the hammock and then settle, well, that was the idea, but cocky Jim said 'easy' grabbed the bar and pulled himself up, stuck his feet into the hammock and let himself 'drop'? down into this moving piece of canvas, the only trouble was it was swinging from side to side, also he had his feet stuck in one end, and as he dropped, it swung, and he missed it completely, fell, hit my hammock, rolled around it and hit the deck with his feet still wrapped up in his hammock, everyone around just cracked up with laughter, so I just said 'easy? and untangled his feet! For the first couple of hours that night it was hilarious, there was swearing and cussing, then a gang of 'Matloes' (sailors) came in, they were the ship's crew and had been sent down to teach us 'Brylcream' boys how to use a hammock properly, so they went around giving advice and tips on how not to strangle yourself, surprisingly after a while you began to get the hang of it and surprisingly and once you had, they were surprisingly comfortable, and when you were at sea you gently rocked back and forth and side to side and you would sleep like a log. The ironic thing was that all of the Navy blokes who were going abroad the same as we were. Were actually sleeping in bunks! I bet somebody arranged that for a bet.

Next morning the ship was due to cast off, so most went up onto the top deck to watch. There was actually a band playing on the quay, but not many people watching or waving, probably trying to get rid of us quietly. I know the 'Fowey' is a large boat, but I couldn't make out where the 2 or 3,000 troops who were supposedly on board were. I know the decks are large but there weren't thousands on deck watching us depart, could be watching from the portholes I suppose, as I found out that there were 3 decks below us, so if there were 3'000 troops on the top deck, wouldn't the boat tip over? o.k. I'm stupid. On the other hand perhaps they only open the cages a few at a time. It was interesting watching the ship slowly inching its way out pushed and pulled by the tug boats, then slowly moving along under her own steam and out into the Irish Cannel, and when the horn blew it made the hairs on the back of your neck stand up. You could feel the rumble of the engines under you feet also. We stayed on the deck until lunchtime watching places slipping by, and the thought struck me that not many people of our age would be able to have the chance to experience something like this, so you have to look on the positive side and acknowledge the fact that it's going to be a once in a lifetime experience.

I used to love going up on deck as much as possible, even just to get some fresh air and chat to the other troops on board. It's hard to remember what actually went on when we were on board during that nearly 4 weeks we were at sea, and how do you keep that many troops occupied all of that time. I know there were lectures, film shows, lots of messes and rest rooms, deck games, fitness classes, more lectures, housey, housey, card schools going on all over the place, there would of course be 'inter forces competitions' on some of the things I've mentioned. There was weapon training off the back of the ship, target floats were towed off the back, and you could fire all sorts of weapons at them, now that I enjoyed. One thing I didn't enjoy was that it was a 'dry' ship! I might as well have signed the pledge! I would have thought that at least they would have let the Navy lads have their daily 'Tots' then perhaps we could have bribed them for a drop!.

We sailed down the channel and around Lands End and across the English Channel towards Western Europe, past Brest in Northern France and into the Bay of Biscay. Now according to our Naval friends, this was the bay of all bays, and if you wished to experience sailing at its worst the B of B was the place to do it, it was, according to them, notorious for its storms and rough seas, so if you wished to get your sea legs, the B of B will give it to you. So with some trepidation we awaited the inevitable. Strange though it seemed pretty calm at the moment and as time went on it remained calm, in fact the sea looked like a mirror, then we were told that we had just crossed the B of B! And were now passing down the coast of Portugal, so if that was a rough sea, it should be plain sailing from now on, goody. We passed Lisbon and were heading towards Gibraltar, it was strange as we passed through the straits as you could see land on both sides of the ship, Gibraltar on one side and Africa on the other as it was a beautiful clear day, then through the Mediterranean past Sicily and on to Malta for our first stop. We anchored in the harbour and quite a lot of RAF chaps disembarked (I got that term right, 'not got off'!) and were ferried ashore for their postings. Looking across the harbour towards Valletta you could see that even after the war had been over for seven years you could still see a lot of devastation and destruction. I think it was the most bombed island in the whole of the war, but it still did not fall to the Germans, I think I'm right when I say it was bombed continually day and night for something like 80 or 90 days, that's why the island was awarded the 'George Cross' because if the island had fallen to the Germans they would have been able to command the whole of the sea of the Mediterranean shipping routes. We stayed overnight but no shore leave, so we just watched the lights of the old town.

Next morning again down the Med and across to Cyprus, we anchored off limassol I think, and a lot of RAF and Army personnel left the ship as there was a big base at Nicosia, and then a short hop to Port Said in Egypt, which is of course is also the entrance to the Suez Canal, we entered the Suez basin and tied up alongside the quay. A lot of Army personnel got off there, and when they were all on shore, the gang planks were pulled up and the boat eased its way away from the quay for about 10 yards, stopped and anchored, there we would be staying all day and all night until it was our turn to join a convoy of ships through the canal as it was one way only. the Suez canal isn't just one long canal but a series of 2 or 3 canals that open up onto large lakes, that act as sort of traffic lights, so you travel one way only down one canal into one of the large lakes and then anchor up, also on the lake is another convoy that has been waiting for you to arrive, then it is their turn to travel up the canal that you have just come down. Then you wait until another convoy arrives from the second canal and anchors up, then you go down the canal that they came up, and so it goes on, I'm not quite sure but I think you wait 3 times on the various lakes before you are though and enter the Red Sea. It's really weird travelling through the canal, as in parts it is only just wide enough for large ships with what seems like only inches to spare on each side. The desert is completely flat as far as you can see and sometimes you will see a train of camels in the distance and if there is a slight bend in the canal you will see a train of camels and right behind them just a few yards is the top of large ship passing them as if it was sailing in the desert.

The reason our boat was anchored a few yards away from the quay in Port Said was because of the 'Bum' boats, as they call them. they are little boats and dinghies manned by Arabs that come alongside the ships and try to sell you all sorts of things, of course all the lads thought it was great fun bartering with them, the boats were 40 or 50 ft below the decks but they would throw up a rope and if you fancied anything they were selling, you asked to see it and they would put it in a net or a basket and you pulled it up, and if you wanted it and you reached a price by shouting at each other, you put the money in the net or basket and lowered it back down to him. There seemed like hundreds of these 'Bum' boats surrounding the ship. The decks were full of blokes leaning over the rails bargaining with the Arabs. We had been pre-warned about these Arabs and were told that it was against orders to try and cheat them, say by asking to see something and when it came up trying to keep it without paying, also, as it was a dry ship you weren't allowed to buy alcohol, besides you don't know what you are buying, it could be lethal. One of our bunch bought a couple of pineapples as he had never seen a real one before, and indeed quite a lot hadn't as well, and he proceeded to cut it up there and then on the deck and stuffing it into his mouth, what he didn't know, and neither did we, is that you are supposed to peel away the outer skin first as chewing that makes your teeth and gums bleed, there he was enjoying it then suddenly blood started pouring out of his mouth and dribbling down his chin and onto his clothes, he wiped the back of his hand across his mouth as he thought it was juice, then realized it was blood and stopped chewing and ran over to the side and leant over the rails and spat everything out, a shower of pineapple and blood, I don't think the Arabs below thought much of that! I think most bought some sort of souvenir anyway.

I forgot to say that we were all now changed into tropical kit, khaki, since we had passed down through the Med and into Egypt, and of course shorts were the order of the day. The only trouble was the heat, as obviously we weren't used to such temperatures and below decks at nights it was really hot and humid and very difficult to sleep and you sweated a lot, even the water in the showers was warm. So Jim and I thought of a solution. So some nights if it was calm and no wind, we would grab a couple of blankets each and creep up on deck and find a tucked away corner somewhere and sleep there, a few of the other lads cottoned onto this and did it as well, it was great, just laying there looking up at the stars, and it was nice and cool, and with the gentle throb of the engines you soon went to sleep, but we went back down before anyone was around in the morning. We passed through the canal and out into the Red Sea and then around the Gulf of Aden, which is in Yemen, and into the Port of Aden itself. Here we were finally allowed shore leave as they were taking on supplies, a lot of personnel were dropped off here as well. The ship was gradually being emptied bit by bit, anyway, shore leave, once all those who were staying here had disembarked and were gone, we were told to muster on deck and file off down the gangplank, after being checked over by the 'Snoops,' oh! yes, there were 'Snoops' on board, only Army ones, M.P.s, We had already been lectured on how to behave in and around the town, and that patrols of M.P.s would be on constant patrol.

As this was our first foray into a foreign land it was quite exciting and absorbing and the sights and the sounds were strange but mesmerising, and also the roads were just dirt. So God knows what it's like when it rains, or perhaps it never rains here? The shops also had strange and exotic things in them, and of course the shop keepers were trying to temp you into the shops with all sorts of offers, why do they call everyone 'Johnny'. I did go into one shop and went mad and bought two tea towels with Port Said on them to send home to Mum! She never did use them, but laid them out on the sideboard in the front room so that everyone would see them! So after that frantic shopping expedition we reckoned it was time for a beer, if we could still remember what it tasted like. We found a bar that already had some troops in and ordered two beers, it was bottled of course and according to the label it was Belgian beer, who knows, but it was nice and cold and it went down a treat, We were advised not to eat out in case you got a dose of 'Montyzumers revenge', anyway the beer was too good to waste time eating. After about two hours there suddenly appeared from behind some curtains two women scantily dressed in local costumes, some Arabic music came on, and they proceeded to belly dance in front of us all, of course everyone cheered and clapped to the music, and boy! Could they swing those hips, all this of course was all new to us, strange lands and people and cultures, which you perhaps you had only seen at the pictures. Also the British seemed to be very welcomed and liked, perhaps it was because of the war.

It gets dark here very quickly and we had to be back on board by 9 pm, so we had another couple of beers and stuffed some of those funny foreign notes into the waist bands, or much lower than that of the dancing girls and then made our way back, everyone was warned not to come back the worst for drink, but we were o.k. swaying a little maybe. As you went up the gangplank your name was ticked off, and as you stepped onto the deck you turned and faced the flag, came to attention and saluted and then walked on. The night was hot so Jim and I stayed on the deck watching all the other troops coming back onboard. There were lights on all over the place and also down the street opposite the gangplank so you could see personnel walking down the street towards the ship. As we were watching we noticed something was going on at the top of the street, and you could also hear a lot of shouting and commotion, you could then make out, as they got nearer, a small herd of goats coming down the road towards the boat, and they were being herded by two or three sailors who were doing the shouting and waving. It was obvious that from where we were that they were p----d out of their brains. Following the sailors and goats were a crowd of locals, who were also shouting and waving their arms at the sailors, the lot of them swarmed onto the quay and stopped at the end of the gang plank. By this time the 'Snoops' were taking an interest in the proceedings at the top of the gang plank, and now there were a half a dozen of them there standing and watching, one the sailors, shielding his eyes from the lights looked up, saw the 'Snoops' at the top, grabbed the rails each side and started to sway his way up, he got nearly to the top, stopped, stood to attention in front of the 'Snoops', and then saluted, nearly going over the side, he then said loudly" Sir, permission to bring aboard next week's dinners, Sir" Well, everyone watching just cracked up, even some of the 'Snoops'. The sailor still stood there at attention, swaying though, by now half of the boat was watching and laughing. The other two sailors at the bottom were drunkenly trying to round up the goats and keep them together, and one would run off to great cheers from everyone watching, it was hilarious, and the one on the gangplank was still standing to attention, and every few seconds, again he would salute, and everyone would cheer. It was better than any comedy show, I think the 'Snoops' thought that by this time enough was enough, two of them grabbed the one still at attention under the arms, lifted him and carried him backwards, still at attention, down the gangplank onto the quay, then the other two stood to attention and saluted, more cheers, but then the goats decided to do a bunk with the locals chasing after them. A couple of the locals stayed and were chatting to the 'Snoops' whilst the rest of them grabbed the other sailors and frog marched them away up the street, more cheers and clapping. I bet we won't see them again for the rest of the trip.

Evidently what came out later was that the sailors had been in a bar all day drinking, and when they were legless, one of the locals came in and asked them if they liked goats meat and milk, in their state they said of course, he then said that he could get them some for such and such a price, so they had a whip round and gave him the money and he said he would go and get it. He came back and said that he had left it outside as it was too hot in the bar, and went. When they managed to stagger outside, of course there were the goats all tied up! So they stupidly thought that as we have paid for them we'll take them back with us, but as they started to make their way back herding the goats in front of them, some locals came running after them shouting that they had stolen their goats. It turned out that the bloke who sold them the goats, they weren't even his, he had pinched them and sold them to the sailors! So the 'Snoops' told them to take the goats away, mind you, by this time they had disappeared somewhere! But it was all smoothed over in the end, but it was so funny.

We stayed there the next day and were allowed ashore for 5 hours as we would be casting off in the evening, we went ashore for a couple of beers as we didn't know when the next would be. So we cast off in the evening out into the Arabian Sea and then into the Indian Ocean, and headed towards the tip of India to an island called Columbo, nowadays called Sri Lanka, but the port is still called Columbo. Going across the Indian Ocean we slept most nights on the deck as it was pretty stifling below decks. On our first night out we were woken at dawn by a lot of scuffling on the deck, and there were the cooks, the native ones, running around the decks picking up fish, hundreds of them, fish I mean. not cooks! I thought they must be pretty good jumpers, the fish, not the cooks! But we found out that they were flying fish. Evidently there are huge shoals of them and if they are being chased by predators they leap off the top of a wave and into the wind, start their engines, not really, they spread their large fins, which act like wings, and they can travel quite long distances and heights to escape. We now know what's for breakfast!

Halfway through the second night everybody had to scamper below decks as it started to rain quite heavily and there was a swell getting up. We swung into our hammocks, getting quite experts at it now, and with the gentle swaying I was soon asleep again. However a rude awakening woke us with crashing and banging and the hammocks were now swinging nearly horizontal, some were being tipped out of them as the deck was going up and down and side to side, things were now rolling around on the floor and big crashes were coming from the mess. The doors to the deck were locked and no one was allowed onto the deck, you couldn't see out of the portholes, just water, it was obvious we were in a storm, and some sort of storm at that! You hung onto what you could. The chairs and the benches in the mess were fixed to the floor so we made our way into the mess and just sat and hung on. I then recalled the tales that were told us about the Bay of Biscay being one of the roughest seas, when it was like mill pond, and then, how the Indian Ocean was usually calm and peace full. I think they got their seas mixed up a bit! But I did learn from one of the old sweats on the boat, a merchant seaman, that if ever you hit rough weather, even if you feel seasick. keep eating, kippers if they are on the menu, and I think he was right, I know the last thing you think about is food when you feel queezy, and it looked as if everyone is going to be seasick by the colour of some! even some of the crew, and so was I, once, but Jim and I made a point of eating when we could, also drinking lots, and I think it helped, glad we took the old boys advice. You couldn't stand properly, so you sat on the floor to get dressed and leaned against your locker so that things didn't sway too much.

The storm went on all day and half the night and I must say the cooks and the medical staff did a great job providing food and looking after the really bad cases of seasickness. By the dawn the storm passed as quickly as it had arrived and we were now allowed on deck to great excitement, as every one was pointing to something in the distance, it was a huge waterspout, it was a long way away but it still looks colossal and with the red sun just coming up on the horizon at the side of it, it looks as if it was on fire. I bet there's not a lot of people who can say that they have seen a waterspout. Nature is wonderful and inspiring, but it can also turn around and kick you in the face, and mostly when you don't expect it! Also there were some helicopters hovering around the stern of the boat, landing on the pad and taking off again one by one, about 4 of them, they were Indian Navy choppers, Sikorsky 55s, and we were told later that some of the troops on board had been so ill that they had bought up the linings of their stomachs and had to be transferred to hospital as soon as possible, Nasty.

Whilst we were travelling across the Indian Ocean towards Columbo, we were finally told our destinations, some would be getting off at Columbo, the remaining lot of Navy personnel would be getting off there, not us, so that just left two more ports of call, Singapore, and Korea. The remaining lot of RAF and Army would be split amongst those two. I wasn't keen on Korea what with the war still going on, so Singapore seemed the best posting after all it was a British colony so perhaps a bit more civilised, and sure enough Jim and I and some RAF lads were to disembark when we reach Singapore in a few days time. We docked at Columbo and all the Navy blokes left, then the boat did the same thing as it did in Port Said, it backed away from the quay about 10 yards and dropped anchor, and immediately the ship was surrounded by a fleet of 'Bum' boats. I did buy some fruit as it looked tempting but was advised to wash it first. Jim bought a Hawaiian shirt, Why? It was great watching all the shouting and bargaining going on. I suppose standing off from the quay was to prevent any one trying to get aboard after dark, and another thing we noticed was that when we were tied up at the quay, all the ropes that went from the boat to the shore had halfway up them a cone shaped metal collar, the sort you would see on a dog to stop it scratching something, and evidently it was to stop rats climbing up the ropes onto the boat.

We stayed overnight in Columbo, there was no shore leave but there was a film show up on the deck and there was a nice cool breeze blowing. Jim and I slept on the deck that night and you could hear all sorts of noises coming from across the dock, also Indian music and there were loads of dockers sleeping out in the open as well as us. Just before dawn the hustle and bustle started on the docks as our boat was getting ready for departure so we decide to retreat and have a shower and go for breakfast. As the ship had unloaded so many personnel by now, there seemed to be plenty of space around, no queuing up for things, plenty of space on deck, also we on our deck were given the choice now to move to bunk sleeping if we wished, but we declined as we had got quite used to the hammocks by now, also there's only about another 1,800 miles to go before we reach

Singapore. So we headed out again into the last stretch of the Indian Ocean before we enter the Malacca Straits and down the Malaysian Peninsular with Malaya on the left and Indonesia on the right hand side, then into the Singapore Straits. Whilst we were on the last leg we had a few lectures and info about Malaya and the situation as it is at this present time, so I will give a brief synopsis as told to us.

During the 2nd world war Malaya fell to the Japanese, but in 1945 it was won back by the Allied forces and was once again a British colony. There then began a period of unrest as there was a large proportion of Chinese living in Malaya at that time. The Malays were quite happy to be back under British rule after the horrors of Japanese occupation, but there was growing unrest among a small proportion of the Chinese, especially the younger ones, who were members of the Chinese Communist party, and they, with the help of the communist government were starting to instigate unrest amongst the population with protests and meetings to the effect that they wanted Malaya to be a communist run country for the simple fact that not only that, but control of Singapore as a very strategic position on the South China Seas, also of course all of the natural resources of the mainland, rubber, tin, and minerals. So the idea was to install a communist government through the local elections, so a communist party was set up to contest any elections, and people were drafted in from china to assist in the endeavour, but as I've said the Malays were quite happy the way things were, so the 'commies' turned to intimidation and threats against the local population as straight forwardness wasn't working. So businesses and politicians were threatened plus the rubber plantation owners and the mine owners who were mostly British, but then it escalated into a campaign of violence. That started off with the bombings of anyone who opposed them, businesses and such, so in the end the communist party was banned and it's most active members jailed, so they went underground and so began a terrorist Gorilla movement. Trained communist terrorists were brought in from China and smuggled across the Siam border (now Thailand) and even put ashore from submarines along the Malacca Straights. These were trained jungle fighters who could live off the land and in the jungles of Malaya, where they carried out atrocities and intimidation of the local people and rubber estate workers. They would strike in bands of 30 or more, murder the village elders, steal food and slaughter cattle and take what they wanted, also carry out hit and run bombings in towns and cities, they murdered British plantation and mine owners, blow up their bungalows and then hack at the rubber trees and render them useless, ambush and murder anyone in authority.

This carried on and it further escalated until in 1948 when the British government declared an Emergency and went to war against the C.Ts (communist terrorists). Troops and equipment arrived from Britain, especially the specialised career troops who already had experience, probably fighting in the jungles of Burma during the war, also troops like the S.A.S who could be covert operatives, and could parachute into the tops of the jungle trees, sometimes 200 ft high, on search, seek, kill missions, but I will expand upon their actions and logistics later.

We now entered the Singapore Straits and proceeded slowly into the harbour bay and docks. It was just after dawn and we had been up since 4am. We had packed our kit bags the night before and were dressed in our khaki uniforms. The sea chests that we were given before we left England now had the rest of our stuff in it and they would be forwarded to us when we were on our permanent stations. We were told that buses would be waiting for us to take us to the RAF airport at Changi where we would be told exactly where our stations were. Jim and I hoped that we would be staying at Changi as it was a big place and sort of integrated with the private airport of 'Singapore Airlines', anyway we all assembled in a big hanger and divided into groups when your name was called out. Sadly I was put into one group of about 12, and Jim into another. My group were told we were going over to Singapore railway station, and going up country to Kuala Lumpur. Jim and his group were staying here at Changi, so we were finally being split up, I suppose it had to happen sometime. So we said cheerio and maybe see each other in 2 years time when we go home! Before we got back on the bus we were issued with a rifle and a bandolier of 20 bullets. The rifle was a 303 Enfield, a shortened version and much lighter and the end of the barrel was flared (anti-flash) as it was a jungle rifle, I didn't like the sound of that! We were told by an Army Officer at the railway station that we would be travelling up to Kuala Lumpur which is up country and would probably take around 6 to 7 hours as it was over 200 miles and as it's not a very fast train it can be susceptible to ambushes which do happen frequently so keep your wits about you and remember now that you are all on 'active service' so be vigilant at all times. There are Malay police on the train as escorts, but keep your eyes open and alert, also load your rifles with a clip of 5 when you get on the train and keep one up the spout, oh and by the way there is also a packed lunch for you. Now the second part was o.k. about the lunch, but it was the first part that worried me a little! one up the spout, ambushes, and then, the 'active duty ' bit, thanks very much, first, 5 weeks on a troop ship and now we are in a war zone waiting to be ambushed! Then he said (can't wait for what's next) "As you all might be a little nervous here is your weeks ration of cigarettes which you get every week as you are on 'active service" it was a round tin of 50 cigarettes, mind you they were 'Senior Service'. I only hope I get the chance to smoke them! So with a good luck goodbye we went through to the train, did I say a Train, I thought that I had walked onto a film set of a cowboy film, the train looked like something out of a western movie, there were 4 carriages, no windows, at least I don't think so, at the end of each carriage was an open platform with a rail around it, inside the seats were wooden with a piece of cloth over them, no lights, as they weren't allowed to run at nights because of the 'Emergency'. The engine was a ' Stephensons' replica, and bellowing black smoke. It must, it just must have come from the Wild West!

We piled onboard but split up between the 4 carriages, we piled our kit bags on the seats for something to hide behind should any lead fly through. Also on board were some of the locals, a couple of goats and a pig, I couldn't see any chickens, but I could hear them. the locals kept looking at us and smiling and jabbering, I hope some of them were carrying guns as well, The train started off slowly with a blast on the whistle, it made me think, was that to let the C.Ts. know that we were coming!!! We went across the 'Causeway' onto the mainland and started up country and our first look and introduction to the jungles of Malaya, which you could touch on each side, ideal ambush territory! And I wondered what life had in store for me next!

Malaya is quite hilly and the train followed the valleys, you could soon see that rubber was a main produce of the country with mile after mile of rubber plantations on each side, interspersed with thick jungle, then occasionally tin mine workings with mounds of earth and tipping tubs rattling on overhead cables. If we came to a downward slope the train could reach a speed of at least 20 mph but uphill it would be quicker to walk, as we got further away from civilisation the jungle was touching the side of the train, so you could see how easy it would be to ambush the trains. You could see the police realize this as they were crouching on the platforms with their guns resting on the rails, so when we saw this we instinctively did the same, or rather hid behind the kit bags and not showing our heads above the windows, well you were a sitting target. The locals just looked at us and smiled. Yes, o.k. we were the British who drove out the nasty Jap's out of your country, but that was years ago, but, and a big but, at the moment, we are a different generation here to drive out the nasty 'commies' you could hear a trumpet fanfare I'm sure, ---bollocks, heads down, roll on demob!!

That journey was the worst I'd ever done on a train, it shook and rattled I'ts way along, and stopped dozens of times, but only at a few stations or sheds, it seemed that when a local shouted on the train, it stopped, and off they would jump, pigs and all, and vanish into the jungle, after about 7 hrs we began to see buildings along the way, and guessed that we were approaching a town or something, then we saw the sign 'Kuala Lumpur', made it in one piece. As we went further in there were some quite modern buildings but most of the roads were dirt, mind you that was over 60 years ago, as then it was just a biggish town or small city. The surprising thing was the railway station, it was a magnificent Victorian building and also another beautiful place was the General Post Office with a large padang in front of it (green), where evidently the upper classes and planters used play cricket. Outside the station was a RAF truck which was waiting to take us to our new squadron H.Q. which was based just outside of K.L. which was called Noble Field, So now for a bit of information about my new squadron.

The squadron is called 656 A.O.P./ L.L. Sqdn RAF, The A.O.P. stands for Air Observation Post flight. and the L.L. is Light Liaison. The H.Q. and airfield is at Noble Field, Kuala Lumpur, and the squadron id divided into flights, five in all, each flight has a number such as 1905, 1907, 1911, 1914, 1917, the flight at Noble Field is called H.Q. flight. each flight is self contained and completely mobile, usually consisting of about 30 to 35 personnel, plus about 6 pilots, all Royal Artillery pilots, or glider pilots, and one senior Officer who is the C.O. of that flight. The aircraft are Austers. then, they were Mark 5, 6, and 7s which are spotter planes, and general dogs bodies, although the squadron is RAF all the personnel were mainly Army, with just about 8 RAF who maintained the aircraft. The rest were all sorts of Army trades, motor engineers, clerical, electrical, armourers, drivers, radio operators, signallers, cooks, one RAF cook. We RAF consisted of 2 engine mechanics, 2 or 3 airframe mechanics, 1 electrician, 1 radio and instrument technician, 1 corporal, 1 Sergeant, both Engineers, sometimes a photographer. Each flight had its own transport, i,e, 3or 4 3tonners, 3 land rovers, couple of pickups, a scout car and a Bren gun carrier, as I've said each flight is self contained and mobile for a reason. All over Malaya were several little airstrips cut out in the jungle by engineers, most were isolated, some more than others, one in particular where you were almost native, called Benta, near Kuala Lipis, the jungle post, or outpost!, more about that later. Each flight occupied one of those strips for about 6 months at a time, and so that everyone didn't go stir crazy, you up and moved out and went to a different location, so the whole 5 flights rotated every 6 months or so. When I say move out, you took everything with you and left your camp empty for the next flight to move in. As I've said to keep everyone sane, and there is nothing to do, as some of the airstrips are completely isolated, stuck in the middle of the jungle, not allowed out of the perimeter without an armed escort.

Now the object of each flights aircraft was to fly over the jungle trying to spot and locate the terrorist camps and movement in the jungle below, a good time of day was just after dawn when the mist is lifting just above the trees and you might see a spiral of smoke rising up from the trees, it could be a C.T. camp or a Malay camp, or even members of our own forces out on patrol, so you have to fly low to investigate it or photograph it, sometimes you might get shot at so you know they are not friendly, so you radio back with the co-ordinates, the message is passed to RAF Changi in Singapore, if it's deemed to be a big camp, Canberra bombers are scrambled, you then drop a flare, fly up high and guide the bombers in as it doesn't take long for them to fly up, in the meantime a troop of S.A.S. are already on their way there in helicopters. The Canberra 's spread bomb the area indicated, and then the S.A.S drop in and do the clearing up, they only leave the important ones alive to be interrogated later. That sort of strike doesn't happen all the time and it's only lucky if it does, most of the time it's just looking and assisting the patrols that are out, giving them information especially if you have spotted a 'clearing'. a 'clearing is an area of ground that has been cleared by the C.Ts and they have planted something in it, rice or whatever, they mark, and the next time they or some other C,T. Band come that way, as it may have grown and be ready to harvest, as things grow very quickly in the jungle. On the ground you could walk right by it and not see it unless you knew where it was, but from the air if you see a clearing and something is growing, it shows up light green against the dark green of the grass and bush. So if there is a patrol in the area, say a Malay police patrol, or the wonderful Ghurkha's on patrol, or a patrol of Africans, they destroy it. There were all sorts involved in the 'Emergency.' Now back to the squadron as a whole. So as each flight is mobile and self contained you move to one of the other airstrips and commence operations in that spot for say 6 months, sometimes longer sometimes shorter, it was mostly done so that some flights that had really been isolated could be stationed maybe nearer a town so that you could at least get some respite from the boredom., that's if it wasn't suddenly put off limits!

Now back to our arrival at K.L. station. We jumped into the truck that was waiting for us, and drove through K.L. to the outskirts and Noble Field H.Q. It was dark by this time and an LAC had been told to look after us until we are sorted out in the morning, so he took us for a meal in the mess, but before we did he said we would have to change into slacks because of the mosquito's, also take your rifle with you. So we had a meal and went back to the hut to sort out the sleeping arrangements, the others were found beds in the hut but unfortunately mine had to be outside on the veranda, great, The LAC bought me a mosquito net but also told me that the C.Ts had been very active around this area just lately, they had even climbed over the perimeter fence and tried to break into the petrol store, but some patrol dogs had seen them off, now I did notice that the perimeter fence was only about 50 yards from where I was sleeping on the veranda, and right next to the jungle, and the fence was only 4 ft high, plus the petrol store about the same distance! So he told me to me to keep alert as if they tried again they could come and cut your throat whilst you were sleeping!! sleep, what bloody sleep, I was waiting for him to smile and say, just joking, but no, he was serious! I went in and told the others and they said that they had been told that as well. I did not undress that night, just lay on the bed with my rifle at the side of me and my knife under the pillow, and watched the dawn come up! What had I let myself in for, I didn't want to come abroad in the first place, I didn't volunteer like Jim did, and he gets put in a paradise place like Singapore, is there no justice, and another thing the veranda I was on was all lit up! They should have put up a sign saying "here I am, come and get me, but mind you don't trip"

Half asleep we went for breakfast and afterwards were told where we would be going, 2 were staying here at H.Q. And the rest of us were split up amongst the other 5 flights, but I was going on my own up to 1914 Flight, which was at Benta, I did mention this location before, the jungle outpost. Trust me to get it! It was in the middle of the jungle, the nearest little town, Kuala Lipis, an hour's drive away, it was in the State of Pahang, which is a 5 or 6 hr trip by road, and was one of the most active terrorist areas in Malaya at the moment, It just had to be didn't it! Normally I would be flown up in one of Austers had there been one from that flight here at H.Q. but as luck would have it, so I was told, there happens to be one of the trucks from 1914 flight here collecting some supplies,(which they did once a month by the way,) and that I could get a lift back with them in the morning, so I was told to make my way down to the stores and behind it you would see a tent, a biggish one, and make yourself known to the 2 chaps there, they have been told that you will be returning to Benta with them. So off I trundle with my kit bags down to the stores place and sure enough there was the tent, it was closed up, so I pulled open the flap and out came a waft of baccy smoke and alcohol! and a shout of 'shut the bloody door' and then 'God, what time is it' and out staggered an army chap in underpants, army ones, his name was Joe Majesky, an old sweat I could tell that, closely followed by another old sweat named Lofty Steer, I introduced myself and they knew about me and said sorry for their state but they had a night in K.L. last night, so they had better finish loading up the truck, they dressed and I gave them a hand with the stores and then we went for lunch in the mess and then a beer in the NAAFI afterwards, we got chatting and they were great lads and evidently so are all the other lads on the flight according to them, as it was regarded as the best flight to be on as everyone got on well and even the officers. Joe and Jim were both Lance Corporals in the RASC (Royal Army Service Corps) and in their

30s, they had been on the flight for about 4 months, they had come from Korea and would be shipped off back home in about 12 months time, as they were regulars. I went back to the tent with them and crashed out on one of the beds, and after last night, had a kip. Later we went up for dinner and of course then into the NAAFI for a few beers, they were broke after last night on the town, so I stood the beers, to which they said I should fit in well on the flight as there's nothing to do but drink and play cards after work, plus guard duty? pardon! The beer by the way was sold in bottles, over a pint in them actually, and you had a choice of two, Anchor or Tiger, both brewed in Singapore, it's a larger type beer, we called it chemical beer, I preferred the Anchor, as Tiger gave you the D.Ts. (that's the shakes) after too many sessions, and you had to dry out for a while and let your systems re-cooperate, or it would addle your brain as well! The lads filled me in a bit about the flight, it was pretty easy going, your working gear was P.T. shorts and flip flops, and jungle hat. The airstrip was quite a short one, about twice the width of an Auster, and about 100 yards wide with thick jungle and tall trees all around. The hanger was a tin shed with room to get one wing in at a time sideways, everyone slept in 'bashers' straw huts, with open windows, and just a flap to cover them if it rained and blew, and it certainly did in the monsoon periods. The floors were concrete and you slept on camp beds, and there was a steel locker on the side. There was a cookhouse, a big tent incorporating the mess, just benches, also there was the most popular place, a hut where you could get a beer and something to eat, i.e. an egg banjo (sandwich) which was run by a little Chinese guy called Chan and there were a few tables and chairs in there, He must have made quite a good living there as that's where everyone congregated at nights. Anyway I would soon find out with who I was to spend nearly the next couple of years with tomorrow. I bunked down in the lad's tent that night as it could sleep 10.

Next morning after breakfast, no time for a wash or shave and onto the truck, it was a 3 tonner with a canvas top, and as the two lad's were in the cab, it meant that I had to ride on the back, it's a good job it was a fine day, actually a steaming hot day so it would be cool on the back. They pulled the canvas top halfway back and I sat on some boxes just behind the cab as it had a rear opening so I could chat to the lads going along. The only worrying thing was that they told me the road up into Pahang was notorious for ambushes as it was a very narrow dirt road with jungle on each side and at one particular place called the Bentong Gap, which wound its way up and around a sort of small mountain and down the other side, but owing to the number of ambushes that took place on that stretch you weren't allowed to travel without armed escort. I had noticed that the lads had Sten guns in the cab and they had told me to load my rifle with one up the spout and keep it handy as they had done. Before we left they told me to change into O.Gs (olive green) and jungle boots as that's what everyone wore outside of camp. We drove for about an hour and it was rubber plantation after plantation, then they began to thin out and the jungle took over, the roads weren't too bad really, a bit bumpy and you could see where it gets washed away in the monsoons. After about 3 hrs we came to a stop, there was a convoy of vehicles in front of us also stopped. Joe said that we had arrived at the start of the Bentong Gap, and this is where we have to wait for the armed escort. What happens is you go over in single file in convoy with the escort, but you have to wait until a convoy coming down in the opposite direction arrives with an escort, then that escort turns around and takes you up to the top. But the same thing happens at the top of the Gap, the escort turns around and takes the convoy that has come up from the other side down the side you have just come up, and the escort that came up the other side then turns around and escorts you down the other side, blimey, I know it sounds complicated but it works well, and besides it gives you chance for a break, so we ate our sandwiches that the mess had made up for us, and a bottle of beer which was very welcome. The escorts were by the way, Malay police in armoured cars and trucks with troops. last week evidently a convoy was attacked and two lorries went over the side and 5 people were also shot before they were driven off, and here was I sitting on the back of an open truck! I tell no lie's, a certain ring was beginning to quiver!

Our escort had turned around and we were ready to go, the climb up was quite steep and at a crawl. You could almost touch the trees on each side so you could see why it was an easy ambush zone. Then all of a sudden there were two sharp bangs. I nearly s—t myself, I grabbed my rifle and flattened myself against the boxes and kept my head down, we kept going and no more shots, as I had thought, I slowly lifted my head and looked through the hatch into the cab, and both Joe and Lofty were killing themselves with laughter. What the b-----d's had done was to switch the engine ignition key off and on a couple of times which makes the exhaust backfire a couple of times, that to me sounded like a gun bring fired. When they finally stopped laughing, they said sorry but they do that to all the new lads!

We finally made it up and over the Bentong Gap without any further incidents, we then we veered off from the convoy with just a Malay Land Rover escort with 6 troops in it. By now we had been travelling for about 6 hrs over dirt roads passing past the occasional kampong (village). Most of them were surrounded by high mesh fences and patrolled by police as these out of the villages were subject to attacks by the C.Ts, also intimidation, and forced to supply food and anything else they wanted. In the whole of Malaya there were areas that were quantified as to how bad the Terrorist activity was, this was signified by flags on the maps. Red was obviously the most active, and White signified that that particular area had been cleared of C.Ts and was fairly quiet at the moment. Benta in Pahang was a red area and one of the most active as it was so isolated with thousands and thousands of acres of prime jungle (which by the way, I will now on refer to it as 'Ulu' Malay for jungle). So the rubber plantations in these areas were always being attacked and more plantation owners and workers being murdered than anywhere else. That's why there was always a large concentration of patrols out in the 'Ulu' also patrols of all nations, Malay Army and police, Ghurka's, S.A.S. different British army regiments, Africans, Indians, Australians, Canadians, New Zealanders, all of the British colonies contributed to the security forces. The Ghurkas were my favourite people, their loyalty to the British was outstanding, they were more British than we were I think! It seemed the young men of Nepal have one ambition and that was to be able to join the British Army and serve the King, it was a family tradition and passed through generations. One Ghurka showed me a photo of his Great, Great Grandfather who was 92, dressed in his British uniform just to see his Great, Great, Grandson off to join the British Army, he was standing there at attention with a chest full of medals, not only that, but also in the photo was his Great Grandfather, Grandfather, and Father! all in uniform. With the pay they received they would send it back home and it would help to keep a family going. Why they never received the same rate of pay as the British Army did, I will never know. Also the way we pensioned them off was disgusting and still is. Ask any British serviceman who fought alongside them what they thought of the Ghurka troops, and you would get nothing but praise, also any enemy's were totally scared of their reputation, as one of the rituals was, and it was a tradition, they never took captives, or rarely, but they cut of the ears of the dead and sent them home to their wives and families to be made into necklaces, the more ears, the braver your husband or son! The famous knife they wore on their belts, the 'Kukri,' it was also a legend. You never asked to see the knife, as if they took it out of the sheath, by tradition they couldn't put it back unless it had blood on it, so they were pleased to show it to you, but before they put it back in the sheath, they would nick their finger and smear the blood on the blade, but I don't think they are allowed to do that these present days!.

Anyway I digress, just trying to fill in with a few facts and figures to make it more interesting, I hope!

After a stop at a roadside shack for a bottle of beer and a beef sandwich, I say 'beef' sandwich, but it was probably 'S—t' buffalo, (cattle that worked in the rice fields) but still tasted o.k. Joe said it would be about another hour and lofty said he would take a turn on the back so that I could have a ride in the cab, as we were entering hostile territory, but I reckon he felt safer on the back with his Sten gun than a green rookie who jumps at every sound! But it was nicer sitting on a softer seat than a wooden box. After about an hour we turned off the dirt road, and onto a dirt track. The Malay Escort waved goodbye and carried straight on, after a mile we then turned into the camp. More descriptions On the right was the Flight office, a long wooden hut which housed the C.O.s office, then the company clerk, next door,the guard room with 6 beds in it, next to that but separate was 'Chans' the local shop, rest room, for beers and egg 'banjo's' and whatever. Opposite were two biggish tents for the NCOs, that would be George, an army Staff Sergeant, who was in charge of all the army bods, and in the other a sergeant in the Glider regiment, he was also a pilot, can't think of his name, nobody liked him anyway, then behind the two tents and up a path was the cookhouse made out of corrugated iron sheets, and also the mess on the side of it. separate to that was the shower shed, and the water tower, and then a few yards away were the thunder boxes,(loo's), Which consisted of two holes dug in the ground and two wooden boxes with a hole in the top, and lids on, all surrounded by a canvas sheet just high enough so that you could see heads and if a seat was vacant or not! Also when the holes were full, or getting smelly! You filled them in and dug some more, well you didn't actually dig them, they had a tool for just that purpose, it was like an ice cream scoop on the end of a pole with a 't' bar on the top, you stood the scoop upright, then two blokes grabbed the 't' bar opposite each other, then walked round and round and the scoop screwed itself into the ground, when it was full you lifted it out,emptied it, and scooped more out, as you went deeper you put an extension pole on until you had gotten down to about ten feet, job done! back in business. opposite the 'latrines' and about 10 yards away were the 2 personnel bashers, with a long concrete path in front of them that led down to the Flight office. The bashers were again straw, well it wasn't straw, it was called 'atap' it was like long palm tree leaves weaved together. Inside the bashers the floor was concrete, there were windows or rather square holes with a flap to cover them if it rained. There were about 15 camp beds, each with a steel locker, not all the beds were occupied as some had gone home, and there were still some more to come as I was the first replacement to arrive. The airstrip ran alongside the bashers about 5 yards away. It was cut out of the 'ulu' which surrounded the whole camp and was some 100 yards long, perhaps 25 yards wide and covered in short thick grass. Over the far side of the strip and at the top end was the hanger, well large tin shed, just about wide enough to get an Auster in sideways, one wing at a time, you would have thought they could have made it wide enough to get a whole aircraft inside the hanger. Inside was a small office and parts store. At the side of the hanger was the fuel store, right next to the perimeter fence and the 'ulu', well thought out that was, just lob a grenade over the fence into the fuel store and no more camp!!!

From the Flight office there was a path that led up past the hanger and up to the Officers quarters that had its own cookhouse and mess, staffed by Malays who acted as 'armors' servants. I think that's about as good a description of the camp as I can give, So, 1914 AOP/LL Flight RAF, 656 Squadron. Malaya. Here I am for the next couple of years, so like it or lump it !!

Joe helped me to carry my kit up to the basher and I chose one of the free beds. Everybody was still out and about and the RAF lads were still in the hanger, so I went back to the camp office to check in, the camp clerk was there, an RASC lad (royal army service corps) called Robbie. The C.O. was in his office so Robbie took me in and introduced me to him. The C.O. s name was Captain Sumners and he remarked that I was the 2nd highest ranked airman in the flight the other being a Corporal Gothard, who was at the moment basically in charge of all RAF personnel. he said I hoped I would fit in alright, and just make sure all the aircraft are well maintained for me and my other Officers, and he smiled, he also said that because of the posting and the location we were in we were pretty relaxed in most things, we are here to do a difficult job under fairly difficult conditions, so as long as you keep your nose clean and don't cause any problems. I'm sure you will fit in then your time with us should be fairly easy. I know we are stuck out in the wilderness, but you'll get used to it and we try to let you out of camp as much as possible on different runs, and in the circumstances I try to keep it as relaxed as much as possible, so I'll see you over at the airstrip sometime. I began to feel a bit more relaxed and Robbie said later that he was a good C.O. he just left you to do your job and as long as things were running smoothly he left you alone, in any case we are due to move again in about 6 months.

I had missed lunch so I went back to the basher and unloaded my kit into the lockers. Then I heard an aircraft and went outside to watch. It was an Auster making its approach to land, it is the first time I had seen one, it is a small kite, high winged monoplane of tubular framework and covered in canvas, single engine Gipsey, The approach was very low, just skimming the tree tops, once past them, a sudden drop, hit the ground, throttle back, and brake hard, on such a short runway you couldn't afford the luxury of a long run in or you would finish up in Chan's! One of the RAF lads was out on the runway, in his usual daily uniform, P.T. shorts and flip flops, he then marshalled the kite to where he wanted it. The pilot climbed out and went into the hanger to sign it off, also to report any faults, meanwhile the kite is turned around, two chaps can do this, then its refuelled, this entails a step ladder, cans, or rather 'flimsy' of 5 gallon aviation fuel and a funnel, one chap climbs up the ladder, leans over the top of the wing, the chap on the ground cuts open the top of the flimsy with a machete (big jungle knife) then passes the flimsy up to the chap on the ladder who pours it into the funnel and fuel tank. Going by the book you are supposed to carefully prize the cap off the top of the fuel flimsy, but it takes too long, so a quick two slashes with a Machete, job done. I guessed that was the end of flying for the day as all five aircraft were on the apron and bedded down for the night, wheel chocks in place, cockpit tidy, and if it was going to be windy, you secured the wings with ropes tethered from under the wing points to the floor hooks. Just as I had finished stowing my gear, all of the lads came in having finished for the day. The four RAF lads introduced themselves, two of them were LACs Jim and Blondie, the other two were still ACs, Norman and Ted, Jim was airframes the same as me, Blondie and Norman, engines, Ted, electrical. The Corporal, Skinny, was in the NCOs basher, was a bit of everything, I met him later at dinner. We sat and chatted for a while and Jim said that 2 of the RAF lads had just gone home a few days ago and they knew that I was due to arrive, and also in another couple of weeks 3 more RAF lads will be arriving, one of them a cook, another engine fitter and another airframe mechanic like Jim and me, all LACs. As it was now starting to get dark everyone changed into O.G.s, slacks and long sleeve Jackets because of the 'mossies' which were by the way as big as dragon flies I'm sure, more about the wildlife later. We went along to the Mess Tent, carrying our rifles of course, you went everywhere with them, and Jim introduced me to everyone we met. All the cooking was done behind the serving table on wood burning stoves by 2 army cooks and a local native boy, the stoves somehow heated the water in the showers. The food was pretty good, straight from the pan onto your plate so to speak. There was electricity in the camp from a big generator, but was soon to be hooked up to a main supply so the rumour goes. The Flight by the way had only been here for a month, they had come down from Fort Butterwoth which was further up country, quite a big camp I think with a much better social life, and there was a town nearby where they could go whenever they wanted to, so it was a bit of a shock to all the others as well when they came here.

After dinner we went back to the basher and Ted said he had better get ready for guard duty, guard duty? I asked what was that, Jim said that G.D. was he only bug bear with this camp, he and Blondie, and Ted and Norman who were all stationed up at Fort Butterworth and never did G.D. there as it was done by the Malay police, and also here on this camp with only about 30personnel eligible to do G.D. and 6 on at a time and some excused from it such as cooks, clerical. your turn came around every 4 or 5 days!

How it worked was that at 6 pm the 6 on G.D. fell in outside the Flight office for inspection by the duty Officer, there was a guard commander with you as well, usually an NCO. You were dressed in your O.Gs. (olive greens) jungle boots, jungle hat, usually a mesh scarf around your neck, because of the mossy's, your rifle and bullet bandana and machete on your belt. after the inspection you went into the Guard room, and the first two would be selected for the first watch, you didn't go together but separate, one goes on way and the other one the other way. You did 2 hrs on and 4 hrs off so you did 2 shifts during the night from 6pm to 6am. so if you were on the 6pm shift you patrolled until 8pm, then 4 hrs off and then on again at midnight until 2 am, so you didn't really get much sleep, so the times were 6-8, 8-10- 10-12 -12-2- 2-4 -4-6, through the night, I tell you it was a bit scary walking around in the pitch dark later when all the lights went out, and the bloody mossy's buzzing around your ears, snakes in the grass, hoping you didn't tread on one, and knowing that there were terrorists out there somewhere, could even be watching you!! And of course the strange noises coming from the 'ulu', If you happened to see a light bobbing along down the path, you knew it was the Duty Officer, from the officers mess after a few drinks, coming down to check the guards, so you hid from him or you would have to challenge him with the old ' who goes there thing' so you couldn't be dealing with that in the middle of the night!, he would then go to the guard room and shout,' call out the guard', to which everyone in there including the ones trying to get some sleep would have to get out and line up outside for another inspection, he would ask the guard commander if there was anything to report, no would be the reply, so it was 'carry on then' and hewould then weave his way back to his mess for some more drink, you could smell the booze a mile away. I will tell you the routine of a challenge, if for some reason he took you unawares, or he had turned his torch off, and he was suddenly there, you shouted out 'stop, who goes there' you wait for a reply, 'Duty guard Officer ' would be the reply, so you say ' advance and be recognised' which they then should, but if they didn't answer you, or advance, then you slammed a round up the spout, mind you I always had one up there anyway! And if they still didn't make any move, you were entitled to shoot them, but they quickly answered every time. There was one Officer there that nobody liked, did I mention by the way that they were all Army officers, well this particular one thought a bit too much of himself and he didn't like RAF personnel either. Always trying to find some fault with the aircraft when half the time he didn't know what he was talking about, anyway, we sometimes wished that if he was guard Officer, he didn't reply to a challenge, get my drift!!

Anyway, back to the basher and Ted getting ready for guard duty. Jim and Blondie said did I fancy a beer, would I! So we went to Chan's, It was just a wooden hut with tables and chairs, there was a room at the back where he kept the beers and did the cooking. There was quite a few in there and it was again intros all round, and of course some jokes about we have a senior aircraftsman with us now so the rest of you RAF blokes had better watch your step!, I met the RAF Corporal as well, Skinny. There were about 20 lads in Chan's so it seemed that it was the meeting place in the evenings, well there was nowhere else to go, after a few beers and a lot of laughs we made our way back to the basher. On the way back I was hit in the face by something hard. I did hear something buzzing and Jim said it was a 'buzz bomb' as they called them, a big brown flying beetle as big as a packet of cigarettes that fly at night, and there was also another one, a Rhinoceros beetle that also flew at night, a big black shiny hard thing that really did look like a Rhinoceros, and if that hit you at speed it really did hurt. The mossy's we're out so I put up my net over the bed, and had a cigarette and chat and turned in. It had been a long day and interesting and everyone I had met so far had been friendly and liked to joke about, so I think I might fit in quite nicely. I slept in fits and starts trying to get used to the sounds of the 'ulu' and the buzzing of the mossy's. Ted who was on his guard stag came in to get something during the night.

Now I'm not going to give you a day by day report, as that would be too boring, so what I will do is try and explain a normal day's routine to start with, and just highlight other things that go on.

So up about 7am and shave and off to breakfast, sometimes you didn't bother to get dressed for that, just a towel around you, and if you were very posh some even had dressing gowns. After breakfast back and get dressed for work, gym shorts and plimsoles, I could never get used to wearing flip flops for some reason or other, they kept shooting off when I walk, must have funny toes or something. I wore my jungle hat and was

214

strongly advised that for a while to wear a shirt as the sun is very strong and a lot of the time you are working outside. I wasn't too bad really as I already had a bit of a tan with that month on the ship, but I did wear a shirt for about a week. Still a month to go before the humid and wet season starts. Some mornings were a bit nippy as it was the dry season but it soon warmed up after the mists had risen, now Norman I was told had only been over here for 3 weeks and he thought that wearing a vest would be o.k. but after the first day when he took his vest off he blistered all where the vest didn't cover, it wasn't too bad so he was lucky as it was an offence to get sun burned and go sick, as it was interpreted as s self inflicted injury! He was walking around and it looked as if he'd still got his vest on, bright red where the sun burn was and white where his vest had been, it looked quite funny. We walked over to the hanger but Ted had been there already. Apparently the RAF lads had worked it out amongst themselves that if one or two of the RAF lads had been on guard duty the night before and finished at 6am, they would go over and unlock the hanger and start to do the Pre-flight inspections, PFIs, on the aircraft, then when the others came on about 8am or near, they would then go and get their breakfasts and then have the rest of the morning off and go to bed and catch up on the sleep they missed whilst on guard duty. It was a good arrangement for us RAF blokes as the army lads had to go straight to work all day after guard duty. Now a pre-flight inspection is carried out by all the trades respectively, you obviously have checked everything within your scope and then sign to say that everything is in working order. Depending on how much flying is taking place that day, the pilots would come down and say that they were taking such and such a plane and then sign for it and you would walk down to the aircraft with them and help them with any kit they had, Then when they were buckled in and settled down they, would give you the thumbs up. Now to start up an Auster you hand swing the propeller to do so, they do have a battery starter button but only to be used in an emergency or if there is no one around to swing the prop. There is a strict procedure to follow or you could lose an arm or a hand. Before the pilot touches anything you turn the prop 2 or 3 times to prime the engine, then you shout to the pilot "switches off, throttle closed, brakes hard on", he repeats it and gives you thumbs up again, you then shout" switches on, throttle set" he repeats, thumbs up. you grasp the prop with your right hand, shout" contact", he repeats, thumbs up, you then swing the prop downwards, stepping away quickly at the same time, hopefully the engine fires up, if not, repeat everything again until it does, you then stand on one side whilst the pilot checks that everything is working correctly, he then waves to you, and you pull away the chocks from the wheels, you then walk onto the airstrip, check that it clear and that nothing is trying to land, then wave to him to pull out and you give a quick salute and off he goes to the end of the airstrip and turns into the wind, and accelerates up to full speed and lifts off, a quick pull up over the trees and away on his mission.

If all of the other planes had taken off, there would probably be one left in the hanger which is due for a Service. We tried to rotate them as much as possible so that we had something to do during the day! There was nobody bossing you about, you all knew what to do, so you did it. As I'd never worked on an Auster before, I followed the Manual, until it became routine, after all you do have to sign your life away saying that everything is in perfect working order as it's your neck on the line if anything goes wrong, also if it came over on the net that a such and such an aircraft is missing or has crashed, immediately all forms and documents are locked away in the safe, until the cause of any accident is established, so if you were the last person to work on that aircraft, you get really worried until it is solved, or it could be just pilot error, but they never make mistakes do they!!!

So days went on day to day, now and again a water lorry would arrive to top up the tank on the water tower for showering, as I've said hot water came from one of the stoves in the cookhouse which was kept going by a couple of local native lads. There were quite a few local people from the nearby village that worked on the camp. They were great full to the British because the village was secure from terrorists as it was behind a tall fence and was patrolled by police. They are of course paid by the Military, they keep the area tidy, cut the grass, stoke the fires, clean through the bashers, we called them 'armours', they would also clean your kit if you wished, also take away your washing and bring it back next day, all nice and clean and beautifully ironed, it was like having your own servant and you paid them a few dollars a week yourself, (the currency in those days was the Malaysian dollar, worth 2 shillings and 4 pennies) also if you wanted anything, as obviously there was no NAAFI, they would get it for you when they went into the nearest town. Each basher had their own 'armour', ours was named Nanook, and he had a son named Peter, he liked the English name! He was in his 50s and his son about 16. Both lovely people, and I suppose it was a good living for them as they would only have probably been working on the rubber plantations, or the tin mines for a living. They both biked everywhere as well. The nearest town, come village was an hour's drive by land rover, it was called Kuala Lipis, we were allowed to go there every two weeks on what was called the Mail Run,. There would be 5 of you in the land rover and a scout car as escort, all armed of course, with radios, everyone had to take it in turns to go on this run, as it was the chance to see a bit of civilization, you were only allowed 2-3 hrs there just to pick up the mail or have a couple of quick beers or do some shopping. This was evidently just in case there were any C.T. sympathisers in the town who could then contact them and say that there were British troops in the town so they would arrange an ambush, hence only the 2-3 hrs. But it was enough time to do what you wanted to do. Once when I was in there I decided to buy a camera as there was a very good camera shop which was recommended to me by one of the Officers, so I thought I'd have a look. I bought, as recommended by the owner as one of the latest cameras, an Agfa 3.5 lens, top notch, it cost me 200 dollars, well there wasn't anywhere to spend your money so why not, and funnily enough I still have it! I remember once on our way back from the town, one of the lads wanted to relieve himself, so we stopped and he went into the bushes and came out, then just as we were about to turn into the camp, this chap shouted "for Christ's sake stop" He said that he had left his rifle up against a tree when he went to have a pee!! so we turned around as quietly as possible and retraced our steps, he suddenly shouted "that's where I went in" he dived into the bushes and a few moments later came out waving his rifle as it was still leaning against the tree, but he looked as white as a sheet and the sweat was running down his face mixed with the look of relief on his face, and I should think so. To lose a rifle, and whilst on active service as well, would be a Court Marshall Offence, and probably 20 yrs in the jug, or shot at dawn! Well, we told him that just to make him feel better!

Now it was a tradition on 1914 Flight to have pets, just 3 or 4, they were regarded as Flight personnel. We had 3 dogs and a monkey, each dog was looked after by one owner, and when that owner went home he would hand it on to someone else to look after. I was handed down a dog called Oscar, it was a black Labrador, about 2yrs old, he was a lovely dog but I don't think the bloke who had him before took a great deal of notice of him, just fed him, as even before he left, Oscar used to follow me around a lot as I always made a fuss of him whenever I could, anyway it was obvious I would take him on. He followed me everywhere, he had a bed in the hanger, he slept under my bed, and came to meals with me, he would sit at the side of me, the dogs ate the same food as we did, only outside with their own dishes, none dare mistreat them or shout at them. Lofty had one, a bull terrier, and he said if anyone touched his dog, he would kill them, and I think he would have done as well, he was nearly 7 foot tall and didn't suffer fools! My Oscar was really good company, when I was on guard duty he walked at the side of me and he would prick up his ears if he heard a strange noise, he made guard duty a bit more bearable. I had him for nearly 2 years, and it broke my heart when I had to go home and leave him there, but I made sure he went to a good new owner, and I know he did. There were 2 other dogs there, Elmer which was Lofty's dog, and Jessie, who looked like a cross between a terrier and a fox, a fox terrier!! They all got on well together as well. Then the monkey, 'Chico Fire Bug,' he belonged to everyone, he had a house box on a stand in between the bashers, he had a collar with a long lead, he was a Rehus monkey, he was named fire bug as he got loose one day, as he often did, went into a basher and found a box of matches and then sat up on the roof of the basher striking them and set fire to it, luckily we were there trying to coax him down at the time so we managed to put it out before he burned the basher down. Then another time when he got free, he got into people's lockers and bit on tooth paste tubes, so when you went to clean your teeth the paste came out of several holes.

Once nearly everyone started to go down with sickness and diarrhoea and fever, flying was suspended as there was no one to service the aircraft. It turned out to be the water supply that came from a large water Bowser (tank) which was towed by a truck and was refilled every so often from town. Joe and Lofty carried out tests on the water and it turned out to be something called Lepro Spirosis, usually found in jungle streams or rivers, so it was thought that the water tank had been purposely contaminated, as when Joe and Lofty went to town to refill the Bowser they checked the town supply and that was o.k., so from now on the water was tested every day and the Bowser lid was kept locked, After I had been there for about a month I managed to get onto the supply run weekend down to Kuala Lumpur for a weekend break. This time two 3 tonners were going as there was quite a lot of stores to pick up, plus two more RAF chaps. So the two 3 tonners set off early on a Friday morning, one with Lofty and me, and the other with Joe and Jim, and this time we took our own armed escort with us, the Bren gun carrying scout car with Clem and Taffy in it. We got to the Bentong Gap without incident, and joined the convoy to go over, but there was a hold up as some sort of incident had occurred on the Gap. Evidently a bus in the convoy was fired upon, one person was shot and wounded, but also in the convoy was a troop of Ghurka's, and they jumped out and went after them, we know what will happen if they catch them, and they will! We reached K.L. late afternoon and made ourselves at home in the big tent behind the stores, grabbed a meal and a shower and changed into some civvy's that we had bought with us, checked out at the guard room and got a couple of taxi's into K.L. It was strange being in the bright lights of a city again, with cars and trishaws going back and forth and music coming from all directions, but it was civilisation! And I actually saw a white woman, at least I think she was white, it's been such a long time since I've seen one! We told the taxi driver to drop us off at a good lively bar, which he did, from then on the evening slowly became a bit of a blur. I do remember dancing and in a trishaw and eating something with chopsticks at a roadside stall, the next thing was pouring out of a taxi by the camp gates and trying to walk straight and look sober past the guardroom, we were stopped, I say we, there was only Clem and Taffy, and me, so God knows where the others were. I said we were stopped and asked who we were, and we said 1914 Flight from Benta, the Snoops just said "Oh, you lot, o.k. off you go" they must have felt sorry for us. So we made our way back to our tent and crashed.

The next morning we all missed breakfast, but the other 3 had managed to find their way back last night also. I was just trying to get my head together when I swore I heard a bicycle bell ringing, I opened the flap and outside was a Chinese chap with a bike and little trailer on the back with 2 big urns on it he said" coffee Mr sir,? God save the King" He was a life saver for us. We all grabbed a cup each, it was good coffee, and he also had some sweet sticky rice cakes which were very welcome as we had missed breakfast, so he did a roaring trade, he must travel around the camp selling his wares I suppose, we told him to come back again next morning. We all decided to go to the swimming pool, yea, a swimming pool on the camp, well actually next door. Well it is the Squadron H.Q. a civilised post, if you didn't mind the discipline and the bull, and having to look smart all of the time, even at work. No, prefer to go native. We spent the day at the pool and got chatting to some WRAFs but you could tell they preferred Officers and not us erks, and you couldn't blame them as they had been invited to the Officers club that night, and besides we did look like scruffs. That night we decided to stay on camp and go to the NAAFI and have a few beers as we were pretty knackered, got into a bit of an argument with some lads who were stationed here at H.Q. they more or less called us lads from 1914 Flight peasants and a disgrace to the RAF, as we looked so scruffy, but we told them that they were lucky to have such a cushy posting, and when we described to them what life was like, that every where you went you took your rifle with you, even to the loo, and the showers, and that you were on guard duty every 4 days, and that you couldn't wear clothes at work as the humidity was so much that you were soaked in sweat in minutes, which attracted giant mosquitoes, and that the 'ulu' was so thick you could walk past someone a yard away and not see them, and that you weren't allowed out of camp without armed escorts, and not at all at night, also would anyone like to come back with us for a few days, as it could be arranged, so if you give us your names we will arrange it!. Funny, but there were no takers on our generous offer, and they soon shut up.

Next morning we loaded up the supplies with another month of goodies, mostly dry goods as fresh stuff wouldn't last five minutes, any fresh stuff was bought in by one of the locals every few days in the back of a little old van, and if we saw it in camp we would rush over and buy some of the things off him for ourselves, mostly fruit of course. While we were loading we had our coffee from the Chinese guy again, could do with him back at our camp, I wonder if anyone would miss him? When we had finished we went to the NAAFI for a beer, we kept to ourselves and out of the way as much as possible, as we didn't want to attract too much attention as to our method of dress and appearance. I did sneak in between some bashers to have a look at the airstrip. It was about 6 times larger than ours, but they do have all sorts landing here, I could see some choppers, Sikorsky's, 2 or 3 Pioneer, they were a remarkable aircraft, monoplane but twice the size of an Auster, and because of its special wing surfaces and extensions, it could take off and land in about 50 yards, plus carrying 4 or 5 passengers, or big loads, ideal for these little jungle strips like ours. There were 7 or 8 Austers also down by the hangers, in one of the hangers there were two, side by side no working out in the sun and rain, also all the personnel who were coming and going were wearing uniforms, khaki dress as well and berets! Now I did feel out of place with my O.Gs, dirty and crumpled, jungle boots and hat, so I thought I'd better get back into the NAAFI with the other scruffs. Whilst we were there 2 RAF lads came in and were looking around and when they spotted us they came over and stopped and looked at us a bit quizzically and asked us if we were from 1914 flight stationed at Benta up country in Pahang? Lofty said "could be, who's asking" the rest of us just looked at them silently and expressionless, there was a long silence, the 2nd bloke was just looking at us lost for words, and the first one was about to say something else, when we all burst out laughing, and a look of relief came on their faces. I bet they thought who the hell are this lot, any way it broke the ice and Lofty apologised for our sense of humour, but you'll get used to it he added.

They were both 3 year regulars, both LAC,s, Don came from London, his name was Alan Donaldson actually, but as there were some Alan's back at camp we renamed him as Don, the other one was also Alan, but because he had come from a station in Northern Ireland, and was always talking about the IRA, we renamed him Paddy. They had both been told when they arrived to look out for a load of scruffs, they will most likely be in the bar of the NAAFI, typical. As those are the lot you are going back with tomorrow. Any way we bought them a beer and they were easy to chat to so we thought they would fit in well. Don was an engine fitter, and Paddy, airframes, the same as me, they had both been in about 6 months and flew out here, and also up from Singapore, so they missed that wonderful train ride. We went back to the tent, giving them a hand with their kit, and decided it was time for a nap before dinner. Don and Paddy said they would unpack their kit and get out their O.Gs and dress like us, the go for dinner and they would see us in the NAAFI later. After our much needed kip we went for dinner and then into the NAAFI, we decided not to go into town tonight but get to know the two new lads better. When we walked in they saw us and bought us a drink, and another, they should fit in very well. Paddy came from Blackburn, and he was an SAC, but was waiting for conformation. He had been stationed in Ireland and was actually on active service there because of all the troubles, the bombings and shootings, he would often bore us with his tales about the troubles and how life was hard during those times, but we found out he was stationed near the borders of Southern Ireland away from it all, but he was funny at times especially when he had had a few beers, well aren't we all. Don was stationed near London so he went home every weekend so he was a bit p----d off when he was posted abroad. They were a bit taken back when we filled them in about Benta, but they looked forward to the easier life style, but not so sure about the guard duty bit, they were a couple of nice blokes, they smoked and liked their beer so they should fit in well.

In the morning we got ready to leave after breakfast, the two new lads had their O.Gs on but told them to ditch the berets as they would be riding in the back of the trucks, one in each, as armed escorts, but if there were any snipers about the first ones to get it were those wearing forces hats, Clem and Taffy in the Bren gun carrier were laughing. We pulled the canvas sheeting back and made a place for them to sit in on the back, told them to load their rifles and keep sharp, I could see Jim and Lofty smiling and I guessed what the b-----s were going to do. I was with Lofty again and so we set off. Don was in the back of our truck and Paddy was with Joe and Jim. We arrived at the start of the Bentong Gap just at the right moment as one convoy had just gone past so we were able to tag on the end of the one just about to go, we had been going for about ¾ of an hour and were on the steep bit and down to a crawl when lofty gave a little toot on his horn and then Joe gave one back so I knew what the pair of them were going to do, the same thing that happened to me. Lofty then switched the ignition key on and off twice quickly and there were two loud bangs, I was looking out through the back of the cab and I saw Don hurl himself flat against the floor, his hat and rifle went skidding across the back as he tried to crawl under the canvas sheet. Then Joe did the same and God knows what Paddy did but I could see Joe and Jim killing themselves with laughter! I think it even took Taffy by surprise in front as he jumped up and was manning his Bren gun until he cottoned onto what had happened, so lofty got the V sign. The convoy up front must have really thought there was an ambush as they all put their foot down, as you are supposed to do if you are ambushed, get away as fast as you can, but we caught up with them and waved that we were o.k. We shouted to Don and Paddy that everything was o.k. now also, but they were still crouching low in the back and Don had recovered his rifle and was holding it close to his chest! After we had cleared the Gap we stopped for a break, well we had to tell them didn't we, and they both called us all the names under the sun, but then saw the funny side of it, so we bought them a beer, and I told them that that's what they did to me when I arrived. But I'm sure Paddy had a brown stain on his trousers, and he didn't smell too good either!! I bet Jim and Joe were glad he was in the back of the truck!

We finally reached the camp and the two lads went into the Flight office to check in and meet the C.O. and we unloaded the trucks, then I went back to the office and collected Don and Paddy and took them to our basher. There was a bed next to mine which Don took, and Paddy bunked next to Blondie, I introduced them to everyone as they unpacked their kit, and we went for dinner where they met the rest of the guys, and then of course down to Chan's for a beer, you could see that both Don and Paddy were a bit wide eyed and stumped to what had happened to them in the last 48 hrs, a bit of a culture shock I suppose, and I suppose I was the same, although I did have that train journey from Singapore to be able to get a little used to things. But these two on a plane from the U.K. then on another one to K.L. and then 6-7 hrs on the back of a truck, and then being shot at!! Then bang into the middle of the jungle, then sleeping in a straw hut with mossy's eating you alive also walking everywhere with a rifle over your shoulder, even to the crapper! Life doesn't get much better does it!

After a while Don and Paddy settled into the daily routine of maintaining the aircraft, doing guard duties, and getting plastered in Chan's, well there wasn't much else to do, as once you had gotten used to the 'Anchor' beer and became addicted, and after a few hours feeling a little peckish, so one of Chan's fried egg banjo's would go down a treat, then stagger back to your basher and collapse on your pit, remembering to open up your mossy net first, not a bad life really as it numbed the more unpleasant things. There would be occasions when some night flying would take place and most of the lads would be up for that one, it happened about once every 2 or 3 weeks, or if there happened to be an emergency drop to some patrol out in the 'Ulu'. There weren't any fixed landing lights on the airstrip so we used 'Goose Necks', which were watering cans with a thick spouts, filled with paraffin and a wick sticking out of the spout, crude but effective, as long as you didn't kick one over whilst marshalling the planes! You would place them about 10 yards apart down each side of the runway, about 20 in all. Flying would start around 6 pm when it got dark, and the kites would take off one after another and fly off to cover their various areas. After we had seen them off we would sit in the hanger playing cards or writing home as they would be gone for about 2 hrs, or one or two would go over to the control tower, (forgot to mention that) it was a little square hut perched on top of long stilts about 15 ft high, with a ladder up the side, a real 'Meccano kit' effort, it was a bit rickety especially when the wind blew. The Control Tower, funnily enough was operated by the Army bods, REME, maybe one or two at a time, but if there was only one up there, we sometimes would go up and listen to the communications whilst waiting for the kites to return, and it would give us some idea when the E.T.A. was (estimated time of arrival) instead of going outside and listening.

Maybe flying over the 'Ulu' at night may not seem practical, but what you were looking for were fires down below, and if you spotted one and it wasn't one of the native camps marked on the maps it could be a terrorists camp, so if there were any patrols out there nearby, you could contact them and give the map references, if not, give the references back to base and they would forward them on for patrols to go out the following morning and find it, or pick up a trail, very cat and mouse. When we got the nod that the kites were on their way back we got everything ready, the ones who were doing the marshalling had a light lazer in each hand, and you gave special signals with them as to which way you wanted the kite to go and the pilots would follow those light instructions, Then park it on the standing, refuel it and bed it down for the night, sometimes if one or two were on longer flights they could land elsewhere to refuel so it could be late before they returned. The next morning there probably wouldn't be any flying because we would have to do the servicing on the aircraft from the night before.

As I've said before we had 5 aircraft, 1 mark 5, 3 mark 6, 1 mark 7, the mark 7 was my favourite, I can still remember Its No VX 714, I liked it because it had dual controls, side by side seats and I used to love going flying as often as possible. If we weren't particular busy on the servicing side and my favourite Captain was taking my favourite aircraft up, Captain Alum was his name, I would ask him if he minded me going up with him, and he never refused me, in fact sometimes if he came down for my aircraft he would look in the hanger and shout "Warden, are you there, I'm taking 714 fancy a trip" In fact he taught me quite a lot about flying and after a couple of flights he used to let me take control, he would say "take over Warden I just want check something on the map" so he would be checking the map and looking out of the window, and after a while he would say "right, now alter course to so and so" so I would alter the compass and fly on, then perhaps he wanted me to do a complete Port side circle so that he could check something out on the ground with his binoculars, I loved it, after a couple of hours he would say "let's head back now the boring stuff is done, and have a bit of excitement on the way" so if we came to a valley with flat ground and growing crops or grazing cattle, or both, he would dive down to below tree height and roar along flat out and the workers and the cattle would scatter in all directions, then at the end of the valley it would be a sudden swoop upwards, leaving your stomach behind, It was great fun, also when you are that close to the ground you seem to be going at a hell of a speed, we used to call it 'shoot ups', sometimes they would do it along the camp airstrip and everyone would come out and watch. As I've said I used to love going up, and also you got paid 6p an hour for being an Observer!

Captain Alum and I did have a bit of a scare once, we had been flying for about an hour when I happened to glance at the instrument panel and to my horror I saw that the oil pressure gauge was reading zero, I pointed to it and he said "shit", did a tight turn about, got on the radio, gave a 'mayday, mayday, call sign and our position, he told me to take the stick and he got out the map and then told control that he was going to find the nearest road that headed in the general direction of our camp, follow it, and should the engine seize up he would try and put down on it, but give the position before he did, so we climbed to get a bit of height in case we had to glide. He found one road which was a bit narrow, if we did have to land on that it would probably tear both wings off, but luckily it led to a much wider one, where we might have a better chance, I was of cause s-----g myself, and I don't think Captain Alum was too happy either. I kept leaning forward and tapping the oil gauge hoping it was just a faulty gauge, then the thought struck me that we were still flying and the engine sounded o.k. so if there had been no oil pressure the engine would have seized some time ago. I mentioned this to Captain Alum and he said "you could be right, keep your fingers crossed" mind you I think I had already got everything crossed! We got to a point where the road went away from where we heading, and it meant that to get back to our strip, which now was only be another ten minutes flying time, we would have to fly over jungle. So the choice was try to put down on the road now and chance a landing, hoping the road was wide enough and no traffic, as it did look fairly busy from up here, or, risk flying on for another 10 minutes over thick the jungle with all the consequences. The engine still sounded perfectly o.k. and nice and smooth, no stuttering or spluttering, Captain Alum looked at me and said "home?" I just nodded, so we turned and climbed again so that if it did stop we would have a longer gliding range. They were the longest 10 minutes of my life, we were told over the net that everything was in place for our landing, fire truck, an ambulance had raced up from Kuala Lipis, a bit o,t,t, but standard procedure I suppose. then at last we sighted our airfield, and did it look good, there was a large smile on Captain Alums face as he put us into steep dive and straight in, no messing, it was a bit of a bumpy landing, not surprising under the circumstances, as we taxied up the strip we saw that the whole camp was out watching and as we stopped by the hanger everyone clapped and cheered. I looked at Captain Alum and he at meand we shook hands, the only one who didn't look too happy was poor old Blondie who had done the pre-fight engine inspection on the plane, and all the documents had been locked away in the C.O.s safe, but captain Alum told Blondie that there was nothing to worry about as everything was working normally when he had done his pre-flight warm up, so it was just a faulty gauge after all that had just packed up after we had taken off and when I had noticed it. So it was changed immediately and thoroughly tested. We had a few beers that night Chans, and even Captain Alum popped in for one or two.

All of the time that I was on 1914 Flight we did lose one aircraft, but thankfully no casualties, we nearly lost another one when one was landing at another airstrip and as he was taxing along, the propeller flew off, of course all flights were grounded immediately and those flying told to land a.s.a.p. right through the Squadron until the cause could be found, that particular plane had just had a major service done on it, and it was poor old Don who had done the engine side of the inspection and signed it off, so he started to sweat a bit, so consequently there was no flying for a few days, but at least our pilot spent a bit of time on a civilised station, but no rest for the wicked, as we spent the time filling sandbags and building a wall around the fuel enclosure, as it would only take one bullet or a grenade from the surrounding 'ulu' to blow up half the camp, I was surprised it hadn't been done before, taking into account the recent escalation in terrorist activity, I had mentioned it before so someone had decided it needed doing. The outcome of the investigation into the prop failure was that it was metal fatigue on the bolts securing the prop to the crank, I think there were about 8 of them, so we had to wait until new sets were flown up from Singapore, and now checks would be made more frequently on the prop bolts. At least Don was off the hook. So we spent more time tidying up the place and we dug some fox holes at the end of the runway and sandbagged them as Bren gun emplacements. it was also decided by George, the army Staff Sergeant, to get a gang together, about 20 of us and go to the far end of the strip and clear some of the 'ulu', bamboo, bushes, small trees, back about 30 yards so as to make it easier to spot anyone perhaps eyeing up the camp, so he got a gang together armed with machetes and chain saws and such, 2 or 3 to stand guard whilst we did it. It was the first time that most of us had actually ventured into the 'ulu', where we were wasn't actually Primary jungle, but it was thick enough, as I've said before in some places you could walk past someone who was only a yard away and not even see them. So we started hacking and chopping away but within minutes you were soaking in sweat, also you had to careful not to disturb any nests, especially the Tiger ants, as we called them, they were big black things about an inch long, and when they bit you it was agonising, and it would swell up into a big red weal and itch for days, they were all over the place, in the bushes, up in the trees, if you did disturb a nest there would be millions of them after you! They say that when they are on the march a column can be a yard wide and you can hear them coming, a buzzing sound, and they devour anything in their path, even the big animals run away from them. Whilst we were clearing, one of the lads said he had found something in the undergrowth and it was metal, so we cleared away the vines and bamboo and pulled it out, and we couldn't believe what we had found. it turned out to be an old Japanese Machine gun, it was rusty and a couple of bits were missing, but it was still on its stand, so we dragged it out and it was quite heavy and carried it back to the hanger, and a couple of days later we started cleaning it up. It could have been hidden there for about ten years but it cleaned up quite good, and we put some of the bits that were laying around back on it and painted it green and put it in front of the Flight Office as a camp mascot.

The dry weather season was now turning into the monsoon season and the humidity was beginning to rise, especially after a storm. I and most of the lads had never seen rain like it, the old saying 'it came down like stair rods' was true, sometimes if you stretch your arm out into it, you couldn't see your hand, also in minutes there would be flash floods. In the villages and towns, along the sides of the roads were monsoon ditches that were about 6 feet deep and 10 feet wide and they would turn into raging rivers, and after the rain would come the steam and humidity, you could put on clothes, then standstill, and in minutes you were soaking wet with sweat. So you just wore shorts and a towelaround your shoulders and keep spraying the mosquito repellent around! And it smelled terrible. Sometimes to save going down to the shower you just stepped outside the basher with your soap and showered there, and when you went for meals or down to Chan's you just put a towel around your shoulders and cape on top, you can imagine 20 or 30 blokes all crammed into Chan's all sweating profusely mixed with the steam and cigarette smoke, a real dive. The worst was if you were on guard duty, you couldn't walk around in that sort rain for a coup[le of hours at a time, you couldn't see where you were going anyway as you might suddenly vanish down a storm drain, and apart from that, what terrorist in their right mind would be out in this! It's only us mad Brits that do things like that! I know what I used to do, and I can say this now, I would go and sit in the cab of one of the trucks, one where I could see if any Duty Officer was coming down the road by a bobbing torch, so

I would quietly get out of the cab and then challenge him, and say" lovely evening sir" a grunt reply and off he'd go!

I did mention that we did lose an aircraft whilst I was on the Flight. It was whilst it was out doing whatever it was doing. It suddenly lost radio contact and became overdue to land. He had been in contact with one of the other Flights when he had given them his last position and then silence. All Ops were suspended and a search Op was instigated, we had 2 aircraft that were already up and 2 on the ground ready to go. When Captain Alum came down I asked him if I could go with him and he said the more eyes the better, also Jim was going up with Captain Grindon Welch, (we called him wind and belch) by this time a big search operation had been launched, 2 more aircraft from another flight and a chopper from K.L. The pilot, Capt Rickards, had given two map references so the search area was divided around those, we, or rather Captain Alum decided to take a path from our camp to the last map reference on the premise that he may have been heading back to our camp from there as he was due to return. So we flew fairly high to start with as to get a wider scope, we both had binoculars and you just looked for any sort of disturbance in the trees, or smoke or anything shining or silver, broken trees or even an S.O.S. sign. It was a good thing it was still morning as we would still have a few hours of daylight left. If we did see anything unusual we would drop down to tree height and have a closer look. We went back and forward lots of times, we even saw the chopper in the distance once, but evidently no one had seen anything so far, so 4 of the aircraft were told to return to their bases, and resume their search at night as there may be the chance of spotting a fire or something, so the 2 of our flight stayed searching for another hour but frustratingly saw nothing, so in the end we had to return to base, the other 2 took off just as it was getting dark and a couple of the lads went with them as observers. The only trouble with the Mark 5 and 6 is the passenger seat is in the back on an angle, which I thought was uncomfortable. We put out the 'Goose neck' landing lights and refuelled the two on the ground in case we had to go up later.

Anyway the night search turned out to be fruitless all round, so things looked a bit grim, you could see that everyone that night was rather quiet, so at dawn they went up again, I couldn't go as I was duty fitter that day, so they searched all day and night again, still nothing. It is literally like looking for a needle in a haystack. During the war lots of aircraft disappeared over jungles, never to be seen again, Then on the next afternoon the C.O. received a call from the K.L. hospital that Captain Rickard had been found alive and well considering he had a nasty gash on his head and an enormous black eye and probably a broken wrist. The word flashed around, and Chan opened his bar and as it was next to the C.O.s office, he declared the rest of the day a holiday. Captain Rickard should be back to camp in a couple of days. The C.O. was allowed to speak to Captain Rickard's and managed to piece together what had happened.

Evidently he was flying along having completed his mission, he had just radioed one station and given them his position and was about radio our camp and give his E.T.A. when his engine just spluttered and died on him, and dived downwards. He was quite low at the time so he had glide as far as possible but there was nowhere to put down into a clear space so it was a case of belly flop into the trees, luckily the trees weren't the 200 ft ones!, he doesn't remember any more then came too and luckily he wasn't trapped, also no fire, he remembered blood running into his eyes and his wrist hurt like hell, he managed to crawl out, both wings had been torn off and unfortunately the radio was smashed to pieces. He looked for the flare pistol but it was nowhere to be found, he had his compass and maps and his pistol, but nothing to start a fire with, I could have suggested something if I had been there, but I wasn't. There was a terrible smell of fuel so he thought he had better get clear in case it went up in flames, which I suppose would have helped the search parties, looking at his maps and the last known position he was at when he radioed in, and then calculating flying time in distance from then, and he knew his heading, so he thought he may have some idea of his whereabouts, and according to the map a road was shown which he reckoned he could get to in a day and a night. There was a machete in the plane but he could only use it with his left hand. In the emergency pack, which is in every kite, he found some medical stuff so cleaned the cut on his head a bit and covered it with his beret to keep off the flies. There was also water and dry biscuits in there as well anyway he decided to set off on his compass reading, but the going was more difficult than he thought what with his injuries, and he thinks he has a bit of concussion as he keeps going dizzy and has to stop and rest a lot, he struggled on as much as he could before it got dark, he could hear planes but couldn't see them because of the tree canopy. He couldn't remember that night as he thinks he blacked out but as soon as it started to get light he pressed on. By now one had closed completely and his wrist was badly swollen, he had no idea how far he had come or how far to go but he just kept going in the direction the compass said, and by his watch he still had a few hours of daylight left. Then all of a sudden he heard a noise in front of him, so not knowing what the hell it could be he crouched down low, not realizing that several pairs of eyes had been watching him for some time! he was behind a tree and when he took a look there was a group of natives in loin clothes and carrying bows and arrows and blow pipes, there were about ten of them. There was one big guy, obviously the boss, he was holding a dead monkey, One of them came forward and offered the captain a bottle of water in a plastic bottle! Which he gratefully accepted as he had drank all his in the night.

Now the Captain could speak a little Malay and the boss seemed to understand him a bit. although they have their own language. I'm not sure if I have this right but I think I was told they were the 'Semang' tribe, who lived in the jungle and had hardly any contact with the outside world, but because of the emergency, the British had befriended them and some of one of the tribes were working for the British as trackers, hence the plastic water bottle I suppose. Anyway between the two of them the boss indicated somehow that they would take him back to their village for the night as it was getting dark, and then in the morning they would take him to the nearest road where he would be able to get more help from passing traffic so they took him back to their village, little straw huts, and a woman bathed his head and eye and put something on it, and on his wrist she put some green stuff then wrapped a leaf around it and the pain went away, they gave him some sort of soup and meat, probably monkey, then lay down on a bed of leaves and straw and fell straight to sleep.

The next morning at dawn they escorted him through the jungle on well worn paths, which was much easier for about 4 hrs and then they came to a road. It wasn't long before something was coming in the distance, he turned to the boss who pointed to the Captains beret, so he gave it to him and he put it on with a big smile on his face, The captain turned to see what was coming down the road and as luck would have it, it was a truck with Gurkha's in it, so his ordeal was over, he turned to thank the people who had probably saved his life, but they had vanished without a trace! now that was the story as I was told, and I like to think it was true, and I hope I have all the facts correct, if not I apologise to Captain Rickards.

Now when you lose an aircraft the object is to try and retrieve the wreckage so as to determine the cause of the crash, but in the situation of the emergency, another reason was that hopefully the C.T. wouldn't find the crash site and find and use anything that might be useful to them, radio, ammunition, maps, tools, engine parts, fuel, and so on. so it was decided to set up a search party consisting of 5 of us RAF lads also an Army escort of about 12 experience jungle patrollers, plus a couple of trackers, probably from the same tribe that brought out Captain Rickards, as it was in their area. An Army sergeant came the night before we were due to go in and they studied the map now knowing the exact location of the crash site, and by taking a different route they reckoned we could go in, do what we had to do, and then get back out in one day with an early start. So the next morning at 4 am we set of from our camp, there was myself, Blondie, Paddy, Ted, and Norman, from the RAF side, We had our own escort to the departure point, the scout car, 2 land rovers and the Bren gun carrier. We rendezvous with the army lads at the entry point, and after instructions of the procedures you follow when in the 'ulu' we set off. The army lads were from the Northamptonshire Regiment, the Pioneer Corps, about 12 of them armed to the teeth, plus the two trackers. So we set off and it was still dark, but we seemed to be making good progress, the two trackers and the army lads knew what they were doing, sometimes they had to hack a way through but mostly we were following well worn paths, probably made by the natives over time. We once were signalled to stop and crouch down as the trackers had heard something ahead. I know I had my Sten gun cocked and ready. We were given Sten guns as they were lighter and you slung them around your shoulders which made it easier to walk. The noise turned out to be some animals crashing through the undergrowth, probably elephants, yes, elephants in Malaya, but they were much smaller than the African ones. After about 3 hrs we stopped for a break, and ate some energy food bars, then on again. After another 3 hrs we walked straight onto the crash site, those trackers were marvellous!.

The Auster was a complete wreck, how he got out with just the injuries he did have was a miracle, I had been carrying a bag of tools, as did the others, Paddy had the sledge hammer, and Blondie his engine tools. We had to slash the canopy so that Ted could get to the radio, and Blondie and Norman started on the engine, they wanted the carburettor as it was an engine failure, also I took a sample of fuel that was left in the tanks. Ted was dealing with the radio and various instruments, Paddy was removing the wheels, when he had done that, and Blondie and Norman were finished with the engine, and Ted with all the instruments he wanted. Paddy proceeded to smash the engine block to pieces and anything else he could find, I think he was enjoying himself. When we finally decide that we had salvaged everything that may have been useful to the C.T.s. Everyone had to get well away and I went and opened up the fuel tanks and let it run for a while, then fired a flare into the remains of the wreck, it of cause went up straight away. We stayed around for a while to ensure the fire didn't spread anywhere else, but as the undergrowth was wet from recent rains it seemed self contained. We didn't have to worry about the smoke being seen and then being bombed or the S.A.S. being dropped in to finish us off!! As all flights had been pre warned that there may be smoke coming from that location. So we started our return journey carrying whatever we could, I had a wheel strapped on my back, Paddy the other one and the rear as well, and the others had bits of everything, even most of the army lads. What remained of the aircraft would soon be obliterated by the undergrowth as it grows so quickly. I noticed that Blondie was carrying a half of the smashed propeller, didn't know why at the time? but later we had it sanded down and varnished and a brass plate put on it with all the details about the crash, I had it sent home in my sea chest and I gave it to the Aircraft Museum with all the photo's, down at Middle Wallop in Hampshire, whether it's still there I don't know. On our way back we had another scare but there again it was some animal or animals crashing through the 'ulu' but you couldn't see anything. After another exhausting trek of about 5 hrs carrying all that kit we finally reach the road, the army blokes had radioed ahead and said our E.T.A. Thankfully the lads from camp were there to meet us with a tea urn and sandwiches which went down very nicely, and when we went ask the trackers if they like some and to thank them, they had vanished and no one saw them go! We also thanked the army lads, mind you today was a picnic to them as they usually go in for 2 or 3 weeks at a time! Before we left we saw them all taking of their jungle boots and then told us to do the same with the explanation that when we crossed two small streams on the way in also way out there was the chance that you may find some leeches eating your legs, poor old Paddy screamed "leeches" tore his boots off and threw them. We were told that if you find any sucking your blood, don't try and pick them or brush them off as they can leave their teeth stuck in your flesh which will turn septic, so light a cigarette and touch the head of it and it will just drop off which was good advice which we remembered well. Sure enough I had one, Blondie had two, and Paddy had one, but he was nearly having a fit, shouting "get it off, get it off" the big wuz, anyway I had a fag on the, so I got rid of it for him, but he wouldn't put his boots back on.

So, just another example of jungle life, what with bloody Buzz bombs, Rhinoceros Beatles, Mosquito, Leeches, spiders as big as your hands, snakes of all shapes and sizes, what next, I'm expecting a Pterodactyl to swoop any minute!! We had a snake crawling though the straw in the basher once, everyone shouted and rushed outside and two of the lads went in with machetes and dispatched it, it was one of the most poisonous snakes in Malaya, about 6 ft long, there's also another strange one, a bootlace snake, you only find them in the 'ulu' they live under logs and things in nests in a ball of dozens of them, they are called bootlace as they are as thin as a bootlace about a foot long and black, and they can go through the lace holes in your boots, someone said they are poisonous. And of course the Ants, several varieties, the ones that bite chunks out of you, the ones that sting you, and the ones that take up permanent residence in the basher, the ones that you don't see until there is food left lying around, any sort of food, especially chocolate, if you left any anywhere, in seconds it would be covered in ants, so you had put anything like that in tins or jars. We did an experiment once to see how clever they were, I bet you won't believe this. We put some water in a tray and in the middle, an upturned saucer and on it some chocolate, so it was on an island in the middle of a water filled tray, and we put the tray in the middle of a table in the middle of the basher and waited, (the things we did to pass the time) and sure enough, within seconds you could see a black line moving across the floor to the table and start climbing up the leg, then across the table to the tray and then halt on the ledge of it, obviously stopped by the water, some stayed on the ledge but some started going back down and back across the floor to the basher sides, (I said you won't believe this) but then came back out and they were carrying in their little jaws strands of straw, and across the floor and up the table legs, across to the tray, up onto the ledge, drop the strands into the water, climb onto them and somehow paddle across to the saucer, in the end there was a convoy of them going back and forth! It was fascinating to watch (o.k. don't believe it, but it's true) they say that ants are intelligent when in a combined group, well, I know they are !

Another thing that occurred whilst we were still at Benta was when the camp was put on a 72 hr 'stand to'. The C.O. received a call from the Malay police regiment that a number of terrorists had been reported, about 40 or 50 of them, they were heading North, but were being pursued by a company of S.A.S. and Ghurkhas, plus Malay police, but they were still a half a day behind them and in the general direction they were heading on, it would take them directly to our camp., but they were hoping to catch up with them before they reached us, but to be on the safe side we should go to a 'Red Alert', also some re-enforcements of local Malay police should be with us in the next couple of hours.

Well of course all work ceased immediately and all the aircraft were flown straight away to another airfield in case we were the objective, all the aircraft fuel was loaded onto trucks and taken down to Kuala Lipis police station out of the way, in fact it was a complete lock down, we all changed into our combat gear and were given positions around the camp to defend, myself, Don and Paddy were in a trench at the side of the hanger facing towards the end of the airstrip as it was supposed that that was the areas that the C.T.s would approach from. We had between us, a Bren gun, with a box of magazines, two Sten guns, and two rifles, come on then!! Plus a powerful battery spotlight. Luckily our trench was dry and it had sandbags stacked in the front. About 20 yards to the left of us was another trench with Jim, Blondie, and Corporal Skinny in it. Other positions had been set up all over camp. By now it was late afternoon and it was just starting to get dark. The cooks had been going at it flat out all afternoon preparing drinks and take away meals as it was obvious it was going to be an all night effort, the cooks galley was blacked out with tarpaulin sheets and as it got dark, all lights were turned off, but we all had torches, and in case you wanted to go to the loo, or something, you walked pointing it down, and waving your torch side to side, so that everyone knew who you were and didn't blow your bloody head off, as I'm quite sure some were a little trigger happy! Mind you, it did seem rather strange and very quiet, everyone talking in whispers, and as the evening went on there was movement around as the cooks distributed flasks of coffee and sandwiches all around, even Chan made visits with his famous egg banjo's and a little brandy to put in your coffee, I bet that goes on all of our 'slates'. Every now and again an Officer would poke his head in and ask if everything was o.k. but he had nothing to report about the C.Ts. I had Oscar in with us and every time someone came near he would give a low growl, so he was a good guard dog. I did let him off a couple of times and told him to go down the strip, I knew he would let us know if anyone was about down there. I think he enjoyed wandering around down there and when he came back he would scoff an egg banjo for his troubles!

So that's where we squatted all night with nothing but the sounds of the jungle. We did hear some crashing from the end of the strip in the early hours and everyone jumped to alert and manned their weapons with hearts pounding no doubt ! But it was probably some animal. Around 4 am the mist was starting to rise and it began to get a bit chilly, luckily we had our blankets with us and the cooks bought around some nice hot soup and coffee which was gratefully received. Then around 5 am we all heard some bangs which went on for awhile, but it was very far away as sound travels in the night but we kept on alert, also we had tried to snatch a bit of sleep in turns, but it didn't really work. Then finally as the dawn began to break, we noticed the Malay police were climbing into their trucks and heading off out. Then as it got light an Officer came to us and said that the C.O. wants us all to gather over in the mess hut where there's a nice cooked breakfast for everyone, but you can now check in the weapons first, then he will be down in ½ an hour to talk to us. It was certainly good to move about a bit and get the circulation going again after 12 hrs cramped up in a trench. When we got to the mess hut everyone was there, bleary eyed and talking about the night before. There were lots of laughs of course and one lad said he swore he saw his Mother-in-law walking up the strip in the dark, of course everyone said that you should have told us and we'd have got her for you! I wonder how much brandy Chan had given him! After that long night the smell of breakfast cooking was lovely. We all looked and felt crabby, but what the hell. We didn't get bacon very often, being a

Muslin country, so I suppose it had been bought in specially, I don't really know, as it was usually Spam fritters and egg, still very nice though.

When the C.O. and some of the other Officers came in, he told us not to stand up, but just get on with your breakfasts, also he had with him 3 bottles of brandy and the officers went around pouring some into your mugs of coffee, the C.O. said it was just to get rid of the chill. Standing there with a mug of coffee in his hands he then said "I just want to say a big thank you to everyone with the professional and disciplined manner that you all applied to yesterdays, and also last nights 'Stand To'. ' To me that's the joy of being a C.O. of a small group like ours, everyone knows everyone and we all work as a family and everyone pulls their weight and it is indeed my pleasure and privilege to be your C.O. Firstly I think we all owe a toast to all the cooks for their gallant efforts throughout the night and splendid breakfast", so we all toasted the cooks. "Secondly I can now inform you, as you have guessed, the emergency is now over, as the troops who were pursuing the terrorists caught up with them finally, but they were only two miles from our camp at 5am this morning. I can see you all looking at each other, yes, it was a close call! but I had every confidence in you all, once again I thank you, Now I'm afraid the RAF lads will have to go to the airstrip and receive some bodies which are being dropped off by the choppers, and when our aircraft have returned, lock them down and the rest of the day is yours. Also I might, with your permission, come down to Chan's this evening and have a few beers with you all, there will be no guard duties tonight as I have made arrangements with the police and they are sending some officers down to do it for us" That's what I call a C.O. So after breakfast, and just then we heard the choppers arriving, so we rushed over to see them in, and some of the army lads came over to help us, which was great. Also some trucks arrived and came onto the strip, the choppers, 5 of them landed, everyone helped to carry the bodies of the C.Ts onto the trucks, some of them were pretty shot up with bits missing, I did notice some had ears missing(Ghurkhas?) I take it they only took the important ones alive. The choppers lifted off and the trucks moved out as we got the call that our kites were due in ten minutes. The army lads stayed to give us a hand. We must have looked a real bunch of scruffs now, as we were now covered in blood and guts, apart from lying in a trench all night! It was funny as when the kites came in and the pilots saw us they said, God! It wasn't that bad was it! After the kites were put to bed it was a quick shower and a nice kip. Then later on in the afternoon we all played football on the strip, then dinner and into Chan's, well as the whole camp was there it was inside and outside of Chan's, A good night though and Chan must have made a fortune, but give him his due he didn't charge anyone for the brandy he dished out during the night. The C.O. did come down for a couple of beers with another couple of Officers. The night finished off with a good sing song. I think the police who were doing the guard duty thought we were all nuts, crazy English!

It was now getting on to Xmas 1953, and apparently the C.O. and five of the other Officers had invited 5 of their wives to a Xmas do in the Officers mess. I have no idea if the wives had come over from England to spend Xmas here especially, or whether they were living either in Singapore or K.L. but arrangements were made for them to come to Benta, stay overnight and the next night and then a few days in a hotel in Kuala Lipis. Now the Officers mess was more or less the same as ours but the cookhouse was on the side, mind you the furniture was better, more like a lounge with armchairs and such, and a large dining table, they also had their own cooks, but not army personnel, I think they were local, as I don't remember any of our cooks going up to their mess. The arrangement was that there was to be a welcome cocktail party and a dinner for the ladies, and the C.O. asked for 3 volunteers to act as 'Flunkeys' or waiters from the RAF lads, I don't know why it was just the RAF lads, probably because we would have to wear best dress and it would perhaps impress the ladies having RAF lads acting as servants! So myself and Paddy and Don volunteered, as we knew there would be some good food going and plenty of booze available.

So the big day arrived, evidently the ladies had arrived yesterday but they had wined and dined at the hotel in Kuala Lipis and tonight was to be the cocktail party on the camp and to show the wives how the Officers worked and lived, how very civilized, so during the day they were arriving and proceeding up to the Officers quarters. Lots of lads were out and about hoping to catch a glimpse of the women, as we hadn't seen a White Women for about 6 months, from what I can remember. So us three were told to get up to the mess by 1600 hrs and make sure everything was in place, and I must say we looked very smart in our dress uniforms, and of course we got the wolf whistles from the lads! Now one of the army cooks had also volunteered to oversee the preparations, as he was, in civvy street a chef in a top hotel somewhere. Geordie was his name, he was National Service and he was going to prepare the cocktails and canapés and make sure the cooks didn't poison any one, perhaps they should have had one of the locals in as a food taster just to be on the safe side! I think that we could have done with one sometimes,- - -sorry, that's not fair, they do their best with what they have. So there we were waiting in the kitchen for the signal to take in the cocktails and canapés, with a quick lesson from Geordie on how to present them to the guests, as for the booze there was loads of it, the white wines and the beer were in a tin bath full of ice, ice cubes were in a thermos tub, we had already had a couple of beers whilst waiting, we could hear them arriving in the mess, and the C.O. popped his head around the door and asked for the cocktails and canapés to be served now. So in we went with the trays of drink and such, once in we probably did stare a bit too much as the ladies looked extremely glamorous in their cocktail dresses, and also very polite when offered a cocktail. Paddy had the canapés and one woman said they looked very nice, and of course he just had to say that they were something he had just whipped up on the spur of the moment, I was chatting to the C.O.s wife as she asked me where I was from. Now Don, who was a good looking chap, seemed to be in deep conversation with one of the Officers wives, mind you he was a bit of a wimp, the officer I mean, not Don! He was Captain Grindon—Welch, the one we called Wind and Belch! I got the distinct notion that we weren't supposed chat to the ladies as the C.O. said "shall we all sit down for dinner now" and then to us three "serve the wine now please" So when they were all seated, in we went with the reds and the white, serving from the right as told by Geordie, we then went back into the kitchen for a beer, then came the command to serve dinner, we weren't going to serve them individually, just place the dishes onto the table and they would help themselves, then back to the kitchen for another slurp!, well, it was warm work. So we just wandered in now and again topping up the glasses, and there was a Grammy playing some nice music so it was all very convivial. I did notice Don was paying particular attention to the same woman again, you can't blame him as she was giving him some lovely smiles.

Back in the kitchen at this time, Geordie was getting the sweets ready, in between a few slurps of whiskey, so in we swooped and cleared the dinner, dishes ready for the sweet course. I must say the red wine was quite palatable also. So as the evening went on, everyone seemed to be in a jovial mood and getting more so. After the sweet course came the coffee and brandy and liquors. Mostly everyone was now away from the dinner table and sitting relaxed in the armchairs chatting. Two of the ladies asked for G&Ts, and I noticed that we were running out of ice cubes, so we had to take a piece of ice out of the tin bath and break it up.

Just a note of interest, in those days there weren't any fridges or freezers, things were stored in ice boxes of varying sizes, and you got the ice from the 'Ice factory' in the town, big blocks of ice about 3ft by 2ft wrapped in sacks and you broke them up into different sizes and put them into the ice cabinets.

By now the evening seemed to be in full swing, the liquid refreshments were flowing quite freely, there was a lot of laughter, some were even dancing to the Grammy. Paddy blotted his copy book once, one of the women asked if there were any of those canapés left, so he put what was left on a tray and took them out, but as he bent down to offer them to her, he toppled forward and shot the lot onto her lap, he apologised profusely and started wiping her legs down, I don't her husband thought much of that, but she laughed it off and went to change her dress. Knowing her old man though she probable thought it was nice, a man touching her leg! A couple of the Officers had passed out in the armchairs. The woman that Don had been eyeing up had now come into the kitchen and was sitting on a table chatting to him. The husband was one of those flat out. Geordie was also flat out in a chair with a glass of whisky still in his hand! One of the cooks had put his hand into the tin bath to get some ice out, not knowing that there was a broken beer bottle in there and cut his hand quite badly, so we told him to keep his hand in there whilst we found something to wrap around it, and then sent him off to get it seen to. The C.O. put his head around the door and asked for a large whisky and a jug of iced water, but there were no ice cubes left, so I stuck the jug into the tin bath as it was still ice cold but the water came out pink because of the blood that was in it I took it out to him but I don't think he noticed anything, I think he was past caring anyway, and so was I! The woman who had gone to change was back, but her husband had fallen asleep so she sat down and Paddy went and asked her if she would like a drink, and she said yes, so he went and got her one and took it to her and again started to apologise for what had happened, but she said it didn't matter and then ask him to sit down and talk to her, which he did, so I went and took Paddy a beer and left them to it.

I must admit that by now I was wobbling a little so I thought I will get myself a coffee and of course a brandy, just then Captain Alum put his head around the door, saw me pouring myself a brandy and Said "I'll have one of those and a coffee and a coffee liquor for my wife please" I poured them and took them in, and he said "Now fetch yours and come and sit with us" which I did, and he introduced me to his wife who was charming and very pleasant and she said "I hear that you are the one that keeps my husband safe when he's flying by looking after his aircraft, so I would just like to say thank you" evidently he had told her that I was his observer too, which was nice.

It was now 3am and I can't quite remember a lot after that. Except the three of us staggering down the road. I was clutching a bottle of brandy. I do remember Don falling down and saying a women's name and that he wanted to go to sleep, so we left him there, and when I fell into the basher I was on my own, so I don't know what had happened to Paddy. It was all very quiet, and Oscar just wagged his tail as I crashed onto my pit. Next morning there was no flying. I wonder why?, so we sat in the hanger nursing hangovers, well, us three waiters! So evidently another good night down on the farm!! The Officers wives had decided to go back to Kuala Lipis, so the army lads took them back as the armed escort, they drove past the hanger on their way and as we were sitting outside they waved to us, and I think there was a special wave from the two women that Don and Paddy had befriended. We also found out that Geordie who had passed out, woke up and had cooked a breakfast for them all. Men of steel are Geordies'

Christmas at Benta was now upon us. There were no special arrangements to be made, flying was suspended for 5 days, Chan had been busy stocking up on the booze, also the cooks had been arranging the food for the 5 day period. We all got together and put up some decorations in the mess and some in Chan's as it was obvious most of our time would be spent in there. Most of the Officers would be down in Kuala Lipis with their wives, but they would have to take it in turns to do Duty Officer of the day. Christmas Eve arrived and most of the lads took the opportunity to have a bit of a lay in as breakfast is an hour later for the next 5 days, and no PFIs to be done so we would just stroll over to the hanger to check that everything was ok, and there were no leaks from the standing aircraft. After breakfast someone had arranged a football match, but everyone had to play in bare feet! it was only 20 minutes each way but quite hilarious, then into Chan's for a pre-lunch drink, then lunch, then back into Chan's to wash it down. Of course nobody was dressed just shorts and flip flops, around 5 pm wander into the showers and have a soak and sober up a bit, then back to the basher and change into evening gear and look a bit more respectable, and into dinner. The food on the camp was really good. I suppose cooking for only 30 odd blokes you could be a bit more flamboyant, and I know that Geordie was good at wangling rations and so were the other two crooks, Jim and Joe, the ones who bought me up to Bents in the back of their truck. If ever they were on the ration run, which was mostly all the time either down to Kuala Lumpur or Kuala Lipis and you needed something, no matter what it was, they could get it, and at a good price too. They were both old sweats, Jim especially, he was once a sergeant, but was busted down in rank, first to a corporal and then to L/ corporal, nobody knew what for and he certainly wouldn't tell you. After dinner of course back into Chan's. It was a good thing today was Thursday, pay day, cash and ash day, the ash meant cigarette issue, 50 fags in a tin, hermetically sealed, sometimes john Player or Senior Service, and of course the ones that didn't smoke sold theirs to the highest bidder, I was o.k. as I had a prior arrangement with Robbie, the camp clerk, he by the way worked on a farm before he was called up for N,S. Mind you it was his Fathers farm, and could have been exempt, but he wanted to experience forces life,even it was only for two years, as when he is finished and he goes back to farming, his Father is going to retire, so Robbie will then be taking it on, but at least he will have seen a bit of life outside of farming. I had a long chat with him once when I was on 'jankers' my punishment was to help in the camp office one night and he was telling me all the things he was going to do with the farm when it was his and to diversify into other things, I often wonder how he got on, he was a quiet lad and didn't drink much but he seemed to have his head screwed on properly, which I don't think you could say for most of us. I also think the majority on the camp were alcoholics, recovering alcoholics, or learning the trade through permanently practising!!

The next 4 days went by in a bit of a alcoholic haze from what I can remember, we just seemed to play cards or darts and spend most of the time in Chan's, except for one night when I had guard duty, in fact it did me good to lay off the' Anchor' for one night, plus get some proper sleep for a few hours. The Xmas day lunch was very, very, good, the cooks really put themselves out and laid on a great spread, there were even tablecloths on the tables, well paper ones. The duty officer joined us and even Chan was invited, and he remarked in his own inimitable way, "me likey Engwish fud" and he contributed some local wine, well I think it was wine, but it went down well, and also we had Xmas pudding with custard, where the hell they managed to get Xmas pudding from, I don't know!! so we all stood at the end and gave the cooks a well earned ovation, and then retired into Chan's, as usual. Boxing day was a little bit more sedate as the last few days were beginning to catch up with us all, and tomorrow it's back to the routine, probably with a vengeance as I know there are a couple of big services to do on a couple of the aircraft, so must have a relatively clear head mfor the next few days.

the next couple of months went by in a routine sort of way. We had one new addition to the camp and that was a new cook, he had just spent 5 weeks on a troopship the same as I did, and found everything very strange, as everyone else did who had just come out from Blighty, By the way, I forgot to mention, I think, that some of the army lads who were on the flight had come from Korea. There was Jim and Joe, and lofty Steer and a couple of others, evidently they had it pretty rough over there and lost a lot of men, so I suppose sending them to Malaya was a sort of halfway recouping before shipping them back home, and sometimes you could sense a bit of battle fatigue showing, especially with Lofty, as after a few beers he could become a little aggressive but would soon calm down, but he was a great bloke to be with. Now back to the new cook, his name was Bob Pickles, a Yorkshire lad, so of course immediately his nickname was 'Wilf' as in Wilfred Pickles, and his wife Maysie, who were on the radio, 'Workers Playtime' for those who can remember it! Wilf was an LAC and a bit of a laugh as well and he liked his beer so he fitted in straight away, plus he was a bloody good cook and brought in some fresh ideas once he had settled in.

Around May or June we were informed that our time at Benta had come to an end at last, and it was time for another Flight to take over so it was celebrations all round, any excuse, so we all started to make preparations for the big move, lock stock and barrel in 3weeks time and say goodbye to this God forsaken place and let somebody else have a go, mind you we have made a lot of improvements since we have been here, so it is now a little bit more civilized than when we came. The place we are going to is called Seremban in the Negri Sembelan area, it's about 40 miles from Port Dickson which is on the south west coast., and it's in a civilized area, where as Benta was a Red zone, Seremban is practically a White zone, not quite, but getting there as it's nearly cleared of terrorists with just the odd skirmish. Also the town of Seremban is quite big place and only a, ½ hrs drive away, and you don't have to have armed escorts when you leave camp, plus another bonus, Port Dickson is supposed to be a very nice sea side place and that's only about 40 miles away.

So over the next 3 weeks we gradually started packing things up, and some of it was being flown down to Seremban a bit at a time, but the normal routine carried on as usual until 3 days before we were due to leave, then flying ceased and everyone started loading up the trucks, and it's surprising just how much stuff there is to pack because everything appertaining to our Flight has to go, and whoever takes over here has to start from scratch. I suppose that's why we are called a mobile unit. The last afternoon all the aircraft flew down to Seremban, as the last day was spent packing our personnel belongings and then re-checking everything. The last evening everyone went into Chan's for a last drink, but not too much as we had to be on the road by 6 am,. Chan said he was 'velly solly' to see us go as we had been the best Fight that had ever been there, and in one way I think that most of us were a little sad, as basically we did have a bit of a cushy time with regard to discipline, and things were always rather casual, and I hope it continues when we get to the new place, except of course those bloody guard duties! One thing I was sorry about was that we hadn't seen the two 'punka wallahs' Nanook and his son Peter to say cheerio, hope they have them down where we are going. Next morning after a very early breakfast, we all helped the cooks to clear their things and load up their truck, they had also prepared some things for the road trip, which would take most of the day. In the convoy were 5 three tonners, 2 flat backs, 3 land rovers, scout car, and the Bren gun carrier. Everyone was of course armed, I was assigned on the back of one of the truck's, the canvas top was pulled back a bit and I had a Bren gun perched on top of the cab and Oscar had a bed at the side of me, Jim and Joe were driving and Wilf was in the cab with them. Paddy had the same on the truck in front of me and Blondie the same behind, and someone was on the back of every truck. So at around 6 am the signal was made to move out, everyone loaded their weapons and we pulled out of camp and onto the road, up front was a Malay land rover and one at the rear, so it was rather a long convoy so we hoped that any C.Ts would think twice about ambushing us with the fire power we had. After a couple of hours we had a shakedown stop, to make sure the loads were O.K. One thing that really surprised me was that when we stopped, there amongst us was the 'punka wallahs' Nanook and Peter, Evidently as I later found out that being 'bearers'(the correct name) to the flight was a full time commitment to them and as we were going down to Seremban, they had relatives who lived near the camp with whom they could stay, so there they were on a truck with their bikes and belongings, and evidently they earned quite a good living doing chores for all the personnel, and I know I couldn't do without them, and I was pleased they were with us as they were so polite and friendly.

So after a nice cup of tea, which the cooks had made in thermos type urns before we left, and the dogs stretched their legs, and also give 'Chico' a banana, off we went again and onto the notorious Bentong Gap, this time we didn't have to wait for any escorts as we were our own and were waved straight on. It was a bit precarious standing on the back as the road was narrow and the trees overhung the road in places so you had to keep ducking the branches. Once through the Gap we stopped for lunch, it was good to have a break as my legs were aching through standing and swaying on the back of the truck. The cooks had made sandwiches and there was some left over Spam for the dogs.

Finally after about 8 hrs we finally reached the Seremban camp, the town of Seremban was fairly large but we came to the camp from the opposite direction so we never saw it. The actual name of the camp was 'Palloy Camp', we were all a bit surprised at the size of it as we didn't realise that it was also the camp of the Royal 11th Hussars Regiment and as we drove along the side of the road, the airfield was next to the road, and then beyond that were rows and rows of barracks going up a hill, which we initially thought were ours, but they housed the regiment. We got to the gates and turned in, and there was a guard room, we turned to the right and the airstrip was in front of us, much longer and wider than our old one, and it was earth, baked hard earth, on the right side of the strip were a row of bashers, 2 large ones, and at the end, two offices and a control tower, on stilts again, then a guards sleeping quarters, and a big tin shed, the hanger, the same size as the one we had before! Then a fuel storage basher, and then stretching down alongside the road, the aircraft parking strip. Behind the offices were some smaller bashers, showers, a rest room basher, just a small room with a few tables and chairs in it, and then the mess and cook houses. In front of the two large bashers, which were our quarters, was a concrete standing where all the vehicles parked. Now on the left hand side of the strip and up the slope was the Regiments camp, about 200 boot bashers I would think. Next to the airstrip is their medical centre and a NAAFI, hurrah! Behind all of the bashers was the road that we had just come along and which led into Seramban. Behind the flight offices were the ablutions, no not holes in the ground but a tin shed, half covered, with 4 compartments, or rather a long wooden box with 4 holes in it and a lid,one in each compartment, but no doors, and at the back of the ablutions were 4 trap doors, which could be lifted up and the drum inside lifted out and emptied, evidently around midnight every night a little old man would come along and lift out the drums, two at a time and he had along bamboo pole and with one on each end and the pole on his shoulders he walked or bounced down along the airstrip and vanished into the 'ulu' then out again with the empty ones and repeated it again, now as it was always dark and there would be guards on patrol, he had a lit candle stuck in his hat so that no one would shoot him!! true. I think he prayed that it wasn't windy! Quite often if you were on guard you could smell him before you saw him, he was called 'the s—t wallah'. I know I'm digressing but I have to write things down as I think and remember them. so, another thing with the opening flap behind the ablutions was, that before you sat down, you lifted the seat to check that there weren't any snakes inside, also no balls of paper or rags, because one trick we used to play was to soak some paper or rag in aviation fuel, wait until someone goes to the loo, then lift up the flap at the back, light the paper or rags and drop it into the dustbin and then run like hell, my eyes still run when I think of the results.

Right back to the beginning, after we had parked the trucks we grabbed our belongings and went and claimed our beds, inside the bashers, they were a bit bigger and apart from the lockers there was a small wooden locker with drawers in it, all of us RAF lads were in the same basher because of our shift work, Nanook and Peter had already sorted out our blankets, sheets, and mossy nets. The cooks were also busy getting to know their cookhouse lay out, there were two local boys working in the cookhouse with them so they had kept the fires going all day, so they were trying to scramble something up for dinner. The army lads had put the covers up on the trucks so our equipment can wait until the morning to be sorted out, all the kites which had flown down yesterday were all over the place and parked anywhere so 4 of us lads went down and sorted them out and bedded them down for the night, then a quick shower, lovely, real shower heads, instead of a tin with holes punched in it. Then a quick dinner, we didn't expect much, but spam fritters and mash went down a treat. Back in the bashers we were all sorting out our gear, anything that wanted washing, Nanook had taken away and off they went to find their relatives on their bikes. Also in the hut it, was all wired up with a plug point at each bed and in my locker, which someone had left, was a table lamp and a mat, it was beginning to look more like home every minute. Jim said did I fancy taking a stroll over to the NAAFI to check it out, Blondie and Paddy said yes also, and Wilf said he would come across as soon as he had cleared up and prepared for breakfast.

So we strolled across the strip and were about to climb up the steps to the entrance of the NAAFI when a voice called out for us to stop, we turns around and there stood an army Sergeant in full regalia, must have been a duty something or other, he said "where are your hats, and why aren't you wearing them", so we walked back down the steps and he saw our RAF insignia, so Blondie said straight away "we don't have to headgear when we are off duty" I think it took him back a bit, as he said "oh, yes, you RAF boys, carry on" Trust Blondie, I know that we are supposed to wear hats whether on or off duty, but as we were in O,Gs, we didn't class it as a uniform, I know it was really, but we got away with it, and did so for ever more, as there were no RAF Officers to check it out with. We were pulled up about it later on in our lot by a Staff Sergeant who joined our flight, but more about him later. The NAFFI was a bit barren and plain, just chairs and tables, but adequate I suppose, it was run by Chinese, but they had everything you wanted, a shop and food and such. All we wanted was a beer after that long day, so it was 'Anchors' all round. there was a few lads in there from the Hussars, and then a few of our army lads came in, and Joe and Jim had been collared by the same Sergeant and he made them go back and get their berets, and they called us jammy sods because we got away with it.

There was no flying the following day which gave us the chance to unpack everything and put it all away, and then sort out the hanger and the fuel store, it was strange that the aircraft and the hanger and the fuel store were right next to the road the other side of just a fence. It was a good job this area is practically free of terrorists as it would only take someone to walk up to the fence and lob a grenade over it and into the fuel store and it would probably blow up the whole camp, it was the same at Benta, right next to the jungle. Doesn't anybody think these things through. Once we had sorted everything out and everything in its place, a few changes started to happen in the flight, firstly we RAF lads inherited a 'Gofor' A young local lad, I say young but he was probably about 16. He came to work every morning wearing an old RAF shirt and a beret and his name was Chico, the same as our monkey, he used to sweep up and tidy around and clean all the tools and help out with just about everything, pushing the aircraft, refuelling, going to the NAAFI for coffees or cold drinks, he was really handy to have around, hence the name 'gofor'. we all gave him a dollar a week each and he was more than happy with that, he would be there first in the morning, and stay until flying had finished, helping to bed the aircraft down, and he loved it, if there was any night flying going on all his relatives would come and stand by the fence watching him, and it made him feel very important working for the RAF, so we tried to make it look as if he was one of us. ah!

Another big change was that one day an RAF sergeant appeared on the scene, a Sergeant Technician, and now he was to be with us permanently and in charge of all the RAF lads, which I think was a bit of a relief for old corporal skinny Gothard as no longer will he be responsible for us lot!

The Sergeants name was Hutson, a Scotsman, so of course he became Jock Hutson. He did say just call me Jock, but if any of the Officers are about, its 'Sarg'. He had been down in Singapore with his wife and son until he was sent up to, us and now had married quarters in Seremban, he would be around 35 to 40. He thought it a bit of a culture shock being here as compared to life in Singapore, so we filled him in with what life was like where we had just come from, so he appreciated what we had been through and promised to make our life here as nice as possible, aren't we creeps, and we did exaggerate things a little I must admit! He also had a good sense of humour and liked a drink, he bought his son up to the camp a few times and we all made a fuss of him, his name was Peter, aged 13, and he liked football and we had some good footballers in our lot and he used to play with them on the airstrip when we arranged matches, say with the Hussars or Ghurkas. In Singapore Jock was involved with the Canberra bombers, so he said he would have to learn from us, all about these little flying machines, also he took no truck from the army Officers, he was in charge of all the RAF personnel and the aircraft, so what he said goes! Jock was a great bloke, one of the lads, and we had a lot of respect for him. Once one of the army Officers came down for his plane, but it wasn't quite ready so he started to get a bit shirty, the Sarg took him to one side and you could hear him say to him, "These aircraft are mine, and my lads responsibility, and if one of my lads says it is not quite ready, then it's not quite ready, do you understand?" The Officer spluttered a little and said "well, yes Sergeant, it's just that I was in a bit of a hurry" "Then you'll have to wait then, won't you sir" said the Sarg, and walked away. Most of the Army Officers were o.k. but one or two didn't like the fact that they didn't have the same control over us as they did with the army lads.

We also inherited a cook from the last Flight, his name was Sharkey, nobody knew he was here until he turned up one morning, he had just come out of rehab as he was an alcoholic, so they thought it was best that he stayed where he was, mind you he was a bloody good cook, when sober! He used to come down to the cookhouse at 6am in the mornings to start the breakfasts carrying a large bottle of 'Anchor' for his breakfast! a character though. then another two RAF lads arrived, one called Johnnie, a radio technician, as all the aircraft were being fitted with new radios, and another lad called 'Scoop', well our nickname for him, as he was a photographer and came to fit camera's to some of the kites, he was a bit of a recluse as he had his own little hut around the back with all his equipment in, and it was noted that he made regular visits to town in the evenings, we reckoned he had a woman stashed away there, well he went so regular by taxi, that in the end he bought his own car, a Hillman Minx.

The biggest change came when dear old George, the army staff sergeant came to the end of his tour and was going home, he was popular with everyone and he had a great send off in the NAFFI, so good that the next morning when they piled him into the land rover to take him to the station, he was still asleep and also when they had to stay and lift him onto the train. He did write to us a few weeks later calling us all the names under the sun but wishing us all the very best, and that he would never forget his time with us, and we then remembered that all the time he was with us, he never charged anyone with any misdemeanours, and believe me there were lots!

The replacement for George, was another Staff Sergeant, an Irishman, as skinny as a rake, a real regimental man, always immaculate with creases in his uniform that could cut your fingers off. Everyone just looked at him when he appeared. his name was Killayley, I think that's how you spell it, mind you he was called lots of things as it turned out! his nickname became 'chuff chuff' everyone took an instant dislike to him, especially the army lads as they soon found out, and when he saw us RAF lads he didn't know what to make of us, but he saw that we had our own Sergeant so he would have to tread carefully. Robbie, the office clerk, he heard 'chuff chuff' say to the C.O. Captain Musters, when he was introduced to him, that he could see by just looking around that a lot of things needed changing and smartening up around this Flight! The C.O. said to just remember where these lads had just come from. So the reign of terror began, first for the army lads. they were now made to parade outside the bashers at 8-30 am every morning in full working uniforms, no more shirts and shorts and flip flops, everyone was given assignments, washing the vehicles, sweeping the parking lot, and line up all the vehicles to within an inch, barrack inspections every morning, also regular kit inspections, then anyone not on assignments he had them marching up and down the airstrip, but only after having to ask permission from our sergeant, which he obviously hated doing, so marching up and down the strip and marching along side of them calling out the time, one, two, one, two, chuff, chuff. hence his nickname, but our sarg soon put a stop to that, every time 'chuff chuff' came to ask permission to go onto the strip, he would say that aircraft would be taking off soon, or that some were expected to land, or that the RAF lads were going to walk up and down the strip picking up any bits and pieces or filling in any holes, so he was reduced to doing it on the vehicle park, I don't think our sarg liked him either! I think that made 'chuff chuff' want to get even with us RAF lads, especially as we were still going around with shorts and flip flops on. Evidently he went to the C.O. and as our spy Robbie heard, asked him, That as he had smartened up the army lads, the RAF people were spoiling it with the way they still dressed, I think the C.O. said do what you think best, but remember the conditions they have to work under, out in the open most of the time in 100 degrees and sapping humidity, but you can have a word with their Sergeant. So evidently he went to our Sarg and told him that the C.O. had asked him to smarten up his lads a bit, so sarg said o.k. go ahead. I think 'chuff chuff' thought he had got one over our sarg, he called us all together and asked us to go along with whatever 'chuff chuff' comes up with, so we said o,k, He came into our basher one evening when we were all there and said that starting next Monday those personnel who were on duty will parade in full working dress outside the bashers with the army personnel at 8-30 am, then march in order to your place of work, no one said anything. Next morning we told sarg about it and he was fuming, then he said that he would like us to go along with it as he had a plan. So the following Monday we dressed in our khaki working dress, shorts, jacket, long socks, and boots. and a beret, and lined up next to the army lads, they all thought it was funny. He came along, immaculate as ever, inspected the army lads, and then came to us, you could almost see the gleam in his eyes, he walked up and down picking up on this and that, telling Blondie he hadn't shaved properly, in fact he hadn't shaved at all, none of us had, we didn't when we were going to work, and he then then called us to attention, left turn and quick march, we tried to make a mess of it on purpose, and he shouted at us to stop, and he said that if we march like that he would have us on the airfield one evening, marching until we got it right, anyway we marched in a fashion past the C.O.s office, he was in there already and looked up when he saw us marching past, rather puzzled, until we were out of site, then ambled on down to the hanger, sarg was there waiting for us, so he said "I want you all to go back to your bashers now and change back into your usual working gear, as there is no way I'm going to let you do any Pre Flight Inspections on the aircraft dressed like that, oh! and take your time! So we did, we ambled back and changed into our usual gear, shorts and flip flops and jungle hats. and then strolled back, by this time it must have been around 9-30 and as we got to the hanger there were a couple of Officers who had come down ½ an hour ago to go flying, but there were no kites ready as no PFIs had been done, and sarg was explaining to them why, so back they went to the Flight office to see the C.O. I suppose. We just got on with doing the PFIs as usual, although a little bit slower than usual. Then we saw the C.O. coming down and go into the hanger to see sarg. Then after about ten minutes he came out again and went back to the office, Jock (sarg) came wandering down the strip to the aircraft to see us, and said "o,k, lads, everything back to normal, now get those kites ready to fly" So end of story, signed, sealed and delivered.

Anyway 'chuff chuff' seemed to leave us RAF lads alone after that so we don't know what the C.O. said to him, but we knew that at the slightest chance 'chuff chuff' would be looking at the slightest excuse to have a go at us. Some of the army lads said that they wanted a transfer to the RAF section! And one heavy night over in the NAFFI after a few 'Anchors' Lofty Steer said he was going to kill him, I think he would have done if he had been around knowing how stressed Lofty gets.

Another interesting character who appeared was Buster, the cabbie, he suddenly came into the basher one night and said to everyone" good evening gentlemen, my name is Buster and I am your personal taxi driver for the camp, very cheap taxi into Seramban or anywhere else, also if you are short of money at any time, come see me for a loan, only 2% commission, if you like girls,I take you to best places, very clean, or anything you want, absolutely anything, come see me first, I get for you" he was a Sikh, a big fat jolly fellow, always smiling, you couldn't help but like him. We did use him quite a lot to get into Seremban, and he was cheap compared to other taxis, and he gave us his home number to ring if we ever wanted him, if he wasn't there his wife took any messages, and she spoke beautiful English also he just about knew everyone, as when he was driving he was always waving to people. Once Blondie and I decided we wanted some civvy clothes, as we heard that you could get a suit made really cheap in town, so we asked Buster and he said of course mem sahb, I have a cousin tailor in town, very good man, will do you a good deal, or I kill him. so he took us to this little tailors shop and said that we were his very good RAF friends and they are looking for suits, so he showed us some materials, one was a very nice black light weight cloth, Blondie liked it as well, so he measured us up and we looked at some styles and picked one, and we asked how much, and he told us, which was amazingly cheap, and we were just about to say yes, when Buster said to him," I thought I told you they are my very good friends, so you can do much better than that" the tailor thought for a minute and then said another figure, which was amazingly another third off. and buster said "that's much better" so we ordered them and two days later we went back for a fitting, and they were perfect, in fact we bought shirts and ties to go with them, we left them there to be pressed up properly. Next day Buster turned up in the basher with them, so we gave him the money to pay the tailor.

After a couple of months things settled down into a routine, I liked Seremban as it was more civilized and all told we had a pretty easy life really, I know we still did guard duties but not so regular as at Benta as there was more bods on the camp now, and it wasn't so intense as before, you just wandered around, walked down the airstrip and tried not to be tempted to shoot at that little candle that kept bobbing along around midnight, (the s---t wallah) then perhaps sit in one of the aircraft for a while, and there was usually someone around to chat to until about midnight, also as you went by the guardroom which was down by the hanger, you could always grab a cuppa. Then around 6am if you were on that shift you could go into the cookhouse and fire up the boiler fires for the cooks. We had the same arrangements as at our last place that when you finished guard duty, grab a mug of tea from the cooks and then go down to the hanger, unlock and then start to do the PFIs on the aircraft, then when the day lads came on, back to the basher, a quick shower and then kip until lunchtime, so it wasn't so bad.

Once, Paddy, Don, Blondie and me decided we wanted to learn to drive, so we arranged with Lofty to borrow one of the land rovers when 'chuff chuff' wasn't around and he would teach us by driving up and down the airstrip, as long as there was no flying which was usually Friday and Saturdays, and after a few lessons we became quite proficient, and as nobody needed any licences and all that, our sarg (jock) commandeered one of the land rovers strictly for RAF use, so now we had our own transport which was very handy for him as he could now use it to go back and forth from home, also it was handy for us for if it was monsoon time we could use it to and from the basher to the hanger, saved us getting soaked!

Now that we were at Seramban we were getting a lot more flying visitors, especially choppers. Some would drop in just for refuelling, or dropping off patrols that had been in the jungle. We once had 3 choppers land at once that had just collected a squad of S.A.S. lads that had been out on patrol in the 'ulu' for 3 weeks, following a gang of terrorists, then finally caught up with them and as usual eliminated them, but they looked terrible after 3weeks in the 'ulu' their clothes were literally rotted off them and they were filthy and haggard, their Regiment must have known that they were being airlifted into us as about an hour before they landed a truck pulled into our part of the camp and it had bought a change of clothes for them, so we took them to our showers and gave them our stuff and towels and shaving things, then they went into the basher next door,the rest room which was of course empty except for the tables and chairs and they changed into their clean gear, also the cooks had rallied round and got a meal for them, the Officer in charge of them had been offered to go up to the Officers mess, but he said he would rather stay with his men, before they went into showers they put their weapons in the empty room, and it was incredible the arsenal that they carried with them whist out on patrol, it seemed each man had his own personal choice as what to take, most had Sten guns, a few Bren guns, some had sawn off shot guns, best weapon in the jungle because of the spread shot, it was either slung on your back or in a special pocket made for it, everyone had their own choice of knife, the favourite being the Gurkha kukri, also some had pistols, they certainly meant business when out on patrol, and strangely enough most of them were Scots. It was said that if an army chap had committed a crime and was due to be Court Marshalled, and go to a Military prison for a long time, he was offered the choice to join the S.A.S. I don't know if that was true or not and whether it only appertained to Malaya. Also the lorry had bought a large glass flagon of brandy which they kept having a tot of, and of course offered to us as well! Incidentally one of the things our pilots had to do sometimes was to drop supplies to patrols that were out in the 'ulu' for long periods. after they had been fed and watered they made their way back to the choppers after lots of handshakes and thanks all round, and off they went back to their Regiment and strangely enough, no one knew where it was!

Just after they had gone, two more helicopters dropped in, Sikorski 55s, and we were told to land them at the bottom of the strip where it was quiet, also at the same time two large black vans drove into the camp and went down to the bottom of the airfield as well. When the rotors had stopped, the doors of the choppers opened and the crew started pushing bodies out onto the airstrip and the blokes in the vans started loading them into the vans, there were about 15 to 20 of them, they were obviously the C.T,s that the S.A.S. had eliminated, the state of some of them was pretty gruesome and the stench made you reach, we helped them to load them and then the choppers took off, we did notice they flew with the doors open to get rid of the stench. I know the smell seemed to linger and you just wanted to have a good shower. I know it put me off my dinner. The bodies were taken to the hospital morgue in Seramban and photos of their faces were taken to try and identify them, well, those that had faces left as shot guns can make a bit of a mess, and also that they were all Chinese.

Another nasty incident occurred at our field. It was that our 'tower' had received a message from a chopper that it was going to land on our strip to pick up a local doctor and fly him out to a patrol that had been involved in a fire fight with some C.T.s and that a couple of our lads had been injured and needed attention, the chopper landed and the doctor was waiting and off they went. About 2 hours later the chopper landed with the wounded men but sadly also with the body of the doctor. Evidently he had treated the wounded lads and had said he wanted them back at the hospital, they loaded the men aboard the chopper, but the doctor walked around the back of the chopper to get aboard and walked straight into the rear rotor blades, which split his head in two and took off one of his arms, tragic, when the chopper arrived we carried his body to the ambulance and one of the chopper crew gave me a bag which contained his arm. At his funeral later there was a large military presence and a guard of honour.

Another thing that springs to mind is that about 20 miles from our camp was a Regiment of Gurkha's and as I've said sometimes the pilots had to drop supplies to the patrols that were out there in the 'ulu, and we used to drop quite a few to the Gurkha patrols as they seemed to stay out there the longest, and us RAF lads had to package up the supplies and fix small parachutes to them and we would put a little note in them saying 'Enjoy, from the lads at 1914 flight' anyway one day we received an invitation to come and spend a day with them as a little thank you. So 8 of our lads, 4 RAF and 4 army and an officer, Captain Alum, my flying mate, went one Sunday to their camp, and boy were we treated like Royalty, Captain Alum went off with the Officers, who were all English in those days and we were escorted around the camp and everyone was coming up and shaking our hands, they are such warm and polite people, but ferocious fighters. We went into their version of a NAFFI, and there was food laid out, so we sat down and were waited on, a drink was poured for us, I don't know what it was, some sort of fermented stuff, but you could taste honey in it, they all stood and toasted us, so we stood and toasted them, then they bought the food, a bit spicy and hot, but not too bad, then they played music and some dancers came on, and we were invited to try, but of course made a pigs ear of it, much to their amusement, then they gave an exhibition of wrestling, that we declined to take part in, then we were taken outside to watch a football match on their parade ground, they sat us in arm chairs with sun shades and the drinks kept coming, we still didn't know what was in it was but it was going down nicely with ice and fruit in it. Finally it was time to go, and it seemed as if the whole Regiment came to wave goodbye, we were a bit merry and so was Captain Alum, but what an amazing day and I have always, and always will have a soft spot for the gurkhas.

Another incident confirming the allegiance of the gurkhas to the British, also their respect and loyalty to their British Officers happened not so long after our visit to their camp. Apparently their CommandING Officer was returning to their camp one afternoon in his car with his driver and two armed escorts, when they were ambushed by terrorists, their car was blown up and all were shot in it. When the news of the killings got back to the camp, every gurkha in the camp immediately took up arms, and I mean every gurkha, office lads, cooks, everyone, they organised themselves into patrols of about 20, jumped into trucks and drove down to where the ambush had taken place, and then spread each patrol out along the road about ½ mile apart and then just vanished into the jungle to try and track down the terrorists, it all happened so quickly that even the Officers didn't know what had happened, and the troops were gone before they could stop them. By this time the terrorists had a head start on the gurkha's of about 4 hrs, but they were expert jungle fighters and they hadn't taken any radios with them so no one could get in touch with them, and order them to return, and it was now dark. Each patrol evidently had walkie talkies with them so they could keep in touch with each other. It was found that there were 6 patrols out there, all moving in a line abreast about 500 yards apart, so they were covering quite an area. We found out about all this at first light next morning, when all of a sudden 4 helicopters landed on our strip to evidently pick up some of the Gurkha Officers who were going to fly low over the 'ulu' with loud megaphones to try to persuade them to return to camp, but one of the Officers said it was probably a waste of time as they loved their C.O. so much, and they won't stop until they have caught up with the C.T.s.

So you can guess what the outcome was to this little story. After a day and a half of pursuit they finally caught up with the C.T.s and surrounded them, there were around 30 to 40 of them, and they annihilated them, they then started to make their way back to the road of course carrying their personnel trophies, which I won't describe! And evidently the bodies weren't worth bringing out. When they reached the road they all lined up in ranks, and smartly proceeded to march back to their camp, the trucks had come to pick them up but they prefer to march back, which was a good 6 miles, and after nearly 2 days in the 'ulu' without any supplies or food! Now every one of those men could have faced a Court Marshal for disobeying direct orders which were broadcast to them from the choppers, but they said to the Officers that they didn't hear anything as the jungle was so thick! One of their Officers said" How the hell can you discipline men like that". They did though everyone was stopped 2 days pay, fair enough!

When I said our trip to the Gurkha camp was a little thank you from them for the supply drops, we also did drops to other regiments who were out on patrol's, We packed the supplies mostly in the empty fuel cans which were aluminium about 18 inches high and a foot square, so they were fairly strong, then we would bind them around with rope and fix a small parachute with a rip cord on it which was to be placed on a hook on the frame of the door by the pilot, which was opposite the pilot on the left hand side, the door was removed of course, then the container was placed by the door inside, so when the drop zone was reached he had to lean over and place the cord over the hook and then lift the container onto the edge of the door and then push it out whilst still flying the plane, sometimes the cord would fly off the hook, so sometimes the pilots would just hold the ripcord, and the supplies would just crash into the tree tops, perhaps if they were dry goods, they may have been retrievable, but not wet goods, and especially the 'extra special' wet goods we sometimes dropped to the S.A.S. which came to us in a glass flagon marked 'gun oil' yeh! The S.A.S. did say to us when they were here, that a lot of the time the 'gun oil' shattered as the chute didn't deploy correctly, so Jim and I decided that it was a crappy system so we got out the drawing board, and we came up with a release hook which we made in the workshop, firstly we made a wooden platform which fitted just inside the passenger door, level with the opening, big enough to stand 2 or 3 containers, so all they to do was push the container out without having to lift it onto the ledge, then we fitted the new hook to the door frame, then on the end of the rip cords we attached another length of cord which wasn't as strong as the rip cord so that once the chute had been deployed the weight of the container would snap the weaker cord, the rip cord itself had to be strong enough to release the chute but not so weak that it snapped before doing so. We ourselves did several drop trials off the top of the fuel store until we found the right type of cord, Then Captain Alum did some drops over the airstrip until, we got it working perfectly every time. We let Jim submit the ides to H.Q. and they sent it out to all the other Flights. Then bugger me, Jim was awarded the M.D. Mentioned In Dispatches, poor old sarg and me, zilch! but it cost Jim a few beers for me and the sarg.

The way that we found out about the 'gun oil' thing was that we received some stores in to be dropped to the S.A,S, so we started to repack them into the tin containers and one of the items was this thick glass flagon which was labelled 'gun oil ' it must have contained about 5 pints, and we thought at the time, that's a lot of oil to keep your guns clean, they must be very conscientious about the cleanliness of their weapons, then we noticed the top was a bit loose so I took it off to make sure,and blimey,the smell, it might have been 'gun oil' but it smelled suspiciously of Brandy! And as they had already complained to someone about losing a lot of 'gun oil' because of the packaging and it being smashed, we decided to package it correctly, we had some sheets of foam rubber so we packed it in the container with as much foam as possible and then wrapped it around the outside, inside we put a little note. "Hand packed by the 1914 distillery Flight, Enjoy" we later received a message back saying "thanks lads, owe you"

Some Saturdays if there was no flying we would change into our civvies, and probably Me, Blondie, Jim, Paddy, Don, and Wilf, and we would get Buster to take us into Seremban around noon to our favourite restaurant which had a covered veranda overlooking the street. We would order a bottle of Gin, tonic water and a bowl of limes, and ice, then we would sit there relaxing and watching the world go by, then around 5, we would order a meal, always a curry, not Indian, but either Malaysian or Cantonese, I think one of them was called 'Nasi Goring' or something, I know it was no 11 on the menu, so after drinking G&Ts all afternoon and then a good curry, we would then decide to go further into town and visit some of the bars and perhaps a dance hall. There would be other troops in town, probably from the 11th Hussars at our camp. Some of the bars were where the Planters used to drink, and it was interesting to talk to them about their lives on the Plantations, and they nearly always bought you a drink as they were grateful for the security that the forces gave them. then after a few 'Anchors' we might head for the dance halls. now the dance halls were a bit wierd, they looked more like a skating rink a big circle or oblong, open at the sides and all the women sat on one side and all the men on the other, so if you fancied one of the girls and you wanted to dance, you went to the little office and bought a book of tickets, for about $5 then go over to the girl and give her one of the tickets and she would dance with you, they were hostesses as you would have guessed, every ticket they got, they handed them in at the end of the evening and received a small sum for each ticket. mind you some were pretty ugly so I reckon they came just to listen to the music!

So after a while we would wend our way back to one of the bars, after probably fixing up either Paddy or Wilf with one of the hostesses,and probably the ugliest, from there on they are on their own. Once when we were on our way back to the bars, we passed a bar where all the trishaw owners drink, and outside were all these trishaws, so silently Don and I and Jim and Blondie wheeled a couple of them away. I sat in the back and Don did the pedalling, Blondie sat in his and Paddy pedalled and we decided to have a race, it was about ½ a mile to the bars and downhill, the streets were hard baked earth and of course down one side were these deep monsoon drains lined with concrete, anyway we started off and were going at a fair lick and it seemed as if loads of people were watching us, we were having great fun, whooping and shouting, we were slightly inebriated, did I say slightly! Anyway about halfway down the slope we heard some shouting and yelling and behind us were the trishaw owners chasing us, so we tried to put a spurt on, but unfortunately Paddy hit a pothole and veered towards the monsoon drain, he jumped off but poor old Blondie went straight down into the drain. Don and I stopped and helped Paddy to drag him out of it, I think it was only because he was smashed out of his brains that he didn't do some serious damage to the bike, no not really, but he was covered in mud so we ran into the nearest bar, shoved him into the toilets to try and clean himself up a bit whilst we sat down at a table as is if we had been there all night, shortly after, two Malay police and an M.P, came in and looked around, Blondie was still in the toilet, thank goodness, and we had got a pack of playing cards and it looked as if we had been there all evening. The police walked around, probably looking for 4 blokes, we hoped and prayed Blondie wouldn't come out of the toilet just yet, but he didn't. Then they left, thank god. He eventually came out and he still looked a mess, and stank to high heaven, but apart from a cut on his elbow he was o.k. As he walked through the bar everybody looked at him, "Had a good night mate" was one remark, I daren't say some of the others! Just then Buster came in and he said he had seen it all, and he thought we were all stark raving mad, and now would be a good time to return to camp as the trishaw blokes were still looking around, they didn't know who they were looking for, just 4 men, so we went out of the back door where he had parked his taxi and back to camp. We threw Blondie into the showers still in his clothes, so he had to walk back to the basher naked. It's a good job that none of the guards didn't see him, sadly no one had a flash camera!

After two or three months here at Seramban we got ourselves organised on the sporting side, we formed a football team, which was pretty good I must say, especially Don and Jim the two strikers. Jim was a naturally skilled player and Don was very fast, also one of the army blokes was a brilliant goal keeper.(I know it's a shame but he was as dim as a Toc H Lamp) I myself didn't play very often, only if they were short. Our reputation got around, so we would play a team from the Hussars and we always beat them playing on the airstrip, some of the local teams from Seramban would invite us to play them on their Padang (playing field) which was in the centre of the town, and there used to be quite a crowd gather, to watch, then we would return the invitation, and they seemed fascinated to be so close to the aircraft. We also formed a hockey team, which I enjoyed playing, and some of the Officers played too. Once again we got a reputation for the hockey as well and again played in Seramban, as it was one of their national sports (I think) as well as badminton, anyway we managed to hold our own, anyway it was nice to get away from the camp sometimes and be entertained by other teams, when we played in town it was on grass, but when we had visiting teams they had to get used to playing on hard baked earth which was like concrete, so if you wacked a hard hockey ball on that surface it really travelled, so there were quite a few injuries sustained. Once there was a small unit of Indians staying at the Gurkha camp, they were Sikh's, turbans, beards, the lot, about 50 in all, good jungle fighters though, as I've said they were Sikhs not Pakistanis, they were both called Indians, as there was no partition in those days. The Sikhs were of course known for their hockey prowess as it was a national sport, so they had heard about our hockey team, so they asked us if we would like a game down on the Padang in town, foolishly our Officers said yes, so we did, and it was embarrassing as quite a large crowd turned up to watch, also all the Gurkhas came to watch as well. well! They completely annihilated us, our shins were black and blue, but they were great lads and we all finished up back at the Gurkha camp for refreshments, Whilst still on the subject of sports, once a year our squadron held a sports competition between all the flights, 6 in all, down at the Squadron H.Q. in Kuala Lumpur. It was held over a 5 day weekend, so each flight would pick a team to represent them in football, hockey, badminton, swimming, and rifle shooting, and tug of war, so presumably about 10 from each flight would take part. We were told to take our best uniforms with us as there would be a Squadron Commanding Officers parade at the end. Also civvy gear for the evenings, so we picked 6 of us RAF lads, plus our Sarg, and we took 6 of the army lads, 2 extra! So one Thursday morning we piled into a couple of trucks and drove up to K.L. which was only a couple of hours away, we only took the scout car as escort as we would be going through an area which was now designated as near enough a 'white' zone (safe) we were all armed of course. I was to represent the Flight in the shooting competition as I had a 'marks mans' badge, a bit rusty though I bet. Also I was in the swimming and hockey.

All in all I think it was just one big excuse for all the lads in the Flights to get together and have one big p---s up. it was well organised and our flight didn't do too bad, we came second overall, the winners of course were the H.Q. Flight, simply because they had everything going for them, a swimming pool next door, football pitches, a rifle range at the end of the strip and all the amenities to practise. If a shot was heard in our camp, the whole camp, plus the hussars would be on 'Red Alert' so I couldn't practise anywhere. We won the football, second in hockey, second in swimming, although I won my two races, won the tug of war, lost the badminton, but proud to say I beat the crap out of them in the rifle and Bren gun shoot out, so not so rusty after all. We had some good nights in their NAFFI though, we weren't allowed out of camp as probably too many would go AWOL, (absent without leave) we still think we were the smartest on the parade ground for the march past on the final day, anyway our sarg and our C.O. said they were proud of us.

One day a strange and completely out of the blue thing happened, I received a letter from Margaret! it was now 18 months since I had left RAF Feltwell in Norfolk and when Margaret was posted to Germany, and of course I was waiting for her to send me her new address when she knew where she was going to be permanently stationed, but of course she didn't know that just 2 weeks after she left I was sent on embarkation leave and then abroad, so she thought I was still at Feltwell, in her letter she said that she was going to be moved to another camp and that she would send me her permanent address as soon as she knew what it was. Well her letter had evidently been chasing me all over the world for the past 18 months, according to the post marks on it, there were two in London, one in Egypt, one in Korea, Singapore, and K.L. it was a lovely letter and of course I had no address to reply to it, and obviously she had written to me again with her new address, which I never did receive, so, as she never heard from me in reply to her letters, she probably surmised that things were over between us, I know that I did have her Mothers address once but in all the moving around I must have misplaced it. It was such a shame, and I must admit it took me a few days to get over it, especially as I felt so helpless as I couldn't do anything about it. I always had her picture in my locker, and I vowed that when I got out of this mob I was going to try and find her and explain everything

The time now was coming up to Xmas 1953 and we decided that the basher next the showers, the rest room, was not being used for anything in particular, there were tables and chairs in there, and the only time it was used was if you wanted some quiet say to, write a letter or read. So we asked Captain Musters, the C.O. if we could turn it into a look alike English pub for Xmas, and he said yes, it was a good idea. So all the lads with varying skills set about doing so. We built a bar in one corner with imitation beer pumps and at the back, a row of optics for the spirits that we conned from the NAAFI, we put a dartboard on one wall and someone made a table skittle board, we decorated everywhere with festive things and lights, which buster obtained for us, and all in all it looked pretty good. All the officers said it was good and looked really authentic and they hoped that they would receive invitations to join in with the Xmas celebrations. Now up 4 weeks before Xmas everyone gave $5 a week towards some booze, even the Officers gave us $100 towards it, so we had quite a good kitty. Buster said he had contacts in town that would be willing to sell us all the beers and wine and spirits at trade prices as a gesture of goodwill to the British troops, great. I forgot to say also that a couple of lads made an imitation stone fireplace with a grating and imitation coal fire effect that flickered it looked really good.

So Xmas eve 1953 arrived, flying had been suspended except for emergencies and tonight was the official opening of the '1914 Flight Bar' all the officers had been invited, but evening dress was stipulated for the officers, not jackets, and all O.Rs. (other ranks) smart casual. The cooks had whipped up a buffet, all the optics were full, and all the bottles of Anchor were in tubs of ice, Johnnie the radio chap had fixed up a gram so there was nice Xmas background music playing, so after dinner we walked around to the door of the 'bar', the C.O. was there with his fellow officers, and he gave a little speech and so did our Sarg, Sergeant 'chuff chuff' was pushed to the background. Then the 'Fight Bar' was declared officially open and running. Lofty and Joe were serving behind the bar and what a great night it was, as far as I can remember. I've said this before that we were just one big family, we lived and worked together so we made the best of it, there were very few arguments or animosity, except 'chuff chuff', we did consider not inviting him, but he would have only got his revenge on the army lads, especially Lofty, who had threatened to kill him, well nobody liked him actually, and perhaps after a few beers even less, but if it happens it happens, but we did keep our eye on Lofty in case he relapsed into one of his dark moods.

The evening progressed swimmingly, the talk got louder and louder as the beer went down and down, there were some good sing songs, you could see the occasional quick exit to throw up, but back in again to replace the loss! Ted heath stood on the table with his trouser around his ankles and gave his rendition of "The day war broke out, my missus said to me" a fag in one hand and a pint in the other, hilarious. a couple of the 11th Hussars Officers poked their noses around the door wandering what all the noise and music and hilarity was, they were of course invited in, I reckon our officers told them about our famous booze ups and told them to pop in if they fancied a beer, but to remember nobody pulls any rank in our do's, just enjoy the way 1914 Flight celebrate things. Also if you behave yourselves, you may be invited back to celebrate New Year. The Hussar's Officers plus another couple showed up, couldn't believe what we had done to the basher also the amount of booze we had! I can remember the first few hours fairly clearly, after that a bit of a blank, I know that I woke next morning actually in my pit, so I couldn't have been that bad, until they told me that Jim and Don had found me at 3 am standing in the showers, naked, singing my head off, and then asking what time breakfast was, mind you they were as bad as me, as evidently they stripped off as well and joined me in the showers and we had a sing song ! No one can recall what happened next as when I awoke, Jim and Don were still asleep in their pits, with two piles of wet clothes at the end of their beds, but mine were neatly folded on my cabinet, so I must have come back to our basher, undressed and then wandered, naked down to the showers, will have to go into rehab after New Year and dry out a bit! Nanook came in and took the lads wet clothes and also mine as they were a bit beer stained, to get them washed and back for the evening. they found Blondie asleep in the back of one of the trucks, and the cooks, Wilf and Sharkey asleep on the tables in the mess, as they wanted to be as near to the cookhouse as possible, because they were going to prepare Xmas day breakfast, with the help of the two local lads who already had the stoves going and the water boiling, so the pair of them staggered into the cookhouse and after Sharky had had his bottle of 'Anchor' they set about breakfast with the help of Ron, no one knows where he slept.

So today was Xmas Day 1954 at Seramban, Malaya, So with sore heads, and when everyone had surfaced, we made our way to the mess and of course the cooks had come up trumps again, the mess looked great, table cloths, napkins, cutlery, glasses all laid out. Breakfast started off with fresh orange juice, then grapefruit, a full English, toast and marmalade. I think everyone felt a bit better after that. After breakfast we all went down to the 'bar' to clear it up and get it ready for the evening. The place didn't look too bad as we reckon Nanook and his son had been in and done a bit beforehand, as all the glasses had been washed and the empty bottles stacked around the back, how the hell did we manage to drink that amount, the tables all wiped and clean cloth's on them. One good thing about the empty bottles was that when you bought a bottle of beer in the NAAFI they charged you a deposit in case you took it away, I think it was about 20 or 30 cents, now we know we didn't get the beer that we drank last night from the NAAFI, but if we kept it quiet, we could take a few at a time over to the NAAFI, and have some cheap beer for quite a time! It did remind me of when I was a kid and we used to climb over the wall at the back of the outdoor beer place, pinch the empties out of the crates and then take them around to the front and get the deposit money on them!

Anyway we refilled the tubs with water and ice, Buster had been to the ice factory and bought back a block of ice which we broke up. As it was nearly lunch we decided to open up the bar, just a couple before Xmas lunch, we sent some into the cooks, All of the officers came in as well, dressed in 'Mufty' they sat with us and said what a good night it was last night, evidently a jeep was sent down to ferry them back to their quarters as some of them were incapable of walking. They had come down this morning and as with tradition, they were going to wait on our tables at Xmas lunch, which they did admirably, after a few Gin and Tonics! The lunch itself was absolutely heroic, how the cooks did it we don't know, there was everything a Xmas lunch should have, Turkey, roast beef, (probably shit buffalo) all the veggies, Yorkshire pudding, stuffing, Xmas pudding and custard, and afterwards coffee and cheese and biscuits and a glass of port, very civilized, the Officers said that they wished they could have had lunch with us but they had to go to the Hussars mess on invitation. The cooks were given a standing ovation and told not to bother with a meal later as the time was getting on, so they said they would make up some sandwiches, put them in the cool box and then put them out in the bar later in the evening, so that they could join in the festivities with the rest of us. I think most of us were so full up, a couple of hours kip was called for so as to charge the batteries up for the evening session!

So around 6 pm a quick shower, our clothes were returned clean and pressed, so back down to the bar for another session, a sing song with Xmas carols, another well deserved toast to the cooks. Nanook and his son Peter, Buster and the kitchen lads, and of course our hanger lad Chico, someone said that they had asked the s---t wallah to come, the old boy with a candle stuck in his hat who emptied the 'thunder boxes' at 2 am every morning. I don't think he came as you would have smelt his presence!! So the same thing happened Boxing Day. It's going to be good to get back to work in the morning for a rest! Not really, as back to the old routine and we had quite a busy period for the next few weeks, a lot of flying at all hours, some Major services to be done on the aircraft, a lot of terrorist activity going on in surrounding areas, but the forces were gradually getting the upper hand as another couple of regions were declared 'white'.

New Years Eve passed in the traditional fashion as expected of 1914 A.O.P. Flight, another couple of hazy days, and we finally drank all the booze, but as I said the empties kept us in beer for a while and the NAAFI never did suspect anything. so here we were in 1955, only 6 months left before I'm home in Blighty and demobbed, in fact a lot of the lads are due for demob, most of us RAF lads anyway and quite a few of the army lads as well. In our lot there's Jim, Blondie, Paddy, Don, Wilf, Johnny, skinny Gothard, and the sarge finishes his tour this year, so over the next few months there's going to be quite an influx of 'whiteys' or 'snowdrops' as they are called, because of their colour, so there's going to be a lot of tutoring to be done to try and mould them into our ways and to keep the traditions of 1914 Flight going !!!

At the beginning of February I was told that I had been selected to go for 2 weeks R& R (rest and recuperation) up at the camp at Frazers Hill. Evidently if you had been stationed for more than a year in what was termed as the 'Low country' and to refresh your lungs from the heat and humidity of the jungle, you were actually ordered to go to Frazers Hill for two weeks rehab. The army lads were the same but there camp was called 'Cameron Highlands' in the Cameroons. The camps are rest centres up in the mountains and because of the heights the air is fresh and more like Springtime back home. I was told to pack my O.G.s and also civvys. I had no idea where the place was and so did no one else, perhaps the place was kept a secret. Anyway Captain Allum flew me to an airstrip, I know not where, and said he would pick me up in two weeks time, and waiting for me was a land rover and also another RAF lad, an LAC. We set off and started to climb up and up on a very tiny track, the driver, another RAF lad filled us in a bit about the camp, he said that as we get higher we will go through a cloud bank for a while and you will feel it getting colder and colder and in fact you will probably start shivering as your body is not acclimatised to these temperatures so there's a couple of blankets to put around your shoulders, and he was right, a little while ago we were sweating in temperatures of 80 and 90 degrees and humidity about 90% and now we were starting to shiver, a strange sensation. After a while we broke out of the clouds and it was fine and sunny. about an hour and a half had passed and we were now in the mountains, not what you would call mountains, but high enough for a dramatic change in temperatures, he said don't worry about it as your body will get used to it in a couple of days. He was stationed here and it had the opposite effect on him when he goes down to pick anyone up.

We finally arrived at the camp. well I say camp, it was situated on a plateau and it reminded us of a Swiss sky resort, there was one large wooden timber place surrounded by small wooden chalets, there were tennis courts, six a side football enclosure, indoor badminton courts, the big timbered building looked like a hotel. We stopped outside it and told to go and check in at the reception, just like a hotel. We were still cold but when we walked into the reception it was lovely and warm, it was all carpeted and on one side a large lounge with armchairs and settees, and what staggered me was a large open fire burning! There was a WRAF at the desk and she checked us in and gave us our room keys, a room all to myself, this was great, she said there are not many here at the moment so it's fairly quiet so you will be staying in the Hotel and not in the chalets. She gave us a list of meal times and an information leaflet about the place, so we went and found our rooms. Mine was a nice size with toilet and shower plenty of cupboard space, it was like 7th heaven and I could definitely get used to this, and the WRAF wasn't bad looking also. I think I'll ask for a posting! Although not much use for an aircraft fitter up here though, although there was a chopper landing pad I noticed. Dinner was at 6pm, buffet style, also one rule was that you wore civvy's all the while, except when you go out on jungle treks, we'll find out what that's all about later. There was a small shop and a bar, a real bar, and not bottled beer, real beer on hand pumps, as I've said, it was just like a hotel.

The WRAF girl was right about it being quiet at the moment, as there were only about 15 blokes here as there is usually around 50 or 60. Also there were all ranks here so you couldn't tell who was who as everyone was out of uniform but everyone seemed to be o.k. After dinner,which wasn't bad, we retired to the bar, there was another room off the bar with 2 snooker tables and a table tennis table in it, most went in to play snooker, but 5 or 5 of us just sat and had a drink and chatted and got to know each other, the lad I came up with, Tim, had been stationed in Malaya for just 12 months and was stationed at Keluang, I think, he was an electrician and worked on Pioneers, the short take off and landing kites, very good on 'ulu' landing strips. after a couple of beers I started to feel very tired and as it had been a long day, I decided to call it a day, but first I thought I'd take a look outside as it wasn't quite dark yet, but when you went outside the cold hit you because you had been sitting in a warm room with an open fire burning and then when going outside you felt it. I don't know exactly how high we were but you could see all the hills and the valleys below you and just jungle for as far as the eye could see. I was glad to get back inside in the warm and also my room was nice and warm as it had hot water pipes running through it.

The next couple of days we gradually got acclimatised, so there was no need to walk around with thick sweaters on. It felt just like an English summer and it was a change from being wringing wet with sweat for most of the day, also sleeping at night was much easier as the mossy's were only little things, so no mossy nets, plus you had a blanket in case it got chilly during the night. Tim and I played a few games of tennis and as it was so quiet in the evenings, I and most of the others seemed to start catching up with the mail back home, or just reading in the comfortable lounge with a couple of beers. On the 3rd evening we were told that next morning after breakfast we were going on a jungle trek, so after breakfast change into your O.Gs as we would be out most of the day. Basically it was to show those who had never been into the jungle before what it was like, so after breakfast we all assembled outside the' hotel.' It was strange that some of the lads had never worn O.G.s or jungle boots before, but I suppose there was no need for them if you were stationed on a proper RAF Station. Tim said he had never worn them before as well, and you could see it, as they were all still brand new, and you certainly could see the difference to mine, as mine were well worn by now. I also had to show a couple of blokes how to lace up their boots. We all piled into a couple of trucks and began to descend down the mountain, then just as we had passed through the mist barrier we stopped and you could feel the heat beginning to take hold. I had told Tim to make sure his water bottle was filled to the top.

Waiting at the stop was our guide, an army Sergeant, and a couple of the obviously native trackers, as they wore only loin cloths, but they did have rifles instead of blow pipes. As we set of the sergeant began pointing out various things, plants, insects, the different types of trees and bush, some trees can grow as tall as 200 ft. The further we went in the thicker the undergrowth became, the trackers up front were now hacking their way through, although this was probably a well worn out trail for us, but the undergrowth can grow back practically overnight, after about an hour we had a short break as everyone was beginning to sweat with the heat and humidity and were advised to drink as much as possible as we can refill our water bottles when we stop for lunch in about one and a half hours time. so off we went again, the trackers did tell us all to stop once and crouch down and be quiet, but the Sergeant said it was probably just animals moving through, perhaps Elephants, you could hear noises, but of course not see anything, To prove just how thick the 'ulu' can be, we went through one particular section where you could only just squeeze through a bit at a time and as I did someone spoke to me, I stopped and looked around but couldn't see anything, and then all of a sudden a hand grabbed my shoulder, it frightened me to death, it was the Sergeant and he standing only a yard from me and I couldn't see him! So It shows just how thick the jungle can be and how easy it is for ambushes.

We finally stopped for some lunch at a clearing where there was a small water fall into a pool, the water was crystal clear and cold and we were told that it was o.k. to drink so to fill the water bottles for the return trip, we all had a small back pack with sandwiches in. The break was very welcome and the water tasted delicious. The sergeant asked if everyone was o.k. some of them were suffering a little bit, but it was just the heat and humidity so everyone was told to drink as much water as possible now, refill your bottles, wet your sweat rags that you wore around your necks in the nice cool water and wipe yourself down and you will feel better. Whilst we had our break I noticed the two trackers weren't with us, I asked the Sergeant and he said they would be out there somewhere probably eating things we know nothing about plus wild fruits, anyway they were back when we were ready to go, on the way back we were once again told by the trackers to stop and be quiet. Then the sergeant told us to creep forward very quietly to see just what we had stopped for, the trackers beckoned us in one at a time to where they stood and pointed to the ground about 5 yards away and you could hear a sort of hissing and rustling sound and there on the ground was a huge column of ants, now I had seen this before and as I said then, the column was about a yard wide and moving quickly, there must have been millions of them, and big ones at that. The Sergeant said we must go back before they sense us, as they will attack. The trackers had gone to try and find a way around them, he then said to make sure none of them had crawled onto your boots or trousers as you will soon find out if they have found a way into your clothes as the bite they give is agony, the acid bite, and they do take a chunk of flesh as well!, So at the double out of there.

By the time we had arrived back at the road where the trucks were waiting for us, everyone looked pretty knackered. I myself knew what to expect as I'd been into the 'ulu' a couple of times before, but some of the lads had found it pretty hard going, much worse than they had expected they said. Going back up to camp we experienced everything in reverse as to when we came down, and as our clothes were ringing wet with sweat, going back through the mist barrier, everyone started to feel very cold and as it was late afternoon and the sun was low it wasn't quite as warm, but there was a nice hot mug of tea waiting for us, which you could take back to your room and get a nice hot shower, change, and into the bar for a quicky before dinner, The talk that evening was of course all about the days happenings and what it must be like for our lads out on jungle patrols for real, as most of them here were either pen pushers or staff on a civilised RAF station. Some of them were interested in the station and unusual Squadron that I was on and the fact that I had been in the 'ulu' a couple of times on aircraft recovery. I hope I didn't bull s—t too much, anyway it got me a couple of beers, I reckon they thought I was an old sweat!!

The following week we went on another of these 'field trips' but this time we all had to carry rifles and larger back packs with water bottles to add a bit more weight, it was evidently to give everyone a taste of jungle life, also this time we had to prepare our own lunch, light a fire and heat up soup and stew. This time some of the lads really felt it. the track back was without a stop, drink while you are walking, I think it was because we were a bit behind schedule, took too long over lunch, as the trucks would be waiting for us to return. I tried to pace myself as I knew what it was like as the time when I had a tool kit and an aircraft wheel strapped on my back, plus rifle, so it was best to pace yourself. Anyway we arrived back o.k. but there was one or two missing at dinner. All in all I enjoyed that couple of weeks up on Frazers Hill, plus I did feel much better for it, now it was back to reality. Again going back down through the mist, shivers, and then the sweating and clinging clothes and humidity. When we arrived at the airstrip Captain Allum was already there chatting to another pilot who had come for Tim, we said cheerio, and it was up and over, and away back to Seremban. As we flew over the airstrip and then around for the approach, Captain Allum said "hold onto your stomach" and we dipped over the trees at the end, then full throttle along the strip 6 ft off the ground and then a mighty swoop upwards at the end, just skimming the bashers, it's called a 'shoot up' it's only done on special occasions, well I was coming back, so it's a special occasion isn't It!! Well Oscar was pleased to see me even if no one else was. So it was once again back to the daily routine, but only 5 months to go. The C.O. called me in one day and said according to records I still have 2 weeks leave entitlement left, and so did Paddy and he was due to go home just after me, so we both decided to take it rather than lose it, also we could have travel passes if needed. We thought about it and decided to go mad and go down to Singapore for two weeks, Johnny, one of the army lads, the one who worked the control tower, heard about us going and as he also had some leave due, asked if he could come too, the more the merrier, and blow me, Blondie said if you lot are going I'm going too, and dam me he managed to get it, so that was 3 RAF blokes out of 7 absent, I didn't think our Sarg would wear it but he said I'll be losing you all soon, and there are two more RAF lads due to arrive next week, so if you can get them up to speed before you go it's o.k. by me. Sure enough 2 lads did arrive, one was airframes and the other engines, so myself, Paddy, and Blondie, gave the two lads a condensed course of their duties, what to do, how to do it, and when to do it, I think they wondered what had hit them. We even had them down in the hanger at nights telling them things. The sarg laughed and called us 3 ' Kernkniving –b-------ds, but I think we got them up to speed in the end. We asked Robbie in the office to book us all in at the YMCA in Singapore and also arrange travel warrants and advanced pay. So a week later off we went, Buster took us to the station and we had a couple of drinks in the bar just to start things off on the right footing. The train was the usual Wild West wagons, but it did have a buffet bar where you could get a cold beer. We of course had our rifles with us so we kept them handy, we can check them in when we get to the YMCA. It took about 3 hrs to get to Singapore, and then as we came out of the station we were stopped by MPs who checked us and our credentials out. We then got a taxi to the YMCA club and checked in, we had two rooms for the 4 of us, quite adequate, we were on bed and breakfast board, and there was a restaurant in there which was quite cheap actually, also we found out that ½ a mile down along the sea front was a 'Union Jack' club for all military personnel which was also cheap to eat and drink in, also it had a swimming pool which was a bonus.

The first night we decided to stay in the YMCA, have a meal and a drink and it was nice wearing civilian clothes again, we got chatting to some Australian submariners who were docked here for two weeks R&R, they told us of some places to go for food and drink. Strangely Blondie asked them if they knew where 'Raffles' is, they laughed and said that place is off limits to the likes of us mate, Officers and plantation owners only, Blondie gave a wry smile, I knew something was going through his tiny brain! The next morning we grabbed our swim gear and took a walk along the front to the 'U,J,' club. The promenade was new and had only just been opened, it was called the ' Princess Elizabeth Promenade', I think that's right, but I think she was Queen by now, I've just checked my memory bank and it was called the 'Queen Elizabeth Promenade' and was opened in 1953. the U,J, club was pretty good, the food was good and the beer cheap enough, plus the swimming pool was great, especially in that heat, and over the next couple of weeks we spent a lot of time in there, and the two Aussies joined us as well so we had some good sessions. There were all sorts from all over the place who used the club, all of the forces and all nationalities, and sometimes scuffles would break out, but mind you some of the lads had come from some hairy places, Borneo, Korea, jungle patrols so you couldn't blame them for letting their hair down occasionally, but the M.P.s weren't far away so things soon got sorted out, the Jocks were the worst, but most of them were S.A.S. just off loading! We also met up with a couple of WRAFs and they would join us sometimes or spend the day with us lolling around the pool and then going for a meal or a snack at some of the stalls in the back streets, in the evenings you could get a good meal for just a couple of dollars, you just sat out in the street on benches and you could eat all sorts, Malay, Chinese, Cantonese, Indian, mind you, you took the risk of getting 'Montizumers Revenge' or not.

One day the two Aussies took us up to the Naval base and we had a guided tour of their Submarine, it was really interesting although a bit claustrophobic and cramped for my liking, they were on a 6 month tour of the Far East, but also patrolling the Malacca Straits as it was rumoured that the Chinese subs were landing communist guerrillas along that coast to help in the terrorist actions against the British, but the Aussies said that they hadn't encountered any as yet, but we hoped they would.

Just about a mile up the road from the U.J. club was the world famous 'Raffles Club' very, very, up market, which Blondie had shown an interest in, and he came up with the craziest idea that one night next week he was going to try and walk into 'Raffles' to have drink, as it would be the only time in his life that he would get the chance to do so! He just wanted to say that he had visited 'Raffles' in Singapore. Mind you I not sure whether it was for Officers and plantation owners only, but it was the unsaid word I think as they said there were always 2 M.P.s on the entrance, and also in the evenings it was strictly black tie, which I know gave Blondie an Idea. I could see that he was absolutely intent on attempting to get in there. Well I daren't let him loose on his own, so I promised the rest of the lads that I would go along with him in his quest, after all we didn't want him to finish up inside a military prison for the next few years, hang on, so could I!! Ah well, in for a pound. Actually I wouldn't mind having a look inside as well. The other lads said we must be mad and don't expect us to bail you out. Mates? The first obstacle was evening wear, so we asked at the YMCA if anyone knew of a cheap tailor locally, as in those days you could get a suit made to measure and ready in 24 hrs and all for a few dollars, as Blondie and I had already found out. So we got a tri-shaw around to some back streets and met the recommended tailor, hoping no M.P.s saw us as a lot of back streets were out of bounds to military personnel, you knew the ones, as at the end of the street was a sign just like a 'no entry' sign in the U,K, The tailor recommended a white sharks skin jacket, shirt and black trousers, bow tie, we already had the shirt and trousers but we also got some gold cufflinks, and a cummerbund, he measured us both up and gave us a price, which we couldn't believe, it was so cheap, he said come back in the morning for a fitting, and low and behold they fitted perfectly, the jacket felt really comfortable and would probably last for years, although I couldn't see me going into my local at home wearing it! They would think I had won the football pools.

So we decided to go to 'Raffles' the following evening, we polished our shoes and had our shirts and trousers ironed, and then got ready, and I must say we did look the part, unmistakably Officer material, we were both sunburnt and we both had blond hair so I think we looked good, and in a dark light and with a following wind we could be mistaken for, ? All answers on a postcard. When we went downstairs at the YMCA, I wanted to go out the back door, everyone was staring at us, and of course it didn't help when Johnny and Paddy and the two Aussies started clapping and whistling, the B------ds, we daren't go down to the U,J, club dressed like this as we would be laughed off the Island. I nearly backed out there and then, but was persuaded to go through with it, so we all went to a local bar for a few bits of Dutch courage. Even then we got some funny looks from the locals, At about 9pm Blondie decided it was time to go, so we got a taxi and off we went with the other shower standing in the road whistling and clapping. again b-----ds, I'll never live this down.

There was a long driveway up to the entrance made of red shale, and then steps up to the large entrance doors, and sure enough there were two M.P.s standing each side of the entrance. Blondie whispered to just act naturally, he was really into the part, one of the M.P.s opened the door for us with a "Good evening Sirs" Blondie answered "Good evening lads" in his posh Essex accent, I just smiled and nodded. I daren't say anything in my Coventry come Cockney voice, they used to say that Coventry was called little London in those days, anyway Blondie spotted the cocktail bar sign so in we went, he ordered two Singapore Gin Slings, which 'Raffles was noted for, but I thought you only drank them at lunchtime or early evening, I don't know, but the bar waiter gave us a funny look and asked if he would put it on account, but Blondie said no, he would pay cash, another funny look, I nearly bit my tongue off when he then said" just keep them coming my good man" oh my God, overkill! After another couple of those gin Slings I began to relax a little and Blondie's smooth talk was winning over the barman, with the tips of course.

The 'Raffle was a magnificent colonial style building, the interior Victorian decor was beautiful with everything top notch, beautiful lounges, and dining room, discretely lit, the place to entertain someone else's wife. There were Flunkeys everywhere, they pulled your chair out when you sat down and when you stood up, pushed it back, if you took out a cigarette, a light was there straight away. If you put an empty glass down it was removed and another full one put in its place. The clients were mostly Officers, young ones, some with beautiful Chinese girls, escorts probably, some older men, probably Plantation owners, knocking back the Scotch, after Scotch. I'd had enough of the Gin Slings so went onto the beer, there was Anchor and Tiger on draught served in long stemmed glasses, I could really get used to this. A woman came in and sat at the bar, she was very attractive and in evening dress, she ordered a drink and of course Blondie started chatting to her. I just smiled and nodded my head, which was beginning to get a bit fuzzy by this time, and I noticed that Blondie was beginning to slur his words as well, but he and the woman seemed to be getting on very well, after another couple of beers I decided to have a coffee and a brandy, the coffee served on a silver tray with biscuits and mints, and real coffee at that, and the brandy was very good, very civilised. One of the flunkeys came and asked if we were staying for dinner, I declined with the excuse that we had to get back to our station.

The woman that Blondie was chatting up, they seemed to be getting on famously, insisted that she bought us a drink, so mine dutifully arrived, coffee and a brandy, god knows what Blondie was drinking but it had a straw and an umbrella in it. I thought I can't really say 'cheers mate, so I just said' your very good health', and mind you she was beginning to look very attractive to me also, she then said put these drinks onto my Husbands account----whoops. I thought,down Blondie down, just at that moment a chap came into the cocktail bar and made a beeline over to us and said to the woman, "Sorry I am late darling, got held up at the bank meeting" after giving Blondie and I a curious look, "that's alright darling, these two charming gentlemen have been keeping me company" The chap got himself a drink and sat himself in between Blondie and his wife, obviously on purpose and started to enquire about us. I thought to myself, he's trying to find out about us as he said he hadn't seen us in here before, and Blondie said that we were new to Singapore and that we were told that 'Raffles' was the only decent place to dine out in. I thought the bloke was a bit smarmy as you could tell with all of his false smiles. He said to his wife that they had better go in for dinner and I said that we had better get back to our station as well. As they left the woman said to Blondie "I hope to see you again sometime" Down Blondie, down!, When they had gone he turned to me, nearly falling off his stool, and said that she was a bit of alright, shame about her husband bit and ordered another drink, this time I had just coffee, as when I went to the loo I swung the door open rather too strongly and nearly smashed someone in the face, and received a rather dirty look.

Then just as I was about to take a drink a Flunky came up to me and said that someone wanted to see us at the entrance door, I thought surely it wouldn't be the lads trying to play some sort of trick on us as I knew they were going along to the U.J. club and it was only just down the main road opposite. So when we staggered to the door there were only the two M.P.s there, so when I asked if anyone wanted to see us, the M.P.s said "yes sir, we do" alarm bells rang in my head, that bloody woman's husband must have had words with them as they asked for our identification papers "please sir" just in case we were genuine, so we had to produce our papers, they examined them and smiled "O.R. fly boys eh, nice try lads and we must admit you looked the part, nice outfits, you fooled us, and normally we should sling you both in the jug, but we are army and the paperwork involved with you RAF blokes won't be worth it, you haven't caused any trouble, so just quietly vanish into the night, o.k." I nearly said that we hadn't finished our drinks yet, but thought better of it! Blondie said thank you very much Sergeant, he was a corporal, and saluted him, the prat. "off you go then, the U.J. club is just down the road, finish your night off in there". So resigned to defeat we started off down the steps, but Blondie missed a step, tripped and crashed sideways into me, our legs weren't supporting us very well, could have been the drink! so we both rolled down the steps and went sprawling onto the red shale driveway! When we eventually picked ourselves up, the two M.P.s were laughing at the top of the steps. I don't think it was because what we had just done, but at the way we both looked, our lovely white sharkskin jackets were now red blotches, scrapes, and stripes, and were completely ruined, so off came the jackets and bow ties and we marched down the drive and out into the real world, for us anyway, I often wonder how many people can say that they were thrown out of the famous 'Raffles Hotel' in Singapore! Anyway you can imagine the laughs we got when we went into the U.J. club.

So ended our two weeks break in Singapore and now back at Seremban and back into the old routine, plus new boys arriving and guard duties, night flying. Getting p----d in the NAAFI, or down in Seremban, the endless jokes and tom foolery, the burning paper in the thunder boxes, beds that collapsed when you lay on them, and carrying lads who were collapsed on their beds out onto the airstrip and leaving them there all night, the insects, and the funny creatures in your boots, beer bottles that exploded when you took the top off, the sweating and the heat, all good fun though. There was one day a month of relief though as we were only about an hour's drive away from the seaside at Port Dickson. in those days it was just a seaside village, but nowadays I believe it is a top notch holiday resort for wealthy tourists, anyway as that area was supposedly free of C.T.s, we were allowed to go there, so once a month on a Sunday one of the cooks, usually Wilf would make up a picnic for about a dozen blokes and we would pile into a 3 tonner, dogs and all, and off we would go to spend a day by the sea, the beach was beautiful and the sea warm and as clear as gin, in the evening we would light a fire on the beach and if you went swimming as it got dark the water would glisten and glow like sparkling lights, it was the fluorescence or the phosphorus in the water, but it looked quite spectacular, also the dogs loved the sea, or we would sit around the fire perhaps cooking something on it and something for the dogs, a few bottle of beer and just chatting, very relaxing and we used to look forward to it. One day one of our lads, Don, was taken ill with stomach pains, the M.O. from the Hussars was sent for and he suggested that he would be better if he was transferred to the military hospital at Kinrara as he had picked up some sort of bug, we wondered if it was from swimming in the sea, but everyone else seemed o.k. the M.O. said they were better equipped to deal with tropical deceases. So poor old Don was flown down straight away, after about a month I did manage to get down to see him, but he had lost a hell of a lot of weight and they were still treating him, a couple of weeks later we were told he was flown home and we had to pack all his kit into trunks and that followed him home later. He was due to be demobbed about the same time as me so I have his address so I shall look him up when I get home.

By this time I was beginning to get demob happy, so I started sorting out my things to send home in my tea chest, all of my English uniform except for the basics for when I get back, I had a spare pair of jungle boots so I put those in as you couldn't get anything like that back home. The chest was sent off with my home address on it, if you were a regular and when you were demobbed you had also to be on the reserve list for a number of years, you were paid, I think it was £12 a year! And you were expected to keep you uniform in good order in case you were called up again. I know my great coat was used to cover up my Dads motor bike in the winter, I know that when my sea chest finally arrived it was months and months after I had been home, and everything in it was mouldy, but after some things were washed I made use of some of them in various ways, especially the boots.

It was now only 4 weeks to my 21st birthday and I began to worry about getting home, as if they sent me home on a troopship I would be way over my 3 years service time, and I was hoping to spend my 21st back home in England, another week went by and finally my orders came through for my repatriation. It was funny as I was working down in the hanger and Robbie the clerk came running down shouting Ray, Ray, your orders have come through, of course all the lads cheered, and someone shouted, 'good riddance'! cheers. The good thing was I was flying home, yippee! I was to report to Changi airport in 5 days time, so panic all around, A lot of the stuff I had amassed over the years I gave away, and the most important thing was my dear friend and companion Oscar, I arranged for one of the lads, Jimmy, one of the new lads to take him on, well actually he had asked me before if he could, so I knew he would be looked after. next day the C.O. Captain Musters called me into his office and said he was sorry to see me go, and if I liked he would put in a recommendation, if I signed on, to go to an Officers training unit as evidently the RAF were short of commissioned Officers in the trades sections. I said thank you very much Sir, and that I would think about it when I got home, no chance I thought, anyway he said it would be on my file and records. I have said it many times since that that was one of the biggest mistakes of my life!!

I think in the next few months most of the original lads on the flight were due for demob, so with only 5 days to go we had some good nights over in the NAAFI. And then the final day arrived, Captain Alum was going to fly me down to Kuala Lumpur, and then train to Singapore. We were to take off at 7-30am so we loaded my kit into my favourite plane, plus rifle and ammo for the train journey. Captain Allum came down and they let me swing the prop for the very last time, it was hard to think that I would never do that again, I walked up to the Flight office to say goodbye to everyone, and blimey everyone one was there, they had all turned out to say cheerio, it was quite emotional, especially saying goodbye to Oscar, my faithful companion for 2 years, it was handshakes and men hugs all round. Captain Allum had taxied up, so it was time to climb aboard, we taxied down to the bottom of the strip, turned and then full throttle back up and away with everyone waving, either that or giving me the V sign, probably glad to see me going. I noticed we were flying in a circle and captain Allum said "let's give them a proper farewell" I knew what he was going to do, a 'shoot up', he came around as if to land but with full throttle, we skimmed up the airstrip just a couple of feet off the ground, everyone was still there and still waving again, we got to nearly the end and I braced myself as we did a huge climb upwards, I think my stomach was left behind, but it was great. On the way down to K.L. he let me take the controls for a while as he used to do when I went up with him as his observer. We landed at K.L. and Captain Alum was going straight back, so we said a warm farewell and I stood and watched as he took off vanished over the jungle.

A land rover was waiting for me and it took me to the H.Q. office where I collected my travel warrant and such, there were two other lads there who were going down to Changi RAF station as well. The journey was uneventful. no armed guards, as it was now considered safe. At Singapore station we reported to the RAF desk and handed our weapons in, I was sorry to see it go actually, also all my O,G, stuff, they asked where were the jackets and I told them they had rotted in the jungle and they said oh o.k. There was a truck waiting to take us to the Changi camp, and there an Officer told me that I would be flying home as soon as there was room on a flight, but in the meantime you will be billeted in the transit section, it should only be for a few days before you go so in the meantime make use of all the amenities on the camp. You will be paid as usual on Thursdays and still receive your cigarette ration. The truck dropped me off at my assigned billet, a wooden one, not a basher, and proper showers and toilets, back to civilisation again, I went in and found a spare bed, and then had the shock of my life, as lying on the bed next to mine was my old friend Jim, the one from Coventry when we joined up together and did our square bashing together, and then our trade training, then stationed together in Norfolk, and also spent 5 weeks on a troopship, and only got separated when we arrived in Singapore! And Jim has spent the last 2 years here at Changi. We both said we often wondered what happened to both of us. It was great to see him again, and here we were both in the transit camp waiting to fly home, we hope both on the same plane, anyway we had loads and loads to catch up on, so the first thing was to get a drink, as he was stationed here he knew his way around and we spent many hours catching up. he laughed when i told him I was maintaining 6 Auster aircraft as he had been working on Dakotas and Canberras, and had only seen an occasional Auster and thought they were toy planes, but when I filled him in on the role they played in this 'Emergency' he changed his opinion as he didn't know what the 656 squadron did up country and was amazed at some of the stories I told him, as nothing ever happened in Singapore, except that he knew some of the Canberas did bombing runs and that was it.

We spent the next few days just hanging around, most of the time down at the swimming pool getting a last minute panic tan, although I wasn't too bad as wearing just gym shorts most of the time back at camp I had a pretty good colour where as Jim had to wear RAF shorts and jackets. there was one interesting thing that he told and that was that just before he was sent into the transit camp, a talk was given by a representative from 'Singapore Airlines' to the effect that they were on a recruitment drive for ex RAF fitters who were leaving the RAF and would perhaps be interested in employment on the civilian airline as they needed experienced fitters and they considered ex RAF were the best, and the package they were offering was really tempting, for a start, as you were being demobbed and after you had been home for a month they would fly you back to Singapore, next, a fabulous salary, far more than you could earn in the U.K. plus free accommodation in a nice flat in a very secluded part of Singapore, plus a car! Also cheap flights to the U.K. on very generous holiday periods you were given. Now those sort of offers would be very hard to turn down wouldn't you think, but Jim said not many were even interested as everyone just wanted to get back to Blighty, and I could see what he meant, everyone in transit just wanted to get back home and I could see what he meant as everyone was demob happy. Mind you that offer was very tempting, and it's one thing I regretted ever since. The other was not taking that offer from my C.O. to sign on again and go to Officers training college. I know now that I should have made the RAF my career and retire whilst still young with a good pension, but there again I would never have met my wonderful Wife!

By this time Jim and I were getting a bit bored as we had been here for a week now and it was only 10 days to my 21st. Another 3 days went by and a lot of lads who had come in after us were gone, but they were going by troopship, another 2 days went by, and then panic stations, we were told that there were 2 seats available the day after tomorrow at 6am so be ready, the trouble was today was Tuesday, so we would miss payday on Thursday, and Jim and I were nearly broke, we went to see someone in the transit office to see if they could do something for us, but we never heard anything, so we were up at 4am on the Thursday, a truck took us to the airport, RAF section, we were given a packed breakfast or lunch or whatever it was, then over to the aircraft, to what we thought would be an airliner, turned out to be a Dakota, an old one at that, Mk iv or something like that, surely that can't get us back to the U.K. Anyway our luggage was stored away and we were told to get in the two empty seats on the port side, seats!! they weren't seats, just webbing on a steel frame! As soon as we sat down in the 'seats, the engines started. I nearly asked if they wanted me to swing the props! The plane was vibrating and you couldn't hear yourself think, it then roared down the runway, for what seemed ages, and then finally we were air bourn, we watched the land disappear and then over the sea. Jim and I shook hands and said bye bye Singapore and Malaya, Blighty here we come. when we finally reached cruising height, the pilot throttled back a bit so you could now at least hear and talk without shouting, there was about 20 on the flight, all O.R.s, there was a Corporal, who I suppose you could call the flight steward, he bought us a cup of tea in paper cups, so we ate some of the sandwiches as we hadn't had any breakfast as everything was done so quickly.

The plane droned on for a while and then the Corporal handed everyone a sheet of paper to read, as it was no good him trying to talk to everyone at once as no one would hear him, hence the sheet of paper, which turned out to be the flight plan and schedule. It was going to take 5 days to get to the U.K. in short hops, as the Dakota could only fly for about 4 or 5 hours at a time as it needed to refuel. 4 or 5 hours at a time on this tub was something not to look forward to! But at least we were on our way home, better than 5 or 6 weeks on a troopship, but sadly I wasn't going to have my 21st at home. The route was Singapore to Columbo (Sri Lanka, ex Celon) then to Bahrain, Cyprus, Malta, and finally landing at Lytham St Anne's, I think that was the way back, anyway 5 days in a Dakota and I reckon our brains will be scrambled. Everywhere we landed was the pits!, It was always at the far end of the runways where we had to doss down for the night. We weren't allowed to leave the airfields as most of them were civilian places. We slept in huts mostly and food was bought to us by civilians, there were no big airports or terminals in those days, very antiquated, mostly tin huts or tiny brick buildings, no amenities or anything, the one I remember most was Bahrain, simply as it was now the 7th July and that's where I celebrated my 21st birthday, did I say celebrate! We landed and as usual, taxied up to the very end of the runway, our sleeping arrangements here were tents, 4 in a tent, and we ate outside, when it started to get dark I said to Jim let's take a walk down to the 'terminal' Which was a small brick building about the size of a house and see if we can get a drink for my birthday, as we had a couple of bob between us, A drink, wrong, it's a Muslim place isn't it. Apart from that there was nowhere to get a drink any way, just a water tap which was warm, so didn't trust the water anyway. Also there were a couple of armed guards there who we didn't like the look of. So we went back to the tents, and a bottle of lukewarm water. So that was the way we celebrated my 21st birthday, I was so p-----d off, I just wanted to kick a camel ! The rest of the stops are a bit of a haze but much the same. The last hop was of course the best, we took off very early in the morning, everyone was looking out of the windows as we flew over France and the channel and we all cheered as we crossed over the shores of England. At last we touched down at Lytham St Anne's, everyone clapped and it felt so good stepping off the plane onto English soil, we were still wearing our tropical gear and even though it was a glorious July day it felt a bit nippy to us, as having been in the far East for a couple of years your blood gets thinner and you feel the cold more, I'm glad we didn't come back in the middle of winter. Lytham St Anne's is a demob and a repatriation centre where we would finally be turned back into civilians, we changed back into our RAF blues which felt strange, and handed in our tropical gear, then a good meal and then afterwards all the usual paper work, travel documents, demob papers, and thankfully some pay at last. A bank draft was given to us if we had saved any money whilst in the RAF. I had quite a bit saved actually as when we were at Benta there was nowhere to spend your money except at Chan's. I reckon I'd be quite well off if I had saved all the money that I had spent at Chan's!! We were to spend the night here at Lytham and travel home next morning, we were shown our billet and after a nice shower we made our way to the camps NAAFI for a drink, surprise, surprise, and there we tasted our first English draught beer for two years, and it tasted awful, I think that drinking all that chemical beer come lager out there had ruined our taste buds! That's why I can't drink lager even now, but after a few pints and a bacon and egg sandwich (banjo) the taste buds gradually started to return to normal, and I am quite intent on aiding that return now that I'm home.!

The next morning with a bit of a sore head we had breakfast, collected our gear and jumped on the wagons to the station. It was going to be quite a journey to get to Coventry, it was a local train to Preston, then to Manchester, on to Crewe, then Birmingham and finally Coventry, most of them were connecting trains so not too bad, two of them had buffet cars so we were able to get food and drink. Some people remarked on how sun tanned we looked and had we been on holiday, and I was quite tempted to say" These are uniforms of military origin, not boy scout uniforms, so we haven't just come back from summer camp" but thought better of it. by the time we reached Coventry we both felt a bit weary with the changing trains and lugging kit about, so we both decide to be a bit posh and have taxi's, as I don't think I could have stood a bus journey, not with all that kit anyway. so Jim and I both said our farewells, and the strange thing is that we both had each other's addresses, we lived at opposite ends of the city, but we never did get in touch with each other for some strange reason. I don't know whether it was the fact that adjusting to civilian life again was difficult and took quite a long time to do so, or the fact that one period of your life has finished, so time to move on get on with the next one, I don't know, maybe it was the fact that I only stayed living in Coventry for a few months before I moved to where I'm living now. But that's another story.

Getting out of the taxi outside our house seemed very strange and I had to stop and look up and down the street, and it felt so unreal as only a week ago I was in a country on the other side of the world, with different weather, customs, and dress. I had to shake myself to bring me back to reality. The front door was unlocked as usual so I walked in and through the front room and into the parlour. Mum was in the kitchen and Dad was in the yard doing something to his bike. Mum looked up and saw me and dropped the tea towel and came and gave me a big hug, then told me off for not letting them know that I was on my way home, she opened the back door and shouted up to Dad "Our Rays home", Dad came down wiping his oily hands, and the first words he said, and he always said this every time I came home on leave were "When are you going back!" Marvellous isn't it, haven't seen him for two years and he wants to know when I'm going back! That's my Dad. Mum started to get some supper and I asked how 'our kid' was. He was now out of the Navy after 7 years service, but he had met a girl when he was last stationed in Weymouth, and they had got married and he was living down there, but they were eventually going to come back to Coventry to live. His best friend Alan, they both went though the 7 years in the navy together and remarkably never got separated, he lived opposite us in the street, had also got married but to a Coventry girl, they were 'best man at each other's wedding. So I suppose that's why 'our kid' wants to come back to Coventry, as Mum said he feels a bit lost there, also the job opportunities are a bit better in Coventry. After supper I took my things up to my bedroom and it's going to be strange sleeping in my big double cast iron bed, after 2 years sleeping on camp beds. Of course Mum shouted up, "bring your dirty washing down" I know she will get the copper going in the morning, and then into the tub and bash it all with the big wooden 'dolly'. I hung up my uniform, never to wear it again and changed into civvies, and remarkably everything that was in my wardrobe still fitted me. I asked Dad if he fancied a pint as it was now 9pm, but he declined as he was still mending his bike as he had to get it working for work tomorrow. He was retired but had taken a job as a Park Keeper to keep himself busy, also he had bought himself a little car, if I remember right it was an Austin Ruby, black of course, he couldn't afford to run it much, so it was in a friends shed in the next street, occasionally he would get it out to go fishing, he had got rid of his motorbike and sidecar, Mum said he liked to just park it outside the house sometimes just to show off to the neighbours as it was the only car in the street, and not many people had cars in those days. Unfortunately one day when it was parked outside and Dad was at work I thought that I would have a little go in it, so I drove it down the street and back and went to turn it around and as I put it into reverse there was a bang and it stopped, and no reverse gear, so I managed to push it to outside the house, it wasn't very heavy as it looked like a big pram. So when Dad came home I did confess to him what had happened and he said don't worry as he would get his friend to have a look at it, so I helped him to push it around to his friends house. I never did know what happened to that car.

So now it was back to civilian life, I have no idea how it's going to be after spending 3 years in an orderly and routine way of life, although a lot of it wasn't exactly routine, and most of the time you knew what to do, how to do it, and when to do it, so you were more or less your own boss, well that's how things were in my lot, so it was a little bit daunting knowing that

I have to go out and look for a job and do as I was told perhaps, that'll be hard, and of course do it to earn a living, anyway that can wait for a few weeks as I intend to enjoy a little respite before that situation arises, as I have been looking forward to coming back to Blighty foe a long time, and having saved a bit of cash as most of the time there was nowhere to spend it, I intend to look up all my old mates and mould myself back into the good life I had before I joined up. I am going to miss all the friends that I made in the last two years of my service. We were like a family, as we were all in the same boat together, and we all pulled together as well. We experienced the good times and the bad times and it always ended with a laugh, I miss my Oscar, and I intended to get a dog just like him at some stage. The fateful conclusion of mine and Margaret's relationship, which I vowed to try explain to her somehow. As for the lads, the RAF ones, we did keep in touch, and in fact we still do after 60 years, some of them have passed, and we are now down to four, but friendships like that are rare.

So there on that note my little story ends, 21 years in the life of Raymond, Thomas, Henry, William, Albert, George, Warden, that's what I was Christened, all my uncles so I'm told. Whether or not my story will be of any interest to anyone, I know not. It's just that I have always had the urge to put to paper the early years of my life, and several people have said that when I tell them of some of the things that happened in my early life, they have said that I should write it all down as it might also be of interest to future generations!, we'll see.

I have considered writing about my life after twenty one, but have been advised by some very close friends who have known me well. as to be careful as a lot of people are still alive who would remember me, ' INTRIGUEING', Well maybe, who knows!!

Printed in the United States
By Bookmasters